Mother Wit

365 Meditations
for African-American Women

ABENA SAFIYAH FOSUA

Abingdon Press
Nashville

MOTHER WIT:
365 MEDITATIONS FOR AFRICAN-AMERICAN WOMEN

Copyright © 1996 by Abingdon Press

This book is printed on recycled, acid-free paper.

Library of Congress Cataloging-in-Publication Data

Fosua, Abena Safiyah.
    Mother wit : 365 meditations for African-American women / Abena Safiyah Fosua.
        p.   cm.
    ISBN 0-687-04794-3 (pbk. : alk. paper)
    1. Afro-American women. 2. Afro-American women—Religious life.
3. Meditations.   I. Title.
E185.86.F675   1996
242 '.643 ' 08996073—dc20   96-33134
                                                                              CIP

96 97 98 99 00 01 02 03 04 05—10 9 8 7 6 5 4 3 2 1

MANUFACTURED IN THE UNITED STATES OF AMERICA

Contents

Acknowledgments

I gratefully make the following acknowledgments:

To Jesus Christ, whose wisdom continues to speak to all of us.

To my devoted husband, Rev. Dr. Kwasi Issa Kena, who read every word more than twice and offered invaluable insights along this journey to publication.

To Dr. Jeremiah Wright of Trinity UCC in Chicago; Dr. Jawanza Kunjufu of African-American Images; Elder Michael Slaughter of San Antonio; and my pastor, Dr. C. Anthony Muse of Resurrection Prayer Ministries in Brandywine, Maryland who has mentored me and brothered me in so many ways.

To Dr. Kofi Ampofah Duodu, of the University of Ghana, Legon; Forster Kwame Boateng of Self-Help, Ghana; and Dr. Jawanza Kunjufu who "named" me. (The family that claims you has a right to name you!)

To my dear sisters, Rev. Janette Kotey of Dallas; Dr. Linda Lee, district superintendent the Detroit District; Barbara Perkins of New Jersey; and Carol Watson Grimes of Dallas, Texas who have interceded, prayed, read, and cried with me.

To Dr. Scharron Clayton of Waterloo, Iowa who encouraged me to pursue publishing these meditations and read through my first draft.

To James (Jimmie) and Louise Porter, and the staff and directors of KBBG Radio, Waterloo, Iowa who provided their first public forum back when some of them were radio devotions.

To Minister Carla Turner, my sister in the Spirit, who served as a sounding board and cheered me along the way.

To Dr. Alan F. Kirton, of the United Methodist Mission Resource Center; Rev. Connie Nelson, of the United Methodist Mission Resource Center; Dr. Carolyn McCrary, of ITC; Rev. Donald Hamilton and Mildred Hamilton, missionaries to Zambia; Revs. Dave and Kristin Markay, missionaries to Lithuania; Dr. Ruth Grumbel, mission to Japan; Rev. Ronda

Lee, missionary to Peru; Janet Buama, Ghana, West Africa; Rev. Regenia Dudley; Rev. Helen Bell; Teresa Honeycutt (Mocha); Marta Reyes; Rev. Pedro and Arsenia Paredes, missionaries to Uruguay; and others who read through early manuscripts and ministered to our personal needs while this manuscript was being completed.

To my sisters LaTosha Smart and Patrice Bishop-Wise who have stood in the gap for me in prayer.

To my "writing sisters" Dr. Linda Hollies and Rev. Valerie Bridgeman-Davis who give me courage to try my hand at writing.

To my mother, Rheta Smart (Maaame Otiwaa), and my "Other Mother" Catherine Calhoun of San Antonio, Texas, all who have served as living models of Mother Wit, and to Daddy (William F. Bishop) who sat up many nights with my manuscript.

To my grandmother, Semilen Black who has gone on to be with the Lord.

Finally, to unnamed and unmentioned women of the Diaspora who continue to shape my definition of Mother Wit. Thank you for shaping the Mother Wit in my being!

Introduction

What, exactly, is Mother Wit? Twenty-six Black women will give you as many different definitions. They will range from rocking-chair wisdom to words of truth from Grandma, Auntie, Big Sis, Big Mama, and Nana. Some will have to mention a particular sister they know, and others will give you wordy descriptions of that which for them has become unfathomable. As you prepare to enter into these meditations that were written with an undefinable wisdom in mind, I leave you with my own mother's definition, which was shaped by her mother's definition:

A person can have all the book learning they can get but without mother wit it's no good. Have you seen people with good education or a good job who can't seem to keep their family fed and clothed? Or who can't seem to keep the rent and utilities paid? It's because they have no mother wit, which is just God-given common sense. Then you see other people with no smarts but they have little fat kids running around and their bills are paid. They may just make it from payday to payday, but they make it. That is mother wit.

What exactly is Mother wit? You decide!

A. Safiyah Fosua
Kumasi, Ghana, West Africa

January

Faith for the New Year

January 1   *Read Revelation 21:5.*

So many things are new in your life. Have you been so in tune with the "same old, same old" that you have been unable to see the newness all around you? Look around you on this first day of the new year.

This year is new. It is a history waiting to be written. Last year's worries and pains are past. There are certain things from last year that you will not have to endure this year. The year holds endless potential. You might just get there this year; you are closer than ever before.

Each day is new. Did you realize that you could create a little New Year's Eve celebration at the end of each day? Why not try this the next time that you feel trapped in an endless twenty-four hour daytime nightmare? It's time to leave yesterday's troubles behind you and embrace today's possibilities.

Praise God that each minute is new! If you happen to get off course during the day, God has given you time to get back where you need to be. There is no need to wait until next year, tomorrow, or even the next hour. You can change directions at any minute.

Not only are you given new time, you are also new. You are not the same person you were last year. You are not even the same person you were yesterday. Last year's trials made you stronger. Previous years' mistakes have made you wiser. Old humiliations have built your character, and life's experiences have made you richer. Don't act old, become new.

God's mercies are new. Baskets of blessings and carloads of grace flow to you each moment. Open them. Smell them. Receive them! This day is but a symbol of a series of new beginnings. Lift your head to greet the year and live!

Taming the Resident Serpent

"Girl, get off the phone!" Johnnie Mae's daughter was on the phone again. "Letha, ain't that much to talk about without repeating something or lying. Get off that phone now!" Johnnie Mae was one of those women who stayed off the telephone. She thought that too much idle phone chatter would eventually lead to trouble.

Letha, by contrast, was one of those teenagers who seemed to have been born with a telephone receiver welded onto their right ears. She and her girlfriends loved to talk. They talked about boys. They talked about the other girls. They speculated about the teachers and their love-lives. They talked about their parents. They just plain talked; and most of it was not good. This time, they were talking about a girl they thought was pregnant.

"I'll be off in a minute, Mama. . . . Mama's trippin'; I have to go; but call me back in five minutes so we can finish talking about Lorraine's baby. Do you think she'll keep it?"

"Letha!. . . ." Johnnie Mae was sounding real serious by now.

"Bye, LaWanda. Don't forget to call me back in five minutes!" *(Pause)* "Mama I'm off . . . been off."

Letha went off to the bedroom to sulk. "She ain't gonna use the phone, why she always need me off?" she thought. The radio was playing so loudly that she could not drown it out with her thoughts. Johnnie Mae's favorite radio preacher was on. She began with these words: "There is a serpent in your mouth. Some people call it your tongue! It's an uncontrollable monster, inspired from hell itself! Let's talk today about 'Taming the Resident Serpent.' "

Letha's face flushed hot with shame. By the time the phone rang she told LaWanda that she had to do her homework.

Are there times when you need to hang up the phone?

Dividing Lines

January 3   *Read Genesis 1:1-5.*

The first thing during the Creation that God did was to divide the light from the darkness. He described their perimeters and set their limitations. Day could not go on forever; night could not drone on endlessly. Your day cannot last forever—your night has an end. The very first day that there was had dividing lines—isn't that good?

We need dividing lines in our world. Something has to tell something else when and where to stop. Something must signal when to get up from our beds of mourning and rise to meet the morning. We need signals that tell us when to climb from beds of depression, and when to dress ourselves for a new day of possibilities. There must be lines that disrupt what might have turned into a bad day, signaling a time to sleep, or to rest. Are there dividing lines in your life?

Some call these dividing lines boundaries. Even little children recognize boundaries. We tell them "No-No," and they respond "Mine!" Boundaries tell us what to touch and tell others what not to touch. Adults also need dividing lines. We need ground rules like, "I won't let you hit me!" Without boundaries, our lives degenerate into chaos.

Creation was a succession of boundaries. Day was divided from night. The sky was separated from the earth. Land was separated from water. They all needed their own place. This didn't mean that one was good and the other bad, nor did it mean that they were not on friendly terms, they just needed their own space.

You also need space. You need your own toothbrush and a place to lay your head. You have been everything to everybody, now you need to be your own somebody. Others need to recognize and respect your need for space. Have they seen your boundaries?

Just as day was not allowed the confusion of spilling into night, those you love must not be allowed the confusion of robbing you of needed space and time. Are you setting the needed boundaries in your life?

Use It or Lose It

Renee could sing so well that the hair would stand up on your arms. She had a remarkable range that both tenors and sopranos envied. Renee also had an attitude. She did not like people who could not sing as well as she sang.

Needless to say, she would have nothing to do with the church choir. The choir was a good one by anyone else's standards, but for Renee, the choir was a source of constant irritation. Every Sunday, when the choir sang, she arranged to be in the church bathroom powdering her nose, or in the church nursery checking on children that she didn't even know. Renee couldn't stand the church choir.

Churches are a lot like small towns. It wasn't long before the choir director heard about Renee's feelings. In a kind way, she challenged her. "Girl, the choir would be better if you would come and help us. God gave you that gift for a reason." Renee, not wanting to appear haughty, made an excuse. "Well, I would, but I baby-sit my grandchild on the days that the choir meets. Maybe another time when my circumstances change. . . ."

When Renee got home, she called her best friend on the phone. "Girl, I am not about to waste my time. Those people are not going to worry me!"

This game continued for several years. It got so obvious that when the choir stood to sing, the ushers just automatically started opening the door for Renee to leave the sanctuary. The congregation made more than a few phone calls to the pastor.

Pastor Brown finally devised a way to stop this madness. She decided to ask Renee to sing for a special program. There was no graceful way to wiggle out of this direct invitation, so Renee agreed to sing on the second Sunday of August. She was so particular that she would not even practice with the church musician; she planned to sing it without music.

On the second Sunday of August, the church was packed. Everybody wanted to hear the notorious Renee sing her solo. At the appointed time, Renee came to the front. She announced her selection. The first note was awful! She sounded like a cross between a sick owl and a stray fingernail against the chalkboard. Members of the choir just hung their heads.

Children in the back began to giggle. Through years of inactivity, Renee had lost her voice!

Isn't that the way it is with us and God's gifts? If we do not use what God has given us, we may lose it too!

Dark and Lovely

Who were you, beautiful black woman? Some say that you were Solomon's chief wife. Egyptian. Black. Beautiful. Bible translators have a hard time figuring out your beauty. Some say dark *but* lovely; others say dark *yet* lovely. Solomon found you compeling and beautiful. Why was it so hard for them to find beauty in a Black woman?

Sisters, why is it so hard for *us* to find beauty in Black women? Why is it so hard for those of us graciously endowed with melanin to recognize that we are also lovely?

The dark maiden in Song of Solomon hints at the answer in verse five: she has been so preoccupied with tending other vineyards that her own has been neglected! Have we, too, been so engrossed with other standards of beauty, other vineyards, that we have forgotten how to recognize our own?

I was a teenager when the "Black Is Beautiful" revolution flowered. That was nearly thirty years ago. We protested about our own neglected vineyards of beauty. We refused to lighten our skin or straighten our hair. We accentuated the hips that everyone else had said were too wide. African-American cosmetic companies helped us learn how to recognize, not hide, the beauty of the Black woman. All of a sudden, we awakened to the beauty of our own vineyards. We challenged America to see what had too often been hidden from its eyes.

We encouraged one another to celebrate. We celebrated our full lips and high cheekbones. We celebrated the roundness of our hips and the strength in our long legs. As we celebrated, the "kinks" were transformed into crinkles and curls, we became black pearls, and every black woman became a teacher. We began to teach the world how to recognize Black beauties. Have you recognized the black beauty within you?

Look into the mirror today, dark and lovely woman. Are your morning beauty rituals designed to help you see your natural African beauty? Are they designed to convince you that yours is "another vineyard," another vintage, another kind of beauty? Are you black *but* beautiful or black *and* beautiful?

Fish Belly

January 6   *Read Jonah 1:17.*

"Do you know what the inside of a whale's belly smells like?" The warning came loud and clear. "When God has something that He needs for you to do, He don't care nothing about your running. Do you know what the inside of a whale's belly smells like?" It did not take three dreams and a vision to figure out what she meant. I was running from God and my running time was just about over.

After our conversation, I began to think about Jonah's predicament—and mine. We obviously thought that we could outrun God. Wrong! There is no place on earth where God is not. There is no place in existence where God cannot exercise His sovereignty. It is a tragic mistake to think that there is anything that we can do to escape.

Imagine what it must be like to be in the belly of a whale. We know how Jonah got there. He knew, without a doubt, that God wanted him to do something—something that he would just rather not do. In an act of rebellion, he ran the opposite way. Now he was in a rib-caged prison, isolated and alone. Jonah was not free to do anything but think about what he should have done. Worse, he was unable to just jump up and do the right thing, because now he was boxed in by the consequences of an unwise decision.

You and I have been there, probably more than once. I heard a wise person once say that we had the power to choose, but we had no power over the consequences of our choosing. Oh, yes, I know the smell of a whale's belly. Read again the words of Jonah's prayer in verses 1-4.

Jonah knew why he was in this most horrible situation. He also knew that God would hear his prayer. The rest of the story is familiar. When Jonah repented, he was released to go and do what he should have done at first.

Being in the whale's belly can take many forms. There are so many prisons that we run to while running away from God. None of them needs to become our grave. God is still yearning to hear a prayer of repentance—unless we happen to enjoy the smell inside a whale's belly!

We Are One

January 7   *Read Ephesians 2:17.*

There is some strange thread that binds us together.
It enables us to set our feet
> In the house of the Lord
> In Mississippi
> Or Los Angeles
>> And feel at home.

This thread is stronger
Than the Baptist Church
Or the Church of God in Christ;
Stronger than an order of worship
Or a theological dispute.
Regardless of the different creeds we may confess,
> Or the names on the front of our churches
>> We are one!

Shouting together,
> We try to make heaven our home.
From the Zion churches of South Africa
> To the New Testament churches of the West Indies,
>> We sing familiar songs.
Choirs sway and rock
> To familiar rhythms in West Africa.

The Mothers of the Church
> Are sitting together

January

> And wearing white
> In Bahia,
> Chicago
> And Egypt.
> They shout their amens in unison.
>
> Children scoot around on splintery floor boards
> In Washington, D.C.
> And New Orleans; while chalky cement floors
> Make ashy knees in Haiti.
>
> The women's choir comes together,
> Dressed like dozens of twin sisters
> And singing like angels on Women's Sunday.
> All the while,
> Pots bubble,
> Fowls fry,
> And old ladies set the table for dinner.
>
> We dance the Peacock Strut,
> The Stretch,
> and the Old-Mother's-Three-Step
> Together, to an invisible beat.
>
> Who taught so many of us
> To form protective circles
> Around one another
> When the Spirit begins to move?
>
> What unseen strings
> Pull that right palm to the sky,
> As Jesus passes by?
>
> We learned these things
> From God our Father, while
> In Mother Africa's womb,
> For we are one.

Tell Us About Your Eyes

> Leah, tell us about your eyes,
>> Were they sad?
>> Were they homely?
>> Were they lovely?
>> Were they loved?
>> Were they searching?
>> Were they hiding from our gaze?
> Leah, tell us about your eyes!

We have gone through a lifetime of Sunday school lessons believing that you were homely and unlovable. We have gone through Bible commentaries believing that it was fine that He loved your sister more than you, because you weren't quite acceptable. It's time we heard from you.

We are like Leah today. We sit silently in the shadows while others try to figure us out. We accept their version of us, while our own version lies hidden. We accept their verdict while they decide our social fate. They cannot decide whether we are acceptable or not. Some days we are called the pillar of the community. Other days they call us "Sapphire's mama." No one bothers to ask us what we were setting out to be. We sit silently on the teeter-totter hoping the balance will tip in our direction.

Maybe "they" can't make up their minds because they need more information from you. Maybe they (whoever *they* are in your life) need to get to know you better. Maybe they just need to understand your story. Maybe they need to hear your definition of you to inform their opinions! You tell us about your eyes!

Today is a day to stop feeling homely and unlovable. Tell us about your inner beauty. Tell us through your eyes!

> Are you loving?
> Are you warm?
> Are you looking for a good friend?
> Are you pleasant to be with?
> Are you silent and steady?

Leah, tell us who you really are, because you are the only one who knows!

Take a Penny, Leave a Penny

January 9   *Read Matthew 18:21-22.*

I smile every time I see one of those containers that says: "Take a Penny, Leave a Penny." Someone who loves Jesus must have come up with the concept. Have you ever stood in line and watched how people react to that little container?

Some people ignore it altogether. They behave as though not having enough is for everyone else. You can almost hear them saying that people without enough shouldn't be in the store. At best, their body language says that the container is for everyone else but me.

Others quickly give to the cause. They shell out pennies with great care and concern for others who may actually need a penny or two at some point in their lives. Those who give pennies, however, seem to also be those least likely to receive one.

Sometimes there are store clerks who want to help us all catch on to the purpose of the penny container. If we fumble, just for a second, looking for exact change, they quickly rush to the group fund and speed the transaction along while we hang our heads in embarrassment. Some of us cannot stand that embarrassment.We hunt until we find a penny to replace what we feel was not rightfully ours.

Forgiveness is a lot like the "take a penny, leave a penny concept." Sooner or later, we all come up short. While we may *think* that we lead otherwise perfect lives, eventually, we are going to need someone's forgiveness. And, as those having received forgiveness, we also need to forgive.

Some of us may have a hard time understanding that decent people will make mistakes. To learn to forgive is as hard as learning to read Egyptian. We want everyone to be perfect, like us, never needing forgiveness.

Others of us lavish forgiveness upon other people like perfume, "cause Lord knows I make mistakes." Yet, when our turn comes, we wallow in the land of shame and regret because forgiveness may be easier to grant than to receive.

Today, I see Jesus, like a store clerk, trying to help us along in the process. "See this container, it's here to remind you that some days you have more than enough, and other days you need help. Somedays you may need to forgive somebody; other days, somebody may need to forgive you. Need a penny? Go ahead, take it. And, don't worry about trying to pay it back!"

Forgotten in the Night

January 10   *Read Psalm 119:54-55.*

The island of Jamaica was only a stone's throw from the New World. These people are my people. I saw my cousins in their faces and my aunts in their head wraps. How familiar it was to see women, my age, huddled together in conversation. I watched the young "brothers" jive with one another and knew that I was at home. These must be my people, their ways are so like ours. They just survived the dark hours of the African holocaust in a different location.

Jamaica reminded me of Ghana. Red clay tiles decorate the roofs in both places. Old English buildings whisper secrets of days long past. Suddenly, it occurred to me that something was missing. In Ghana, nearly everyone carries their packages on their heads. Baskets, buckets, bundles of sticks—everything is carried on the head in Ghana. Only a handful of Jamaican women carried packages on their heads. In the United States, even fewer Black women carry packages on their heads. Did we forget our traditions during the long night of suffering?

The older we grow, the more we learn the value of tradition. We look for the old holiday recipes after the last old woman who can remember it has died. The old folks pass away with the homemade cures for night sweats neatly tucked in their bosoms. Were we so engrossed in making a living that we forgot to teach the grandchildren their table etiquette: "Did you ask to be excused, honey?"

Spiritual things are a lot like that. The pressure of busy times or hard times, when it is night, provides a convenient reason to lose tradition. We are so busy catching planes that we forget to pray for them. We are so busy putting children on school buses that we forget to pray for their safety.

Faith has a culture, just like Black folks have a culture. There are rituals to be observed. So much remains to be passed on to the children of the faith. Hard times can affect us in one of two ways. They can make our faith grow. Or, at other times, we may get so engrossed in "making it through the night" that we forget how to carry spiritual baskets on our heads.

Queen

How must it be, Esther, remembered primarily for your beauty? Sunday school teachers tell young girls that you were the first beauty queen. Perhaps men still fantasize about your form and features. Were you good in school? Were you even allowed to go to school? Did you have hopes for your future? What was your favorite thing to do? We are fooled into believing that your greatest asset was your body.

Esther entered the kngdom because she was a raving beauty; but her mind was what God used to save the Israelites. At her uncle's urging, she developed a plan to see the king and save the nation. She did this without compromising her moral standards.

Unfortunately ladies, we are still being fooled into believing that our greatest asset is our sexuality. We fret over it, use it like a tool, and sometimes even boast of it to our friends. Our great-grandmothers considered it a curse, because it brought many of them unwanted advances. They did not survive because of their sexuality; they lived by *mother wit.* The use of a womanish wisdom that only God could have given, rescued many African-American women of the past.

Esther must have had some mother wit. Mother wit is at work when the impossible becomes possible in some peculiar womanish way. Esther used mother wit to gain an audience with the king. She took advantage of the rules of "queen etiquette." She knew the king well enough to know a pathway to his heart. Her body didn't save the day, it was her mind! It was God-given mother wit making God's plans nonthreatening, noncompromising, and workable.

Thank God that we do not have to use sexuality to succeed. Numerous women in our past did not use their bodies to get ahead. Black women continue to survive because of good old mother wit; God working things out in nonthreatening and earth-shattering ways. From where else could some of our timely ideas have possibly come?

Place of Prayer

January 12   *Read Acts 16:12-15.*

Sometimes life seems so ordinary and routine. Lydia was going to the place of prayer, down by the river as she had always done when she visited Philippi. She was a business woman who sold a product in good demand, purple cloth. There must not have been enough men in town to warrant a synagogue, so these few faithful women, with Lydia, an out-of-towner, gathered weekly to pray.

They were God-fearing women in a region where other gods were more popular. Yet, they continued faithfully in their religious obser-vances—even in the absence of what we would call a formal church or synagogue. Another visitor came one day, a male visitor by the name of Paul. For Lydia, whose home was over 200 miles away, a miracle hap-pened at the place of prayer. All of a sudden, faith made sense. She heard about Jesus and was baptized.

Life might have been quite different for Lydia had she chosen not to pray that day. Life might even have been different for Thyatira, the site of one of the seven churches cited in the book of Revelation, had Lydia not been at the place of prayer. Life might be different for you if you choose not to pray today.

Where is your place of prayer? Do you have a regular time, or a regular group of people with whom you share your joys and concerns as you come into the presence of God? Are you still struggling with where to *place* prayer in your schedule? Don't delay; find your place, for who knows when God might send a stranger your way with a message that will change your life forever.

Hair

Read Matthew 10:29-31.

"Twelve, thirteen, fourteen. . . ."

"Child, stop playing in my head and counting. What you doing, anyway?"

"I'm countin' the hairs on your head, Grandma. I read in my Bible yesterday, that God counts the hairs on our heads. I wanted to see if I could count yours. Twinny-one, twinny-two, twinny-three. . . ."

"I don't think that's what the Bible had in mind honey. I think it really meant that the Lord knows how many you're going to have when you die."

"Thurdy-six, thurdy-seven. . . . Grandma, I'm confused. There's a whole lot of bald-headed men around here. Why don't they die when they run out of hair? Fordy, fordy-one. . . ."

"Hush, child. What I think the Bible really means to say is that God knows everything about all of creation. God knows when the birds jump up and down, God knows where all of the ants are. God even knows so much about each one of us, that He knows how many hairs are on our heads. Ouch, that hurt! What you doing now?"

"Well, I just pulled out a hair to see if I could throw God off. Maybe, a long time from now, He'll let you stay a few extra days while he figgers out what happened!"

"Girl, I give up!"

God knows your destiny. God has already planned the number of your days. Even the hairs on your head are numbered. Relax, nothing can happen to you today that will be a surprise to God.

Sunrise

Read Malachi 4:2.

For the first time in days, Barbara felt warmth. Three days ago, surgery had transformed her once warm, comfortable world into an unpredictable ice palace. Her toes couldn't seem to get warm again. Her fingers felt cool and clammy. Any direction she moved, pain reminded her that she had just had a hysterectomy. She had never realized just how much her abdomen was involved with everyday movement.

The "pain machine" had been taken back to storage last evening. All through the previous night she had been painfully aware of its absence. Her head, however, had cleared enough to think and to pray.

All through the night, she thanked God that she had been well up until this time. She thanked God that her surgery had not been complicated. She thanked God that her family did not think of her as less than a woman because she no longer had a womb. She thanked God for her husband, who had slept in an uncomfortable chair by her side each night. She had fallen asleep, the night before, thanking God.

This morning of the third day, however, brought warmth. The sunlight poured ribbons of liquid warmth through the blinds. The ribbons grew wide enough to touch one another on the white hospital blankets that were piled upon Barbara's chilly sleeping body. The change in temperature was enough to awaken her. Before she even opened her eyes, she saw the brightness of the sun. She squinted as she looked at the ribbons of light pouring through the slanted blinds. She felt their healing warmth bathe her once cold limbs. Muscles relaxed as pain drifted into the background. "Today will be a good day," she thought.

Her mind, which had been on red alert, relaxed as she drifted off to sleep, thinking about the Sun of Righteousness who had come into her room that day, with healing in His wings.

Have you seen the sun (Son) today?

Meditations on Martyrdom

January 15   *Read Romans 5:5-8.*

Martin Luther King, Jr.'s birthday always stirs up certain thoughts. We all agree that Dr. King made many contributions to humanity. He provoked the country to raise the quality of life among Black people in the United States. The idea of nonviolence, though not original, came to America's attention while she still had a conscience. It challenged her to live out her creedal confession. Nonviolence was used as an instrument of change. He made a lasting impact upon the entire world.

I can still remember the height of the Civil Rights movement. My family was glued to the newscasts. We anxiously watched the battle of our age: violence versus nonviolence. We cried. And, we hoped.

I was a preteen at that time. The realities of life had not yet begun to sink in. I knew the threats of physical danger and death. I saw people lose their jobs. I saw supporters terrorized and ostracized. My youthful idealism overshadowed those realities. As an adult, those physical and economic realities are just beginning to gain meaning.

As adults, we look at the concept of martyrdom with awe. How many of us are willing to stand up for a principle? How important is that principle when it could cost us our lives or worse yet, the lives of those we love? It is painful to think that courage and resolve could spell ruin for those we love.

Human history is heavily punctuated with examples of martyrdom. Religious leaders, political leaders, social leaders—we are humbled to be reminded that we live in the corridors where human history is written. At the same time, we sadly realize that our children have little understanding or knowledge of this same history.

How many God-sent martyrs have we forgotten? How much progress do we take for granted? Progress is often disguised as childhood labor laws, worker's safety regulations, or women's voting rights. Much of what we call change is brought about by those willing to stand by their convictions—even face death.

Our relationship with God is founded upon a similar concept. The human condition is such that it required martyrdom to save us. Jesus Christ is a martyr for our sake. How we gloss over the greatness of that sacrifice. We take the miracle of our redemption for granted. God gave His one and only Son to change our lives. Jesus became a martyr for all of humanity! Isn't God's grace amazing?

Dreamer of Dreams

January 16   *Read Genesis 37:5-10.*

You are familiar with the story of Joseph and his brothers. Joseph was his father's favorite. Joseph had this coat of many colors. Joseph dreamed daring dreams. Those dreams eventually came true.

There is something about dreamers that challenges and frightens us. We are challenged to expand the realm of thoughts and to re-imagine things that we had once considered impossible. We are frightened because often the dreams are impractical, seem grandiose, or are even dangerous. No doubt, Joseph's brothers thought these things about him.

Remember the outcome of Joseph's dreams? He eventually became a leader of his people—after having been falsely imprisoned and discredited.

There was another dreamer of dreams. A man named Martin, after his father. This man was born January 15, 1929. As a young man he dared to dream the dreams that few of the other young preachers had dared to dream. His brothers were also frightened. History reports that the brethren were so frightened at first that they removed Martin from a prestigious national office in his religious body in their effort to divert him from danger. Later, some of them joined him.

In spite of the obstacles, Martin Luther King, Jr. still dared to dream those dreams. We heard him dream aloud:

I have a dream that one day this nation will rise up and live out the true meaning of its creed: We hold these truths to be self-evident; that all men are created equal.

Others began to share his dream and began to sing "Ain't gonna let nobody turn me 'round" while they sat down in protest and refused to fight back even when the dogs, the hoses, and the billy clubs were used. The moral conscience of America was awakened. When the American dream became a visual nightmare, change began. Before his death, Dr. King began to see his dreams become reality.

When a dream is shared and captured, it becomes impossible for it to die. We need dreams that will erase our nightmares. We need dreams that will live until they become reality. Where are our dreamers? Are you one of them?

One-Upwomanship

January 17   *Read Proverbs 14:30.*

Valerie had a good job. She worked reasonable hours and received exceptional pay. She and Helen, who was also well compensated, had worked together at the same company for over ten years. They started when their children were still in high school. Their families alternately shared graduations, weddings, birthdays, and anniversaries with each other. Valerie, Helen, and their families, had been inseparable for years.

One day Valerie got a promotion. She was given the retiring assistant manager's position. Helen would soon be under her supervision. They were such good friends that Valerie thought nothing of it. She would never think of mistreating her friend, or misusing their friendship.

Helen, on the other hand, was unsettled by the promotion. She had to force herself to congratulate Valerie. Helen even complained to her husband that she was more qualified for the job. Gradually, Helen began to share her dissatisfaction with the other workers behind Valerie's back. Before long an old friendship was beginning to dissolve.

Valerie loved her friend Helen, but it did not take long for her to discern that this promotion had provoked her friend to envy. She was wise enough to understand that it wasn't money, nor was it power that was creating such a problem. Valerie understood that Helen was really more afraid than jealous. Helen feared that Valerie's success would somehow change a relationship that had been established upon the foundations of equality. When they were no longer equals, Helen feared, they would probably no longer be friends. Valerie wondered how she might have responded had the roles been reversed.

When Valerie and Helen sat down to talk about the promotion, they both cried. Helen enjoyed things as they were. She was unsure what would happen to all of them in the future. After hours of conversation and buckets of tears, they were able to reassure each other that nothing would change. Their friendship was greater than the workplace.

Success often does strange things to the people around us. Are you feeling similar friction from a longtime friend? Perhaps this is the time to swallow your pride and affirm an old friend who just might be having problems with some good things that have come into your life.

Earthly Considerations

January 18   *Read Luke 16:19-25.*

When you stand before the Lord,
In the days that yet will come.

When the final words are spoken,
And your friends have all gone home.
When you ponder your estate,
And observe those all around.
What will you and Jesus talk about?

Will you discuss the weather,
Or the atmospheric shift?
To the air that is in heaven,
From the "airs" you found on earth
As you and angels gather 'round the throne?

Or in your great discomfort
Will you talk about the heat
Hotels you used to visit
And the foods you used to eat
As you warm your sweaty carcass 'round the fire?

Today won't you consider this
While time is not too late
Sharing things that clutter you
Dividing up estate
Lest you end like this old soul
Complaining to the Lord
And hearing the reply:
It's their turn now!

Is That All You Can Remember?

January 19   *Read Luke 8:1.*

Why do we catalog people? We put them into neat compartments like placing books on bookshelves? We justify why they are presently important by referring to their past. Why can't we just accept one another at face value?

How often have we been tempted to introduce someone, or remember someone by their testimony of deliverance? You know what I mean? "This is the divorcee and mother of two. This one is the former prostitute. And this little lady . . . ." God has thrown the memory of who we once were as far away from us as the east is from the west. We, on the other hand, keep those memories alive.

I'm sure that Mary of Magdala must have felt the same way. Her past shows up more than once in the Gospels. At other points, a kind of biblical shorthand is used—"Mary Magdalene (you know who I mean)."

If Mary could speak to us today, I wonder if she would ask us: "Is that all you can remember about me?" What else is there to remember about this Mary? Well, one important thing shows up in today's passage. She was one of the women who helped support Jesus and the Twelve out of her own means. Jesus remembers that she sacrificed to make sure that his ministry had financial support. "Is that all you can remember about me?"

When brave men fled and left Jesus alone in the Garden of Gethsemane, and devoted male disciples hid behind locked doors, this Mary was one of the women who begged to anoint his body with the customary spices. When Jewish law prevented the completion of their task, she was one who was somehow going to roll the stone away and finish the job. I can hear her speaking to us again: "Is that all you can remember about me?"

What do we remember about the Marys in our communities? Do we remember their pasts or are we celebrating their victories? Do we unconsciously look for signs of regression, or are we thankful for God's blessings in their lives today? Why is their business so important to us?

Jesus explained the motivation to us, those who are forgiven much, love Him a great deal more. Is it our jealousy that causes us to repeatedly bring up their past?

Perhaps this is why, of all the people who could have been chosen, Mary of Magdala was the first human being to tell the world that "He's Alive!"

Prince of Peace

January 20   *Read Isaiah 9:6.*

Nothing had ever seemed to disturb Aunt Hattie, who was now 103. She had seen it all. Her husband died when she was in her thirties, but

Hattie kept on raising her five children like nothing had happened. When one of those children died while he was in his teens, Hattie took herself a reasonable time of mourning. Then, she shook the grief off and went back to raising the rest of them. Over the years she had lost her job, had her house broken into twice, and had survived a tornado! Not one of these had succeeded in wiping the serene smile off her face.

Now, Janna, was looking at Hattie's toothless smile, up close, pleading with her for wisdom. Her youngest boy was in the service. He had been sent to a war zone and Janna was worried sick. She just couldn't find any peace.

With Aunt Hattie, you first had to sit for a while—then ask your questions. (You know how it is when you visit the old folks?) Janna sat on one side of the sun porch while Hattie sat in her favorite overstuffed chair. This chair was faded from both age and sunlight, with carefully starched doilies draped over its arms.

As they sat there in the silence, with Aunt Hattie nodding off from time to time, Janna read the lines on Auntie's countenance. The usual whistle-marks and crow's feet were there, but worry had never found its way to Hattie's face. After one particularly long spell of nodding, Hattie sat up in her chair and opened her eyes as though startled. The half smile on her face, confirmed that Hattie had not intended to nod off on company. She leaned forward as though paying attention to a conversation.

Janna, sensed that this was her cue. "Auntie, my boy is gone away to the Middle East. I hear that war might break out while he's there and it's tearing me up on the inside. . . ." Though she had said it, Janna didn't feel like she had finished it so she just hung there, paused in midconversation, waiting for Hattie's answer.

The few seconds that passed before Hattie's response felt like an eternity to Janna. The large old clock ticked so loudly that she had to look at it. The room had become so still and so silent that it felt like no one was breathing.

Without even looking at Janna, Hattie replied in a slow, contemplative way: "Hmmph. Seem to me like the war done already broke out inside of you. *(Pause)* Thought Jesus was the Prince of Peace." Soon the room was quiet again and Hattie had resumed her intermittent spells of nodding.

They were back to sitting again. Before long, with peaceful tears in her eyes, Janna stood up, tiptoed across the room, and let herself out.

Is Jesus your Prince of Peace?

Trouble Don't Last Always

I wonder if the old folks had this passage in mind when they sang their song? They sang while toiling in the hot southern sun. In church, at home, anywhere, they sang of an experience that was not yet theirs. It takes some vision of the future to declare confidently in word and in song that trouble does not last always. The old folks who sang this song had been in trouble all of their lives. Practically everyone that they knew and loved had been in trouble all of their lives. Where did they get such hope? What must they have seen that inspired them to sing the words: "I'm so glad . . . That trouble don't last always."

Did the people of Zephaniah's village sing a similar song? What was the tune? Zephaniah was a son of Cush, a Black man, and a possible descendant of Hezekiah. These people had also seen trouble for most of their lives. Everyone that they knew had seen trouble for a long time. God, speaking through this ebony prophet, encouraged them to sing as though their sorrows were already ended.

> I'm so glad
> That trouble don't last always.
> Oh my Lord, Oh my Lord, what shall I do?

Today's passage tells us what to do. Sing and shout for the joy that is surely coming. Rejoice and spin around wildly because the Lord has already taken away the judgments against us. Rejoice because enemies are turned away. Give thanks because the Lord is in the midst of us. The day of renewal is coming. The days of loud singing are on the horizon. Above all, do not let your hands grow weak. Deliverance is a promise. Hold on tight, for trouble don't last always.

For Victims of Incest

O God, the night was intended to be a time of rest and restoration. We are aware that, for some of us, the night is filled with fear and uncertainty.

We petition you for the healing of the many sisters who are victims of incest. O God, may our sisters be able to realize your supportive presence as they walk in muzzled silence.

Lord, forgive our part in the conspiracy. The mother who knows, but turns a deaf ear to her daughter's pleas for fear of losing a husband, is as guilty as he. The sister in the next bed or in the next room, who is more afraid of public embarrassment is just as guilty as her brother. The aunt who sees no harm is guilty too. When we accuse the victim of somehow causing an act of violence against her, we are also participants in this horrible crime against women who are often too young to articulate their pain.

Forgive us, Lord, and teach us appropriate, liberating responses so that no woman need ever again fear the night.

Makeover

January 23   *Read Matthew 9:16-17.*

I passed by my favorite makeup counter the other day. They were doing makeovers. I am always tempted to stop and let them do my makeup. I always fear that I do not know how to make myself look good; certainly not like they do. I don't know why I have never let the experts do my face.

Perhaps I worry that they may advise a different color lipstick. I have been wearing the same group of colors for years. On television, when they do a makeover, they advise new hairstyles, new clothes. I don't know if I am ready to give up my old comfortable hairdo. Maybe I really want a new look, while holding on to the old colors, the old ways of doing my eyebrows, the old ways of doing my hair. Do I really *want* a makeover?

In today's passage Jesus is appealing to common sense. They would never dream of patching an old preshrunk garment with new, unshrunk fabric. The first wash would ruin the entire piece! Neither would they ever have thought of pouring bubbly new wine into an old cured wineskin. All of that bouncy activity would split an old wineskin; the wine would run out and the skins would be useless.

So, why is it that we think we can pile the newness of our relationship with God on top of the deadness of a previous lifestyle? It makes no more sense than keeping my old lipstick color or hairstyle in a beauty makeover.

Christ comes into our lives to perform a spiritual makeover. He erases the age lines and we become as newborns. The old folks said, "Looked at my hands and my hands looked new. . . ." God revises every aspect of our appearance. He offers us a new personality, more like His; a new outlook, full of bright optimism; and life that never ends. He cleans the closets of our past and clothes us for the future. Unbelievable results!

Will it hurt? Only if you are one of those who insist upon keeping your old lipstick color!

The Joy of the Lord Is Your Strength

January 24   *Read Nehemiah 8:8-10.*

"Have you ever heard but not understood what you were hearing" the sermon began. "Or, have you ever listened to someone without hearing what they said?"

At that point it felt like a pin pricked Maizie's soul. She had been sitting in church for years, listening without hearing what the preacher had to say. She had been more focused on when to give the announcements, or who was going to shout. "What have I missed?" she asked herself.

"When the people heard the words of the Law," the preacher continued, "they recognized how they had offended God for years without even knowing it."

Hot tears poured from Maizie's eyes. She was sitting in her home church, hearing God's word for the very first time in years. The impact of a lifetime of having been separated from God hit her like a heavy weight.

She looked back at the way she had "religiously" attended church for so many years. She had been a "Sunday's only" Christian. She thought about all of the people who must have known that she was not for real—not until today. "They were nice to me anyway," she sobbed. A new deluge of warm tears made tracks down the side of her face.

During the next half hour of the sermon, Maizie was lost in the past. Old sins paraded across her mind in an ugly procession. "Lord, forgive me," she whispered, "how could you stand me for so many years?" The tears gushed with greater intensity. When she came to herself, she realized that the Reverend Winters was still preaching.

Reverend Winters' once delicate female voice had taken on new intensity. "It's time to stop weeping and stop mourning for the day that you finally heard God has become a holy day. Rejoice, for the joy of the Lord is your strength. . . ."

At this point, Maizie leaped to her feet. "Oh, my God," she thought; "*I* am shouting!" She had sworn that she would never get emotional in church. By this time, however, it was too late to do anything about it. Her feet seemed to sprout wings as the Holy Ghost parted a pathway for her through the people who had been sharing her pew. Before she knew it, she was at the altar, with new strength, spinning and shouting and waving her hands. "Praise God!" "Praise God!" "Praise God!" Amen.

Going Through Changes

January 25   *Read 1 Kings 19:19-21.*

Have you ever felt as if you were going through changes? It is hard to read this passage and not feel some of the changes that Elisha went through. True enough, he received the opportunity of a lifetime—to study under Elijah the prophet. But he also went through some major changes like leaving home and career to walk into uncertainty. To this, we would reply: "Yes, but his change was a change for the better. . . ."

We all know that some kinds of changes are necessary to place us in the will of God. Leaving behind bad habits, thought patterns, sins— these are needed changes. There are, however, some major misunderstandings about the meaning of change.

Change does not always mean new and improved. Where did we get such an idea? On the surface, it seems like such a harmless concept— changing for the better. When we hear those words, it somehow challenges us to see that who we were, or what we were doing was incomplete until this new and improved thing happened.

The phase "changing for the better" sets us up for the sometimes faulty notion that we were not doing our best—until now. Or, even worse, we are lured into believing that we had no hope of pleasing God and being a good person—until now. How could we possibly be fair if we said that Elisha, in today's reading, was not in God's will until Elijah's mantle fell upon him? Perhaps, when the mantle fell upon him, it simply signaled another of God's purposes in his life?

How then can we look at our changes? Perhaps the answer to this question lies in our perceptions of God's purpose for our individual lives. Perhaps it starts when you can answer the following questions: What does God need for me to do in my lifetime? How much does God need for me to accomplish in my lifetime?

Could it be that we are so resistant to change because we somehow mistakenly see ourselves as in charge of life's purpose and direction? Are we resistant to change because we forgot who was steering the boat?

Did you know that you are important to God? You are important because of your unique personality. There is none other exactly like you. You are also important because of your unique purpose. Each of us has a purpose and you are no exception. Only you and God can ever understand your purpose. Others may guess about it. You may even guess about it, but God does have a unique purpose for your life. Sometimes, fulfillment of that unique purpose involves change.

So then change is just change. It does not have to be good or bad. It does not have to be for better or for worse. Change might just be in our lives because God's purpose dictates this change at this time. If there are several divine plans waiting to be completed, there also must, of necessity, be several divine changes. This may even give new definition to the phrase, "going through changes."

Lockjaw!

January 26   *Read Daniel 6:19-23.*

What do you mean, "May your Majesty live forever?" Isn't this the same king that allowed Daniel to be thrown into the den of lions? Instead of giving that king a piece of his mind, Daniel blessed the king: "O King, live forever."

According to Daniel's report, he had been caught in a technicality. Under normal circumstances, the king would never knowingly have done anything to harm him. In fact, when he learned of the miscarriage of justice, he tried every means legally available to change the sentence. The king's hands were tied, and Daniel was thrown into what was possibly the worst situation of his life. But, guess what? The lions must have had lockjaw! Daniel walked away unharmed.

Divine interventions like these are excellent times to glorify God. Yet many of us, when delivered from lions often, choose to steal the spotlight from God by calling attention to human error. We blame the system, we blame our lawyers, we look for scapegoats. In Daniel's case, what good would it possibly have done to bash the king for the tense situation that he had survived? The king was as powerless as Daniel. Because Daniel chose to praise God rather than to critique human inadequacy, we remember the situation more for what God *did* than for what the king *could not* do. Perhaps this is a good day to evaluate our responses to the inevitable miscarriages of justice around us.

The mean-spirited people of this day still throw the innocent to the lions. Every day, someone is falsely accused. You may have been in a similar situation at some point in your life. Those who trust in the Lord will continue to see miracles. When this happens, be sure to give God the praise—and remember, lions can still get lockjaw!

Unpressured Time

January 27   *Read Psalm 42:1.*

Thank God for bathrooms! Bathroom time is unpressured time. It makes room for itself. Little children have to *wait* until mommy comes out of the bathroom. Some young mothers look forward to being able to shut that door and put the world on hold. Phones wait, dishes wait, everything waits.

How ironic that this is a time when God chooses to speak to many of us. "It occurred to me, while sitting on the throne," she said. How many testimonies have you heard, describing how God spoke to a sister while in the bathroom? What is so spiritual about bathrooms?

Perhaps it's not the room but the time. Bathroom time is something that cannot be compromised. We can rush almost anything else, but we cannot rush our "necessary time." The way God seems to speak to so many of us in bathrooms must be an indication that He needs some "necessary time" with us.

We all know that we need to make more time for God. How many times do we wallow in the land of frustration and despair because of runaway schedules and uncontrollable demands? Quiet time with God just does not seem to make room for itself the way bathroom time does. There are too many days when our good intentions do not bear fruit, and once again prayer slowly sinks to the bottom of our to-do list.

Thank God for His grace! When we cannot seem to figure out how to allot enough time with the Lord, God often reaches out to meet with us in the unpressured spaces. God speaks gently on the commuter train. God comforts us in airports and cars. Those spaces of time, when we are seemingly trapped and can do nothing else, become opportunities for divine communion. Ironing boards become altars and bathrooms become gateways to prayer.

Lord, our souls long to meet you whenever and wherever we can. When we cannot seem to control our fast-paced world, and on those days when we have not allotted enough time with you, please continue to reach out and meet us in those unpressured spaces of time.

Playing Sister for the Bill Collector

January 28   *Read Genesis 12:10-13.*

Abraham is not the first man to ask his wife to lie for him. This is an old, old story. The Lord had just blessed him. Of all the people on the earth at that time, Abraham was invited into a relationship with the Almighty. Abraham saw the land of the Canaanites that would eventually belong to his children's children. He built an altar and worshiped the Lord there.

Then came the lie. It was not an accidental-backed-into-the-corner-I-couldn't-see-any-other-way lie; this lie was premeditated. "Sarah, you are so pretty. I could get killed over you. Stretch the truth just a little bit, say that you are my sister so that things might not be so hard on me. You know how hard things are for a Black man trying to make it, baby . . . ?" Can you believe his nerve?

Perhaps it is harder to believe that Sarah, whose name was still Sarai, went along with the lie—twice! She allowed the Pharaoh to believe that she was Abraham's sister; and she allowed Abimelech, king of Gerar, to believe that same lie. Each time she was taken into the household and considered part of the harem, while Abraham received gifts. Each time, the king became aware of his mistake through the misfortune that came.

Why did Sarah allow herself to be used in this way? We could point to the powerlessness of women in that day as an excuse, if some sisters weren't still lying to protect their man. Sisters, what still moves some of us to lie for the men in our lives? Why do some sisters lie to the bill collectors, the police, or even to his other woman for him? What causes us to place our lives, our integrity, and even our relationships with God in jeopardy in this way?

Perhaps, this passage has been preserved as a word of warning for all of us. A lie is a sin no matter who benefits.

The Least of These

January 29   *Read Matthew 25:37.*

"Look at that man. He's eating from the trash can!" Willie Mae didn't know what to do. She was in a large city for a conference, and couldn't understand the concept of hungry people. Back in the country, where she lived, there was always enough for everyone. People in the country traded and shared. A bumper crop of greens meant greens for the entire community. A good year's berries meant everyone could make cobblers and can the excess. How could a man be reduced to eating other people's garbage?

That evening in the hotel, the visual image of that man bent over the trash can would not leave Willie Mae's mind. She was hurt in ways that she could not explain. Her thoughts drifted to her oldest son who had just moved to California to "find himself." She was overcome with grief at the thought that he might ever be in a similar condition.

The next day her mind was far from the business of the conference. Willie Mae had been on the verge of tears all morning. She was relieved when they broke for lunch. As she stared at the attractive china garnished with flowering kale and bearing a croissant sandwich, she could bear it no longer. She headed for the door, carrying the hotel's fancy china with her as she mumbled the words. "It's just not right."

Well, you know where she went. She returned to the alley where she had seen the man eating from the trash can. He was back in his regular spot, looking for something to eat. All of a sudden, it dawned on Willie Mae that she might be in danger. She swallowed the lump in her throat and approached the man, holding the hotel's fancy china plate in her trembling hands.

They just stood there for a time, looking each other in the eyes. As Willie Mae looked into this man's eyes, she saw what could have been her son, her uncle, or her cousin's child. The compassion in her eyes said, "I care about you." The man looked past her manicured appearance and saw in her the people from his old hometown who often wondered what had become of him.

Finally, they both looked at the sandwich and the hotel's fancy china plate. She offered it to him with a look that said, "I wish I could do more." He accepted it with eyes that cried, "Thank you, sister."

Is there anything that you can do for the least of God's children today?

Old Drunk Hannah

January 30   *Read 1 Samuel 1:10-13.*

Does anyone ever bother to ask why some old women who are not drunk stagger? We see them, even consider them odd, but does anyone stop to pray? So many sisters suffer the inconvenient or embarrassing effects of bodily conditions and hardly ever seem to receive the support they need from us.

What happens when diabetes creeps up to the doorstep of an otherwise healthy woman? To whom does she report the resulting robbery? Can she really talk to me? She is condemned to hide the strange odors that come from her mouth, knowing that I may not recognize or appreciate them. I often miss the warning signs. Have I really been my sister's keeper?

When a sister becomes incontinent, who teaches her to ignore the all too familiar rustle of adult diapers? Who encourages her to come to lunch anyway? A chronically ill sister is often left to wonder: "Does anybody care?"

Of course we care! We just don't know what to do. We are afraid for them and for ourselves. We run from our mammograms, and clinisticks, and blood pressure checks because we are afraid that the health robber may creep up to our doorstep too. We are uncomfortable with colostomy bags, and insulin shots, and prosthetic devices.

Our fearful silence renders them taboo. Avoidance transforms them into exiles. Then, we sadly spy on the exiles we have created, fearing that, one day, we may join them.

Lord, what can I do? Can I work around the schedule of a woman on dialysis? Could I sit beside one with cataracts and describe the passersby? Is it possible for me to resist staring at the balding head or the empty chest so that she and I might share life on that day? Teach me Lord to see beyond the body's shell.

Lord, teach us to support one another. Help us to learn how to care for our sisters with chronic diseases. Let intentionality and awareness flower into new liberty for them and for us. Set our captive sisters free!

The Missing Link

January 31   *Read 1 Corinthians 12:4-7.*

Eva never could get it into her head that all Christians had gifts. She would look at the singers and wish that she could sing. She would look at the shouters and secretly wish that she could shout. She was too shy to try to usher, and she had never quite figured out how to work with some of the ladies in the kitchen crew. Witnessing on first Saturday's was absolutely out of the question. So, when she'd go through her list of church gifts, as she periodically did, she'd sigh and tell herself that she was the one person in church without spiritual gifts.

This thing was a sore spot with her. She felt like she was dead weight and didn't really do the church much good. She couldn't even give good money she thought—after her husband died she was on a pension. Dutifully, she would scrape a few quarters together to give in the mission offering. Each week, she would drive home, in her old struggle buggy wishing that there was more that she could do for the Lord.

One day, the new minister came to her with an idea. "Eva," he said, "my wife and I are about to have a new baby. Would it be a big inconvenience to ask you to turn on the heat on Sunday mornings before Sunday school?" Eva's heart leaped with joy. "Yes, of course, I'll be glad to."

Before long, as usual, Eva was going down her list of missing church gifts again. As usual, she came to the same old conclusion: "I'm the only one in the church without a spiritual gift." In the meantime, she was faithful to turn on the heat on rainy days, on snowy days, or on days when the building just had a slight chill.

Then, one day, the inevitable happened. Eva caught the flu and couldn't do her job. She called Sarah, who was too busy with small children to make it there ahead of time. She called Jeffrey, whose car wouldn't start that morning. She called Louise, who hesitated too long before she answered. It wasn't until she had made six more futile phone calls that she realized how important it had been to the church for her to arrive early and turn on the heat. "Maybe I do have a gift after all!" she thought.

One hundred and three cold worshipers definitely thought so as they struggled to keep their minds on singing and praying. Needless to say, church was over an hour earlier that day.

February

A Field of Hope

February 1   *Read Job 13:15.*

There is a desecrated graveyard in New York. It was discovered, purely
by accident, as humankind was expanding its building project. As far as
people have determined, it contained the bodies of countless slaves that
were buried during the time of slavery.

Archaeologists of color have flown in from all over the country. They
are carefully removing the remains of each body. The artifacts buried
with those bodies are being contemplated. They are studying the bones
and trying to make sense of the lives that are represented in this field of
hope.

Most people don't think of a cemetery as a field of hope; but I suspect
that for these slaves it was a place full of hope. The songs that they
sang indicate that the grave was their only place of hope. You see, they
felt that going home was either back on the boats that brought them
here or back through the grave. Either way, they had hopes of going
home.

Job, when his life all of a sudden did not make sense, continued to
hope in God. The entire story revolves around the fact that righteous
Job continued to hold on, in faith, in spite of what happened to him.
Those bones of our ancestors also continue to speak of hope. Those
who hoped to go home, one way or another, perhaps only hoped that
we would be free. Now, here we are finding their bones and contemplating their lives.

When we rebury them, in a new field of hope, what will we use to
mark their graves? We don't know their names. We only guess at their
stories. All we know today is that they believed in God in spite of their
harsh reality.

Today, I mark their graves, in my mind, with the words: "Though he
slay me, yet will I trust in him."

Africans in the Church

You were there from the very beginning—worshiping in Jerusalem as the Jews do. You were there hungering to hear about Jesus, along with everyone else. You had come and gone, as you had always done, still not fully understanding what you heard. Is the prophet talking about himself or about someone else? No one had known how to interpret what he said. But, you were there, trying to understand the Bible, hoping for someone to explain it to you, Ethiopian brother of mine.

You were a dignified man, tending to your queen's treasury back in the time when African queens like Sheba ruled with diligence. Your queen trusted you to go and see about your religion and you came back with revelation to share with all.

The news of Jesus made it to Africa quite early, you see. You were one of the first African missionaries to Africa. Others had gone to Egypt and Libya near Cyrene (Acts 2:10); but you were going to your home to tell the news.

God heard your cries for understanding. Many more people would be in the church if they could just understand. America is full of people who have heard the good news. Practically everyone here has heard about Jesus, yet few understand. God wanted you to understand, Ethiopian brother of mine, kissed by the sun of Africa. He sent a young prophet on the run to open your eyes.

That same God provided water for your baptism in the desert. There in the presence of your driver, and Philip, and heaven itself, you sealed your covenant with Him. You testified by your baptism that Jesus had truly come into your life. Then you went home burning to tell the news. Quite early, there were Africans in the church.

I Love You . . .

We live in a world filled with uncertainties. We are not sure of the economy. We are not sure of the government or the government of other countries. We also are not sure of ourselves. So much of what we hear about us is negative. Is there anything good about me? The deafening silent response creates overwhelming feelings of insecurity. These insecurities cause us to worry about the ways that others secretly regard us. Insecurity breeds more worry and more worry breeds more insecurity—a vicious cycle.

In human relationships, insecurity causes us to do things to somehow compensate for the reasons that we feel people should not want to be around us. We make ourselves indispensable so that we can feel needed. We try to supply others with reasons to love us.

Moses addressed Israel's insecurity in Deuteronomy 7:7-8. He reminded his peers that they had no special merit that commended them to God. They were not a large powerful nation with which anyone would have been delighted to be associated. Quite the contrary, Israel was a small and seemingly powerless country. God simply chose them because of His love.

Most of us feel small and powerless. Whether we are heads of corporations or janitors, we often feel that we have to be phenomenally good and efficient in order to justify our position. Like Israel, we feel that we must point to some status symbol or achievement in order to earn love and positive regard. The phrase "I love you because . . ." strengthens our insecurities because we often translate that to mean if we cease to be a good cook or a good provider, or an available listener, or a good anything, somehow the very foundation of our relationships will be shattered. We have a hard time with unconditional love.

God's love is unconditional. God speaks to us today in the same way He spoke to Israel. He did not say that He loves us because we are great and prestigious. Accomplishments and merit are not the basis of God's love. God does not love us because of our phenomenal giftings. God does not love us because of a flawless past. God does not say I love you because . . . . God just says I love you. UNCONDITIONALLY!

Belongingness

February 4   *Read John 15:19.*

One of humanity's basic needs is to feel like we belong somewhere. For people without a country, and often without a community, this need becomes intense. There are so many places where we feel uncomfortable. Where do we belong?

Perhaps, this issue of belonging is part of what troubles us about a shaky marriage or a family in crisis. When personal relationships are fractured, where do we belong? This might also be one of the strong motivating factors that drives us to join all kinds of groups. We need to belong.

African scholar John Mbiti is known for the quote, "I am, because we are; and since we are, therefore I am." This points to the fact that people of African descent are known for their need for one another. Without the quotation, most African-Americans know how important it is to belong somewhere. Remember the ritual ways that our ancestors once introduced themselves to others? "I am So and So and I belong to. . . ." With the rapid disintegration of so many African-American communities, where, now, can we find a place to belong?

Ultimately, we all belong to God. As members of God's family, the Bible teaches us that we will be isolated from and in tension with much of the world's system. When those times inevitably come, do not lose sight of the fact that the community of faith is a place where we can all belong. This faith community consists of an intricate web of people with whom we can share our lives. We are all connected to one another and to God through Christ. Perhaps in time, God will use some of us to transform the African-American community into another place to belong. Who knows, God might eventually use us to rebuild the world community.

Until then, are you feeling connected with others? Where do you belong? It is not good for any of us to be alone. Today, why not ask the Lord to show you a safe and comfortable place to just be.

Memorials and Monuments

February 5   *Read Joshua 4:1-7.*

The Lord did not want them to forget. Joshua commanded the soldiers with him to build a monument. It commemorated the way that God parted the waters of the Jordan River the same way God had parted the Red Sea. Once again, the people passed through on dry land.

Monuments are important. One obvious function of monuments and memorials is to remind us of past moments of glory. This particular monument was to remind Israel of God's supernatural intervention. When times are rough, we need the memory of those glory days of the past to propel us into the future.

Monuments have another function. They are strategic markers that keep us from turning back. They remind us where we have been. Israel's soldiers would have to look at this particular monument on the way back to the wilderness if they decided to turn back. Monuments can commemorate both good events and bad events. Both kinds are important.

Some years ago, I had the privilege of visiting one of the concentration camps in Germany. I saw a monument of some places where humankind has been. Though World War II was over more than thirty years before this visit, the smell of charred human bodies still filled the buildings. We looked at the pictures of Hitler's experiments; we saw vivid pictures of the human incinerators. I'll never be able to erase the sights and sounds of the BBC film that showed a mangle of bodies that looked like a grotesque bone pile. Outside the main building, which had become a museum, stood a thirty-foot wrought iron statue of that mangle of bones. They looked like something from Ezekiel's valley of dry bones. They were not connected to one another, just horribly piled together. Underneath the wrought iron sculpture was a sign, written in several languages, for all the world to read: "Lest We Forget."

Human beings have come from some horrible places. You and I have come from some horrible places. Sometimes looking backward is healthy. Lest we, too, forget.

Race Matters

Read John 4:3-9.

Racial problems are at least as old as the Bible. The Jews felt that they were God's chosen people. They were proud to be a pure race; they had not intermarried with other nations. They thought of intermarriage as sin. At one time they were in exile. Away from their land, their temple, and many of their kin, some of them broke the taboo and intermarried with the groups of people among whom they lived. When the time of exile ended, these racially diverse Jews were considered inferior. They called them Samaritans, and they lived in a different section of the nation of Israel.

It almost sounds like an allegory for America's racial climate, except this feud with the Samaritans really is part of Israel's history. The Samaritans never lost their stigma. Their ghetto was named Samaria and the Jews not only avoided their territory after dark, they also often refused to go through Samaria unless it was an emergency! The normal detours between Judea and Galilee could have added from twenty-five to forty miles to an already tedious journey. Jesus chose to go through Samaria.

How shall we interpret verse 4: "But he had to go through Samaria"? Imagine how the disciples, who were not necessarily inclusive, might have shared this information. How did the folks back home in Galilee look at his going through Samaria? The important point is that Jesus was not worried about popular biases; he went through Samaria. He was not bound by partiality; he had work to do there on his way home. There were souls to save, and a particular conversation was scheduled at Jacob's well with a woman there.

Jesus chose to cross racial boundaries frequently in his ministry. He went to Samaria because the people there needed Him as much as anyone else. For Jesus, race did not matter.

Prayer: Lord, deliver me from the sin of partiality. Amen.

Songbird

Songs are powerful. They reflect our innermost thoughts. We learn a great deal about people by listening to the songs they sing. If you listen carefully, you can hear familiar refrains from the television programs and commercial advertisements that impact some folks. Fast food, soap operas, airlines, and sitcoms; you may hear them on the bus or in a grocery line. What kinds of songs are you singing these days?

Songs also reflect moods. Those acquainted with heartache will help you sing your somebody-done-you-wrong song. Love songs are hummed by lovers, or those who want to be loved. National hymns are sung by misty-eyed patriots. There is so much to hear in a song.

The protest songs of the sixties and the liberation songs of the Civil Rights movement revealed the heart pangs of those who longed for liberty. "Ain't Gonna Let Nobody Turn Me 'Round" and "We Shall Overcome" rang like battle cries for nonviolent warriors. Even today, when the old soldiers gather, throats get lumpy and tears begin to roll when those songs are sung.

What then is a song? Is it a wandering piece of soul? It seems as though the essence of our being walks around the room when we sing some songs. A mirror? A song reflects our mood and tells on us; it shows people what's inside when we don't want to talk. A barometer? Yes, a song can be a barometer. Fight songs work us into a frenzy, while peace songs calm the soul. What's your favorite song?

The psalmist knew the power of song. Today, the psalmist encourages us to sing a *new* song—to the Lord! Perhaps the Lord has only heard our songs of complaint; headache, heartaches, back-broke-under-the-load aches. It could be that our songs only report the news; he said, she said, look-what-they-did-to-me, I said. Examine the content of the songs you sing. It could be time to change your tune!

Got What You Wanted?

February 8   *Read Numbers 11:18-20.*

Dr. Jawanza Kunjufu, well-known educator and Christian teacher, once gave this assignment to his students: What was the year that we, as African-Americans, got what we wanted and lost what we had? I was one of those students and it was not the first time that I had heard that phrase. Quite often I had heard "the old folks," as we call them, try to stop us from making foolish decisions by the use of this proverb.

Israel also knew the meaning of this African-American proverb. While in the wilderness, they began to complain to God about not having meat. They had manna but they didn't have meat. Well, these people grumbled and complained to Moses again and again. He took their complaint to God. The results were tragic. Quail came, and the people ate themselves silly! Then, they died because they got what they wanted and lost what they had!

Returning to Dr. Jawanza Kunjufu's question: Did we get what we wanted and then lose what we had? You decide. We got desegregated schools, and lost extracurricular activities that had been safety zones, free of the pervasive pressures of racism. We lost some of the extras that gave our youth self-worth and a sense of accomplishment. We lost teachers who lived with us and knew us well enough to treat our children as their own. We gained the right to frequent any business establishment, and lost a multitude of Black restaurants and retail stores.

Friends, how will we ever return those things to our children that were lost in a necessary struggle? How will we provide avenues for youth self-esteem and the much needed sense of accomplishment?

Life often feels like a series of compromises. Every major victory has its cost. But, can we not regain *some* of what we once had?

Finding Faith

February 9   *Read Luke 18:1-8.*

Can't you see her? She is wearing an old, outdated wig and overcoat. It has been a long time since her youth flowered; the petals have fallen to the floor unnoticed. Here she is, seasoned for the battle by the denials and the disappointments of the past. Persistent! Not brash, not impolite, just persistent. Again and again persistent. I'll be here again tomorrow, persistent. She achieves her goal because the judge knows that if he doesn't give in, she will never give up.

That woman has been around a long time. Society calls her persistent and pesky, but Jesus calls it faith. Others might have thought that she was wasting her time because she kept petitioning a judge who didn't fear God or public opinion. The widow didn't care. She didn't care if he was the hanging judge, or the racist judge, or the incompetent judge, or the idiot who came to office because no one else was available judge. He was the judge; and she was going to have justice—even if she had to show up again, and again, and again!

She didn't care what others thought of the judge, nor did she care what bystanders thought of her. She needed something. Her resources were few. She had no choice but to hold out in faith for what she needed.

Are there ever days when you need something and your resources are few? You may not be a widow; you could be any of a number of women with limited resources. Perhaps you have no other choices. God's message for you today is: Persist!

It takes faith to keep on keeping on. How did the widow keep the faith? Certainly she encountered the inevitable rejection and ridicule that we fear so much. What motivated her to persevere? The widow was moved by what she knew without question. She did not seem to care to know the judge, or to know the system, she already knew God. She knew, instinctively, that God always sides with the righteous. She found faith to persevere because she was sure of God who is faithful.

God continues to side with the righteous. God is faithful and God's will eventually prevails. It does not take an old woman to grasp that truth. Hang in there!

Do It Yourself

February 10   *Read Proverbs 6:6-8.*

Some of us feed the squirrels or the birds in the wintertime, but who feeds the ants? Without a taskmaster to crack the whip, or a supervisor to direct them, ants manage to take care of their needs year-round.

By contrast, when we feed certain animals for too long, they forget how to care for themselves. Domesticated animals have difficulty when placed back in their natural environment. Some birds, that become accustomed to the kind souls who feed them, forget to fly to warmer climates. Even the ants, given the opportunity, would probably learn to let someone else take care of them.

Since the Emancipation, we have collectively struggled with issues that revolve around self-care. Slavery was a disruptive institution that interrupted some of the normal ways that we responded to basic human needs. We cannot, however, allow the past to paralyze us. Together, we can make better provisions for our elderly and our poor. Together, we can educate our children, supplementing what we complain that they lack in modern school systems. Together, we can create jobs for the jobless in our communities. Together, we can house our homeless. Now is the time to rise and relearn the ways that God intended for us to care for ourselves—in community!

An old community proverb reminds us that God helps those who help themselves. There comes a time when all of us, from birds to people, must employ the means of self-perpetuation that God has given us. There are just some things that we should be doing for ourselves.

Malcolm, Martin, Mandela, and Me

February 11   *Read Exodus 3:15.*

When Israel heard the familiar refrain, "the God of Abraham, the God of Isaac, and the God of Jacob," they were reminded of the original covenanted agreement that Abraham entered into with God. In exchange for Abraham's obedience, God promised to make him a great nation (Gen. 12:1-3). God promised Abraham that his offspring would be numerous, and that all of the earth's families would be blessed through his family (Gen. 22:18). His son Isaac inherited these promises, as did his grandson, Jacob. Individuals in Israel were reminded that they, as descendants of Abraham, were also heir to the tremendous promises that had been made to their ancestors. Every time they heard the names Abraham, Isaac, and Jacob, they were reminded, male and female alike, that they were standing in line to receive long-awaited blessings.

Corretta, Winnie, Betty Shabazz, wives of martyrs living and dead; these three women are historical reminders of recent struggles, sacrifices, and victories. These names represent a dramatic change in human history. Annelle Ponder, Dolly Raines, and Fannie Lou Hammer were great contemporary women engaged in the struggle for civil rights. African-American women all over American continue to reap the benefits of their faithful stance. We African-American women have our own reminders.

Our history with God goes beyond the mention of a few names. There are hundreds of names that serve as reminders of God's promises, some not so famous. Add your own names to that list; perhaps a noble great-grandmother or aunt who taught you to love God and value freedom. You have a history book inside of you. Keep these memories alive and close to your heart. Place them on display in the galleries of your mind like ancient heirlooms; they are reminders that we are heirs to God's promises.

Some time ago, I saw a T-shirt that read, "Malcolm, Martin, Mandela and Me." It reminded me that in the African-American community, as in Israel, God is remembered from generation to generation.

Affirmative Advocate

February 12   *Read Psalm 72:11-14.*

Long ago, in the days of affirmative action, you were a double minority —Black and female. The presupposition was that both women and African-Americans had no one to advocate for them. For most of us, this was true. Did you find yourself boasting, unconsciously, that you had a greater chance of getting a good job, even more than a Black man because you were a double minority?

During those days, were you a single parent, another minority? On a first-name basis with poverty, did you feel weak, defenseless, and needy? So many Black female single parents worked for minimum wage, some while attending school, thankful that each day had an end. Affirmative action was king. He was our friend, he championed our cause. Who will be our champion as affirmative action wanes?

Did we forget that Jesus was our Advocate before affirmative action every appeared? He continues to be the King of kings and the Lord of all lords. The psalmist today reminds us that all of the nations will heed him. What kind of advocate might he be?

Our Advocate hates violence; that means violence on the streets as well as domestic violence. Our blood is precious in his sight. He is a champion for the defenseless and the needy. Jesus also hates oppression. Oppression comes from many places. Everyone knows that government and systems unwittingly birth oppression. However, we also create just as much oppression within our communities and within ourselves. God is against all forms of human oppression. We have an Advocate who cares about the totality of our being.

The King, our Advocate, has never been powerless. One day, Jesus will transform human history in such a way that he will cause affirmative action to look like a bandage!

Light of the World

February 13   *Read Matthew 5:14.*

This little light of mine,
I'm goin'a let it shine.

Just how *little* is that little light of yours? Jesus compares it to a light capable of providing illumination for the city. Sounds like a big light to me. Just how *big* is your light?

That light of yours, little as it may have seemed to you, can challenge the darkness of an entire city. Just like salt, referred to in the verses prior to this one, what seems like a little can go a long way. In a dark cave, even a match is startling. In similar ways, your light is striking, notice-able, and life changing. Just how big is your little light?

My God gave it to me,
I'm goin'a let it shine.

That light of yours came directly from God. Jesus is the Light. He placed his light in you so that others might find him. That's why your light shining among men and women has the ability to point the way to Christ. What an awesome light you have!

Jesus gave you His light, so that you could light up things for Him in this dark old world. That light is precious. That light is godly. Shine light. Shine.

Won't hide it under a bushel basket,
I'm goin'a let it shine.

Just why would anyone put a light under a bowl? Some scholars say that the bowl or the basket was used as a candle-snuffer. This meant that a light under the basket or bowl was destined to go out! The obvious lesson here is that your light will go out if you don't shine! You are inef-fective unless you choose to shine. That light was only given for one pur-pose—to shine!

I won't let Satan blow it out,
I'm goin'a let it shine.
Won't let Satan blow it out,

I'm goin'a let it shine.
Won't let Satan blow it out,
I'm goin'a let it shine.
Let it shine, let it shine, let it shine!

God Is Love

February 14   *Read 1 John 4:7-9.*

"Fold your hands, Baby. No, can't touch your food yet; we got to give thanks. Fold your hands, close your eyes, repeat after me: 'God is Love.' "

"God is love."

"Look at how that child smiles when she says God is Love. You think she understands yet?"

"No, Lucille, but one day she will. You starting her out right."

"Baby Girl, if I don't get you to understand nothing else about the Lord, understand that He is love. He loved you enough to make you, pretty girl. All of God's girls is pretty; don't let nobody tell you nothing otherwise. Now smile and say it again nice and loud: 'God is Love.' "

"God is love!"

"There you go, Baby Girl! He loved you enough to give you a mama that loves you and a big mama, and a brother, and a daddy. He didn't want you to get scared at night because you was alone. He put you in a warm house with no holes and no big mice! God is Love!"

"God is love!"

"Look a there, I didn't even have to tell her to say it this time. You sure she don't understand yet?"

"I don't know Lucille . . . ."

"Baby Girl, I know you don't understand this yet, but one day you are probably going to do something wrong. Don't feel bad about it because we all do. You'll know it when I spank them little fat legs and say no-no. That's called sin—when you do something wrong, especially after you know better. But, you know how much God loves you, Pretty Girl? He love you enough to send his little boy and trade him for you. He let hisn die so you could live. Now say it again with me, Baby Girl, 'GOD IS LOVE!' "

God is love.

Give Me Your Heart

February 15   *Read Proverbs 23:26.*

Take my hand, child of my village. Follow me through the paths that have been carved through the thickets. Look at the well-worn soil and know that the paths that brought me to this place will also take you to your destination. Observe the travelers who diligently put one foot in front of the other. Look at the calluses on their feet. Look at the feet that know the way home.

Give me your ear, child of my village. Listen to the stories of how we arrived. Some on boats, some in baskets, others carrying brown paper sacks. We were determined to get there. Hear how we arrived. Listen to the songs of freedom and gladness. Hear the moaning in the brush arbors. Let your ears mark the cadence of clapping. Listen to the stories that describe the journey home.

Here, look through my glasses, child of my village. Clean off the dust spots and see what I see. See my perspective, study my rule book, read from my Bible so worn and so true. Look at the warrior women that others cannot see. When you look through my bifocals you can see Ida and Mary and Nanny and Anna are over there too. Look at those angels who they stand guard over you. Now, look closely for the road that will lead the way home.

Give me your heart, child of my village. Place your heart next to mine while the beats find their synchrony. Remember your mama's heartbeats, the first you could hear? Today, let our hearts beat together like drumbeats that scare away fear. Come close to my heart and hear about Jesus. Come closer and feel the Spirit of God. Stay close to my heart, child of the village. I have much left to teach you before you go home.

A Living Heritage

February 16   *Read Psalm 23:1-6.*

When I was in the fifth grade, long before prayer and Bible readings were banned from the public schools, I had a teacher named Miss Johnnie

Mae. She was a devout Christian woman who taught all the usual subjects—and required memorization. We memorized bits and snatches of
the great poems of the world including some of the Psalm.

Of course, my fifth grade mind-set thought that all of this was quite
unnecessary. I did, however, find quite a sense of accomplishment in
mastering pieces like Psalm 100, and Psalm 23. I still remember struggling with the King James Versions *maketh, leadeth,* and *taketh.* I was
too young to really understand what those words meant, but a sense of
peace filled my young soul when they were repeated.

At this time of my life, my family was unchurched. Somehow, in
memorizing several of the great landmarks of Christian worship, I felt
closer to God. As I matured I forgot the great poems of English literature,
but I never forgot those psalms.

There were a few years between the fifth grade and age twenty-
eight—the year of my conversion. In that space of time, memories of
those homeroom devotions ran periodically across my mind. In times of
adversity, I was reminded that, "He leadeth me. . . ." In times of weariness of stress I am still reminded that, "He restoreth my soul." In times
of insecurity, I am reminded that, "We are his people, and the sheep of
his pasture" (Ps. 100).

My memories, like many of yours, are sprinkled with the pain of the
sixties unrest and the tension of the Civil Rights movement. But I am
also nurtured and comforted by the beloved texts of the church.

I confess, sadly, that I have forgotten the last name of my fifth grade
homeroom teacher. I have forgotten the other literature that we memorized in grade school. The Psalms, however, are a living part of my Christian heritage. Through these I am reminded that the Bible is a living doc-
ument, lovingly transmitted to us through the ages. I am reminded that
it is the ever-spoken word of our living Lord.

Wet Feet

February 17   *Read Joshua 3:14-17.*

This river was no mere trickle. The Jordan River, possibly at flood-
stage, stood between the Israelites and the promised land. A strange

thing happened on the day that they crossed over. As soon as the priests got their feet wet, the waters of the Jordan parted and the entire nation crossed the Jordan on dry ground.

We've also had rivers that separated us from the promised land. Wide formidable rivers stopped passage from slavery to enfranchisement. A strange thing also happened to us. We have crossed over some parts of our Jordan on dry ground while some of the priests got their feet wet.

Those priests were untold hundreds of preachers and teachers, nurses and garbage collectors, domestics and unemployed, women, men, and even children. They were people who heard God's call to do something about the plague that hindered all of us. They got their feet wet, sometimes in their own blood.

We have only crossed over parts of the Jordan. There are many areas where formidable rivers of racism, sexism, and classism divide us from God's promises. In the distance, I hear God calling for His priests to be the first ones to challenge the waters. Listen carefully; the Lord may be calling you to get your feet wet this time!

Old Time Religion

February 18   *Read Acts 2:42.*

The new converts practiced, what we would call old time religion. It occurred to me that I need some more religion. In all the confusion over the differences between religion and Christianity, and religion and spirituality, I had allowed religion to become the bad guy. Those ritual observances called religion, that are often mistaken for spirituality or Christianity, are a necessary part of our faith life. We also need religion.

This revelation came to me while reviewing an assignment that I had given to my religion class. I asked them, at the beginning of the semester, "What is religion?" Toward the end of the semester, I was combing through those short essays looking for signs of growth. While the majority of them had done the expected and anticipated thing—confuse Christianity or personal spirituality with religion, others had defined religion as a set of ritual observances that reflect faith. Their definitions made me long for more regular religious observances.

Among their short papers, I found my own personal hunger for religion.

I hunger for more of the regular spiritual rituals that are reflective of my faith. My soul hungers for a morning signal. The toothbrush and washcloth tell my sleepy body when to start the day. What prompts my spirit to pray? How does a soul that feels hungry all the time know when to expect nourishment? My spirit yearns for some tangible way to know when to break into spontaneous praise. I need holy habits—I need an old-time religion.

Many of us have forgotten how to physically kneel in prayer. Yet, many of our fondest memories are of mothers and grandmothers kneeling on splintery floors. The childlike list of people for God to bless is often replaced by the sophistication of modern or meaningless prayer techniques heard on our favorite evangelistic channel. Where are the rituals of old?

Rituals help to bring order to chaotic lives. They provide meaningful ways to make sense from nonsense and quiet a troubled spirit. On days that life seems out of control, they provide a familiar point of connection with the Ground of all Being. We all need more rituals in our lives.

The older I get, the more the old songs make sense, perhaps they too have become a part of my rituals.

> It was good for my old mother
> It was good for my old mother
> It was good for my old mother
> And, it's good enough for me.

Passionate People!

February 19   *Read 2 Samuel 6:12.*

David was a passionate man. Everything he did was with fervor. He slew Goliath because of a passion he had to visit his brothers on the battlefield. He was too young for war, but he had an intense love for Israel that caused him to step forward when men cowered.

David loved his best friend, Jonathan, deeply; not in an inordinate way, just deeply. He fell madly in love with Bathsheba; enough to risk his relationship with Israel and with God, enough to kill her husband. David was a man that could do nothing without passion. In this context, it seems most natural to see him leaping and dancing in what was the equivalent of his underwear when the Ark of the Covenant, which represented the presence of God, was brought home.

African-Americans are also a passionate people. What happens at family reunions and gatherings? Some are partying, some playing cards, some talking loudly, others are eating. Children are playing, old men telling tall tales, women exchange recipes while music gets ignored in the background! Wedding receptions are a beehive of activity and funeral luncheons are times of exuberant affirmation. Plus, don't be at a house party on a Friday night when someone calls a six no trump!

This just goes to reinforce the truth that it is most natural for us as African-Americans to approach our relationship with God with vitality. If we love God at all, it will probably be with the same intensity that we love one another. Some of us must search the Scriptures fervently, sing spiritedly in the choir, and pray until both heaven and earth are shaken. Some preachers have no choice but to preach until hell is disturbed, with us helping him or her along the way. Some of us must dance before the Lord, as David danced, publicly and shamelessly, until yokes are broken or victory fully celebrated. To insist that we sit still and worship quietly would be like rubbing the spots off a leopard—painful and futile!

Grandma's Bones

February 20   *Read Genesis 50:24-26.*

Such a long way from home! Joseph had learned to make the best of what could have been an unredeemable situation. God had taken him from the prison to the palace, yet something in him still longed for home—a home that he would never see. The Bible tells us that one day, hundreds of years later, the Israelites were able to honor their promise to him. Someone along the way felt obligated to remember Joseph's dream of going home. I can imagine the musings of their promise to Joseph while bitterly oppressed in hard forced labor. Maybe thoughts of keeping that promise kept them going. Eventually, they were able to take his bones to a home that he had never known.

Joseph was not the only person to die with unfulfilled dreams. When we think of Joseph's bones lying in Egypt for hundreds of years we must wonder about other bones and other dreams waiting for fulfillment. What bonelike dreams are you aware of? Perhaps your grandmother would have simply loved to drive—alone? Maybe your great-grandmother dreamed of freedom? Some simply dreamed of going home.

This passage inspires thoughts about homes that we have been unable to know, unfulfilled dreams, and delayed answers to prayer. So many of our mothers and grandmothers left their bones for us to bury at home. Are we, like Israel, obligated to our ancestors? We understand the concept of being obligated to the next generation. Somewhere, an African proverb reminds us to be careful with the earth because it is not inherited from our mothers but borrowed from our children. Popular thought reminds us to work toward a better world for our children. We spend a lot of energy preparing for the unborn—but, what of our ancestors?

We have stopped tending graves and sheltering dreams. We have forgotten what we owe but we carry our ancestors inside of us. We carry their hopes and dreams and unanswered prayers. Some of their prayers will never be answered because we are unwilling to suffer just a little while longer. Some dreams will die because we refuse to dream with them. Who will bury their bones at home?

Their dreams were given to me as part of my inheritance. I dutifully carry them into the future. Let me wrap them carefully in kente and give as many of them as I can to my sons and their wives and to their children not yet conceived. As I pack for my missionary term to Africa, I am reminded of dreams that ought not die.

I carry the ancestors inside of me,
   they are going home to Ghana.
Mama's pots, Grandma's shawl, Great-grandma's crystal
     packed and ready.
   I carry them with me in my being.
  Great-grandma's sense of community is going home,
Grandma's dream of touching African soil is going home.
Mama's misty-eyed thoughts about an all-Black country go to
     Africa with me.

I carry the souls of *my* Black folks inside of me. I must share them with the ones to come in hope that one day someone will take my pots, and hankies, and butterfly-dreams to a home that I have never known.

Window to the Sky

February 21   *Read Isaiah 42:5-9.*

Who knows what they thought about as they looked at that small opening in the sky? The tour guide had taken us into the woman's dungeon. The musty room still smelled of human excrement. We could feel the anguish of those who had been held there—waiting for the room to fill up so that they could be taken to the Americas.

As a woman of African descent, born in America, I thought I was well aware of the horrors and injustices of the "peculiar institution," as scholars have called it. Visiting the slave castle in Cape Coast, Ghana, was like discovering slavery for the first time.

My legs grew weak as we walked from room to room and heard descriptions of the slaves, conditions. The trenches in the floor that served as an inadequate latrine, the closeness of the quarters, the governor's quarters, in sight of the women's quarters with a convenient staircase leading to his bedroom, all contributed to the knot that rose in my stomach.

Then, there was this window aimed at the sky in the woman's quarters. It provided the room's only visible source of light and ventilation for the three hundred women who waited for the boats to come. It was so high. If several women had stood on one another's shoulders, they still could not have reached this window. It looked so small that none but a small child could have squeezed through.

The knot in my stomach gave birth to a deluge of uncontrollable tears as I began to wonder what my grandmothers must have thought as they looked at this window to the sky. Its rays of light must have reminded them that daylight was somewhere in the world. The rain that must have at one time or another fallen through this window must have been a reminder that all of creation was not out of control. Somehow, the hope of a coming deliverer must have wafted through this window to the sky.

There are many modern dungeons and many prisoners. And, thank

God, there are yet many windows with a sky view, reminding us that prisoners will be set free.

The Feeling Is Mutual

February 22   *Read Isaiah 35:1-4.*

We are responsible for one another. We've known this ever since Cain asked, "Am I my brothers' keeper?" We are our sisters' keeper and we are answerable, in some ways, to God for our sisters' well-being.

Isaiah refers to this kind of mutual responsibility when he foretells the future of Israel. They would not always be a wasteland; they were destined to become an Eden. In the process of waiting, some had become weak and feeble; their hands were weak, their knees wobbly. Some were just about to lose their grip. "Talk them through their fears," Isaiah encouraged. Remind them that God, their inner strength is, coming to save them. They were mutually obligated to keep one another encouraged while waiting.

Times are no different. Some sisters seem to live from one trial to another. Be encouraged; the lives that we lead will not always resemble wastelands. During long sieges of pain, some people forget that help is on the way. We are all waiting through this siege together; take responsibility for encouraging someone today.

So, how shall we strengthen one another? Encouragement takes so many forms. For some, a phone call will do. Others may just need a sympathetic ear. Another sister may need a few hours of your time every now and then. Some may need bandages and a word of reassurance. Then again, some dear sister may just need to see your smile, from a distance.

Cloud of Witnesses

February 23   *Read Hebrews 12:1-2.*

We know that we are not alone in this world. We live in community with all that God has created. We are surrounded by soil, water, sky, plants, bugs, and beasts. These are but a portion of creation that we can see. We are also surrounded, the writer to the Hebrews reminds us, by a great cloud of unseen witnesses.

Who are these witnesses? Long before Christianity came to the West African world, our ancestors recognized the cloud of witnesses. They are a natural part of our culture. Our lives are enriched by consciousness of the elders, those the West Africans call the living dead and the ancestors.

Our elders are precious to us. Maya and Mari, Angela and Alice, Big Mama and Aunt Betty Jean, all are important in encouraging us to be. They came to be our elders by virtue of the impact the sum total of their lives makes upon our human existence. Our lives are changed forever because of the insults they endure, the banners they raise, the splash they make in the pool of life.

For the West African, the living dead, those who have died in recent memory, are still remembered in the community. Their lives continue to inspire the living. We, African-Americans, are no different. We call Jareena's name as though she were still here. We quote Sojourner's truth as our own and great-grandmomma's shout is rehearsed in the secrecy of the children's bedrooms.

Some of us only dream about the ancestors. We imagine what our African foreparents must have been like. As we look at today's Native Americans, we can only attempt to imagine the Native Americans of the past, who often shared their teepees with our African mothers and embraced our African fathers as brothers. We look further to see the pyramids and the ancient empires of Ghana, Mali, and Songhai. Looking even further into the past, we see glimpses of the Africa that provided refuge for Joseph and the Christ Child, or for Joseph and his brothers. The dead are not sleeping; they are very much alive in our midst.

There is life on the other side of death. God is a God of the living, not the dead. The cloud of our ancestors' witness is here surrounding us. It continues to whisper God's wisdom to our open ears.

Don't Be Ashamed

February 24   *Read Psalm 71:1-6.*

I am so glad that the psalmist chose to pray about shame. Shame is almost a taboo concept in American culture. We are also quickly losing shame in African-American culture. Yet over the years, shame has been powerful and influential in preserving the morality of our community. We heard admonitions like, "Don't make your parents ashamed of you." It was the antithesis of pride. We were once ashamed to be caught in the act of adultery. We were once ashamed to do things that brought dishonor to the race. There was a time when we were ashamed of past sins.

What does it mean to be put to shame? Enemies know how to put us to shame. The 1992 presidential campaign was an exercise in shaming opponents. Faces flushed hot with shame as we revisited each candidate's past. The American public was subjected to one sordid detail after another. It was a tug-of-war between campaign issues and the candidate's character. We were all put to shame. "In you, O LORD, I take refuge; let me never be put to shame" (71:1).

Who doesn't have some aspect of the past from which we have been delivered? Perhaps the greatest fear that the American public, and leaders in the African-American community, experienced is the fear that someone will come along and unearth the unsavory aspects of their pasts.When wickedness rules, we all suffer.

Perhaps the psalmist faced a similar ethical dilemma. He appealed to God to deliver him from the grasp of the wicked. He petitioned for refuge. Today, we have one to whom we can also petition. His name is Jesus. Though he did not have a sordid past, he is acquainted with the shame of sin. He delivers us from shame. He stood in defense of a woman who had been caught in the act of adultery. He dared to be seen with Mary of Magdala, from whom he had cast seven devils.

The Garden of Eden gave humankind two fierce enemies—guilt and shame. Adam and Eve committed the gravest offense—they were guilty, they were both to blame. The cross of Calvary cancels the death penalty for the guilt in our lives. Our bill is paid; a repentant soul is no longer guilty—no longer to blame.

Adam and Eve's acknowledgment of guilt revealed another problem. They were sorry that they had sinned and they were sorry that God knew about it. They were ashamed. For the moment, they hid behind fig leaves. Of course the fig leaves were not enough; humans need more. On Calvary, Jesus also became our hiding place. His presence in our lives even covers past scandals. Don't be ashamed.

Remembering the Ancestors

Unborn children and ancestors figure prominently in traditional African thought. We prepare life for the unborn. We work hard to ensure that both the world and the community are better places for them. One African proverb asserts that we must be careful how we treat the earth because it is borrowed from our children.

We learn from the ancestors. Though the common trend is to focus upon their successes, we also learn from the reality that they made many mistakes. They had to find God; they had to learn to live with one another. Yet, they struggled for equality, they fought to make a better world for children who were not yet conceived. We look at their imperfect lives and learn some of the ways that God continues to work in our lives. There is so much to learn from the ancestors; if only the children could hear them through the generation gap!

Even Israel had its generation gap. They struggled with many of the same issues that plague the African-American community. Israel's children, like ours, were in danger of making the same mistakes repeatedly. The psalmist's remedy—teach them about our history with God.

The concept was simple. Reach back into the history of our ancestors. There we will find numerous examples of our stubbornness and failure and examples of God's love and deliverance reach forward into the lives of our children and even further to their children unborn. Instruct them so that they might learn from our successes and our failures.

What, then, shall we teach our children about the past? Shall we teach them about the betrayal of the chiefs so that they are prepared for the many betrayals that continue in the community? Should we break our silence and explain the burning of Black communities during the riots of the sixties? Have they really understood that some courageous Whites participated in the Underground Railroad? Do they know where you were, politically, when King was assassinated, or when a later King was beaten? Some of your children still have not heard your success stories. Have you told them how you got over?

We share the same ground with the ancestors, our children, and the unborn. We have so much to learn from one another.

Ain't Scared of Nobody

February 26   *Read Psalm 27:1.*

Gye Nyame, in the Akan language, means literally, *except God*. The Akans are the predominant ethnic group within Ghana, West Africa. In 1957, Ghana was the first independent sub-Sahara African nation.

The Ghanaians use Gye Nyame, the symbol of the sovereignty of God, everywhere. It is found on clothing, in architecture, and adorns everything from key chains to bumper stickers! It was so prevalent that I determined to learn more about its meaning.

Except God. To my Western ears, the phrase sounded incomplete. I attempted to obtain a more explicit definition from the people I met. Pressing, I thought I heard the translation of "Nobody but Jesus!" Another said something akin to "God and God alone!" Still another essentially communicated, "If it had not been for the Lord, on our side. . . ." The definition that most resonated with my soul, however was, "Fear no one but (except) God."

Seen through the eyes of West African culture, the writer of Psalm 27 could have been Ghanaian. "The LORD is my light and my salvation, whom shall I fear?" Turn those words around and they say "I fear no one except the Lord, who is my light and my salvation."

What of our fears? If we could only begin to recognize that those who often strike terror in our hearts are not light or salvation, fear would disappear. Look closely at the words of Psalm 27:1. Open your heart and receive them. Then, why not proclaim to the skies "I ain't scared of nobody—except God!"

Having said all this, I ask: "Is there anything in your life worth fearing today?" Gye Nyame.

Doubly Blessed

For so long, we have regarded our need to be culturally bilingual as a curse to be borne for the sake of survival. We winced and flinched as we studied Chaucer when Hurston and Hughes were really running through our veins, and harbored a pained look when Bach was played.

Look, however, at Daniel, Moses, and others who were similarly forced by the mandates of a society that was lopsided. Examine the ways that God used their curse and turned it into a strong point for their communities and His.

So now, here we are; celebrating God's presence in every manner from the "Hallelujah chorus!" to *Hallelujah, Anyhow.* Causing people to wonder what makes us so flexible and comfortable with God's people from Appalachia to Beverly Hills; while all the time we retain the reason and the rhythms that have caused our kinfolk to sing praises to the Almighty for a very long time.

May I propose today a cure for the vexation that inevitably comes when forced to learn two history lessons instead of one. Consider this mental cure for the sense of overextension that comes from being forced to think from both the right and left sides of the brain. When the classics and gospel music collide and do battle on the keyboards of your mind and you need peace, remember Daniel. And know that you, like Daniel, are not cursed, but doubly blessed.

Moonlit Nights

"The elders are the ones authorized to communicate culture." The man from Cameroon was describing the social structure of his native land. "We rely upon the old ones to teach the young ones our stories. On moonlit nights," he continued, "we gather around our elderly people and listen to stories of the past. The griots tell their stories at night when the workday has ended. How many of you have noticed that the moon has light?"

Thoughts of the moonlight began to drift through my mind. Harriet Tubman regarded moonlight as a friend. Eyes spying freedom quickly adjusted to the moonlight as they followed the North Star home. The eyes of those in pursuit were mentally restricted as they waited for the light of the sun. Of course when sunlight came the fugitive slaves were well hidden, waiting for the moon to rise again and light the path of their escape.

God gave the moon to rule over the night. Granted, the moon is a lesser light—but it is light. Nighttime, according to this Bible passage, has its rightful place in the rhythm of life. Does this mean that those periods, the ones we call seasons of night, do after all have light? Perhaps the night seasons of our lives have their place as well. Could it be that there are some stories, some lessons of faith, waiting to be told in the night seasons?

The fact that we have stopped telling our stories at night does not stop the night from having its own light or its own stories to tell. The next time your season of night comes, quiet yourself, and allow your eyes to adjust to the beauty of your moonlit night. Then, listen; there are stories to be heard in the night.

March

The Second Time Around

March 1   *Read Jonah 3:1-5.*

"Don't make me have to tell you twice!" These are words that make many adults shudder as they remember their childhood. Most of us knew that if one of our parents had to reprimand us twice, it would not be pleasant.

Having to hear these words for a second time was not pleasant for Jonah either. The Lord had already told him to warn Nineveh. Instead, he ran and ended up in a whale's belly. The second time he decided to do what the Lord said. I wish things were so simple for us.

In case you find yourself struggling for the courage to do what the Lord has been telling you to do for a long time, I invite you to look at what happened in Jonah's case the second time around. Where was the mean-spirited Gentile city that he had dreaded? We find no record that anyone made fun of him. He does not seem to have been in physical danger. Instead, it appears that God had already prepared them for his visit. The people of Nineveh listened, repented, and the city was saved.

Can you trust God to do the same for you? Perhaps the situation that you dread most will not really be so bad either. God is able to take the cruelest or the most impossible situation and turn it into a haven for you. Finally, keep in mind that you may be the key person that God needs. It seems that Nineveh could not repent until Jonah went there to preach.

It is never too late to do the will of God. God can even use you the second time around.

Phone Call from the Furnace

Wait a minute! Isn't Nebuchadnezzar the same king who put them through the fire in the first place? Now we see him calling them to come out of the fire and testify! Then, they are not fired, they are promoted. What made the difference?

How well we know this story. The same king who persecuted these young men observed how they withstood all that he had done to them. He was forced to look at his madness and acknowledge a Power greater than his own. Their God had done the impossible and it was time for him to reevaluate his lifestyle.

Notice how he watched them. Those who persecute us often do. He was furious, the Bible tells us, and he wanted to see them suffer. He heated up the flames so hot that he did damage to his own workers. Then he watched, like a cruel little boy who sets bugs on fire, to verify their complete destruction.

To the king's surprise, they were not destroyed. Quite on the contrary, they were unharmed. The very fire that had destroyed his soldiers could not even singe their hair or scorch their robes! They were not bound. They had been tied and thrown into a hot spot. Once there, they were seen walking around! They did not even seem to be uncomfortable. Finally, they were not alone! Three were thrown into the fire but four were seen walking around!

There's a lesson in this passage for us today. Perhaps the fire comes to prove to our oppressors that they are not God. Could it be that these three men were allowed to go through the fire so that the king could recognize God? Nebuchadnezzar was forced to acknowledge that God was the greatest power he had ever encountered. Could it be that we go through some fires in our lives so that our bosses, or those who want to boss us, can learn who God is?

We need not fear the worst that anyone can do to us. Like these three young men, we cannot be destroyed; we need not be bound; and we will not be alone! The fourth person in the flames will be with you too!

Can God Take a Bad Thing and Turn It Around?

March 3   *Read 2 Samuel 12:24.*

It was just a plain old affair! David took a woman from another man, and they had a baby. This is an old familiar story. How many modern lives share this story? The question for today is: Can God take a bad thing and turn it around?

So few of us lead perfect lives. I'm so glad that God chose to record the struggles of David and Bathsheba. They mirror the lives of so many people we know. The lady down the street is married to a man whom she took from someone else, while all the gossips wonder if their roof will fall in as punishment or if their child will ever amount to anything. "They didn't start out right" they say. They wait for the other shoe to drop in their lives, and applaud when it does.

Life was no easier for David and Bathsheba. Everyone in the kingdom knew the scandal. They had an affair. They lost their first baby. The entire family fell apart under the pressure; sibling rivalry became bloody sibling war. Nothing was ever the same again. They had a second child named Solomon. Could God, did God, take a bad thing and turn it around?

The Bible reminds us that of all the children David had, Solomon was chosen to rule the kingdom. This was not without great national and internal controversy, nevertheless, Solomon ruled. History tells us that he was the wisest king ever to rule. History also tells us that the days of King Solomon were considered the golden years of Israel. Solomon was allowed to build the Temple for God that his father's hands were too bloody to build.

In similar ways, God is still salvaging the wreckage of our lives. How He must grieve over some of our lifestyle choices! Since the Garden of Eden, we have been error prone. As long as there are people, there are going to be mistakes; but, if we hold onto God's unchanging hand, eventually something good will come to our lives.

Today's word is a bittersweet word for those of us in impossible situations like this one. Though people may never forget your untimely journey to this place in your life, persevere, get on the right track, and God will eventually turn it around.

God's Strength for You

How many times have I tried to be strong all by myself—thought I could handle it? "Jesus, I'll call you if things get out of control." Of course, things never appear out of control until they are really out of control! Each time, I vowed that I would call on the Lord sooner; and each time I foolishly fell on my face.

My strength is not sufficient, neither is yours. We cannot make it on our own. The stresses of this life do not originate with human beings and cannot be solved by human strength. The Bible reminds us that the real war is in the spiritual realm, therefore human weapons are ineffective. God's strength is the only plea that we have.

God offered us His strength when He offered His Son. Jesus took the form of human weakness that we might be able to become strong. He exercised power on earth, in a limited way, in order to grant us access to heaven's unlimited power. If we could only receive Christ's personal invitation to abandon our own inadequate efforts!

Armed with God's strength, we are able to withstand the fiercest challenges with patience. We can handle children that we don't understand, people who don't understand us, and tasks that we can't stand. Joy is possible again. Our female ancestors did not experience our constant bouts with depression; and they withstood greater trials. How? They leaned on the Lord and gave thanks that they were able to prevail.

We often marvel at the ways that our foremothers endured hardship and were still able to experience joyful lives. Faced with obvious limitations, they made the only choices available to them. Do we modern women somehow think that we have more choices than they had? The list of human hindrances contains more constraints than the American past. How blind we have become to our obvious limitations.

Have we been fooled into thinking that life is more manageable for us? Life is not manageable, it backs us against the wall. Then we are often unconsciously, and often unwillingly, forced into relying upon God's strength. Why does it take the last resort, or the end of the road to get us to rely upon Him?

Today, may we consciously rest in His strength and receive the patience and joy that comes from knowing that God has everything under control.

Holy Women

The holy woman in today's passage, Anna, had been a widow for a very long time. Somewhere in the midst of her loss, she retreated to the temple. She served God with prayer and fasting, night and day. Luke calls her a prophet. She is remembered for speaking God's thoughts out loud about the baby Jesus. She is a reminder of the holy women who have always served God.

African and African-American culture are filled with examples of holy women. They are set aside in the churches of Africa just as they are in the traditional African-American church. They wear white there too and they take responsibility for nurturing and instructing the younger women.

We don't see holy women as often as we once did. As a non-Catholic little girl, I remember being fascinated by the nuns. They were visible reminders that holy women existed. I often imagined what it would be like to wear a habit and live in a convent living my life serving God and people. When I was young, I wanted to be a holy woman.

As an adolescent, I met holy women in the Baptist church. They wore white to represent purity and they always sat together. They were called the mothers of the church. There was a holy aura about them. There they sat, as visible reminders of those who live for God.

Where are the holy women today?

Have we shut them out? Forced them underground? Have we failed to listen when they came to correct us and nurture us? Perhaps the defiant individuality of our day has caused them to hide from criticism. Or, could it be that we, the holy women of tomorrow, are afraid to hear that particular calling?

One thing is certain. We will always need the godly influence of holy women in our lives.

Seventy Times Seven

Read Matthew 18:21-22.

I cannot do this anymore
I told the Lord one day.

She stepped upon my little toe
It was not in her way.

She'd done this crime
Time, and again.
It's time I called
Forgiving's end.

Or, so I thought.

It was all well
Till end of day.

I bent my body
Down to pray.

I say:
Our Father
Who art in heaven
Hallowed be thy name
Thy kingdom come
Thy will be done
On earth as it is in heaven
Give us this day
Our daily bread
Forgive us our trespasses
As we . . .
As we . . .
As we forgive . . .

(Sigh!)

Lord, I forgive this lady
For the sixty-ninth time!
Amen.

Pretty Feet

"Lord, don't let her plant her feet on my doorstep! She has always got something bad to say about somebody!" Have you ever found yourself breathing those words? There are days when I feel like Evilene from the broadway musical *The Wiz*: I want to stand defiantly and proclaim, "Don't nobody bring me no bad news!"

The sin of gossip and talebearing hurts all of us. The person bringing bad news hurts themselves by committing sin. The person who does not know how to shut it off also hurts. How many of our spirits have been wounded by hearing something bad about someone that we know?

Human beings have been spreading bad news about one another forever. The ninth commandment, which deals with false witnessing, was designed to address the often ignored sin of gossiping. The Israelites received the Law in the desert, before they entered the promised land. They were encouraged to develop new habits so that the promised land would not become another version of slavery.

While we were in the wilderness of sin, just like the Israelites, we were enslaved by a number of vices. As those redeemed from the hard bondage of sin, we have also been given the perfect law of love that encourages renewed habits. We need to leave our enslaved habits behind, especially the sin of sensationalism and gossip. Why? Because nothing poisons our spirits like bad news.

Our hearts yearn for good news. "Tell me something good girlfriend. What's the good word?" The world is so full of trouble that good news is refreshing. Good news lifts our spirits and gives us hope. Good news reinforces our belief that God is on our side. Is there any good news from the Lord? Isaiah's world was full of bad news. They were so eager to hear some good news that he made a strange declaration. Even the feet of the good news messengers are beautiful!

Do you bring good news? Come on in, pretty feet!

Alone with God

Turn off the television. Unplug the telephone. Pull down the shades. Shut yourself in with God. Alone is not a synonym for lonely. Alone means opportunity. Alone means respite. Alone can mean retreat.

There are times when we must be alone with God. Life is so full of things that tire us spiritually. We must have an opportunity to stop the merry-go-round. We must make time to break the routine that threatens to ruin us.

Moses was known for being a man of the mountain. He was summoned to the mountain to be alone with God many times. We traditionally think of him as a man eager to be alone with God, but actually he may have gone reluctantly. Do you think, perhaps, he worried about the displaced people in the wilderness? "What will my absence now, do to them?" He may even have worried about his workload. "If I leave today, who will do the things that I usually get done?" Maybe Moses even felt guilty about getting away for a time of refreshment when others seemed to need it more. What are some of the struggles you have when the Holy Spirit subpoenas you to the presence of God?

To be honest, Moses was the busiest he had probably been since deliverance of the Israelites began. He had thousands, perhaps millions, of disoriented people in his care. They were hungry, they were stressed-out, and they were afraid. He was the person they both looked up to and complained to. Does any of this sound familiar to you? The busiest moments in our lives are the times when we need most desperately to hear from God. They are also the times when it is most difficult to hear because of the relentless activity. God's solution: Take some time alone with Him.

How can I be alone with so many people constantly around me? There are times when the bathroom must become a prayer closet. There are other times when a car becomes holy ground. In the busiest of places, God makes a way for us to be with Him.

Often, we do not recognize opportunities for miniretreats. We are so accustomed to having people around all the time that we feel lost without them. There are times that many of us feel lonely, when God has simply made a way for us to be alone. So, turn off the television, close the blinds, and spend some time alone on the mountain with God.

The Lord Is in His Holy Temple

"The LORD is in his holy temple; let all the earth keep silence before him!" I first heard these words as a little girl in church; they were used to open the worship service. All the people would stand reverently and acknowledge the presence of God in the worship service. Each week, I imagined that God was coming, at that moment, into the building in all of His majesty and glory. I could feel Him looking into each heart and noting each person's need for Him. Something about hearing those words quieted my spirit. Suddenly, everything was in order as it should be, when the Lord came into His holy temple on Sundays.

When God is in His holy temple, everything should feel like it is in order. God is the one who brings order out of chaos. His Spirit hovers over the chaos of broken lives and brings order. In the beginning, there was a place for everything and everything was in its place.

This God of the temple is the one who fills the void places with created order. When the earth was formless and empty, He spoke and the formless void became the Garden of Eden. When He is present, empty-headedness becomes a mind filled with praise; empty, aching hearts are filled with His love. There is peace, when God is in His holy temple.

Did you realize that God is in your temple? "Do you not know that you are God's temple and that God's Spirit dwells in you?" (See 1 Cor. 3:16). Let your spirit rise, reverently, to acknowledge His presence. Your body is the temple of the Holy Spirit (1 Cor. 6:19). You are a holy people serving a holy God, and He comes to receive your worship.

Because you are a place of worship and praise, there need be no chaos or void places in your life. The Lord of the temple is the Lord of your temple and comes to set your life in order. He comes to fill the emptiness of your life.

"The LORD is in his holy temple; let all the earth keep silence before him!"

Sign Language

Has your head ever been so congested that you couldn't hear? Did you feel frustrated, awkward, and alone? Thank God if you can hear today.

It is hard for some of us to imagine not ever being able to hear. Who knows how long this man had been deaf? We only read that he was deaf and had a speech impediment.

Have you thought about the connection between being able to hear accurately and being able to speak properly? I know several hearing impaired persons who speak well, but there are many more who struggle with words because they have never heard them clearly. Perhaps some of our crazy-sounding-talk is because we aren't hearing God clearly and find it impossible to respond to life's challenges correctly.

How was this man ever to know that Jesus was about to change his circumstances? He had not heard of Jesus. He couldn't hear. People who loved him brought him to Jesus for healing. How could he possibly have any hope when his life had been quiet, awkward, and he had been alone for so long?

God's healing invades every world. The world of the hearing impaired is no exception. Jesus chose to build this man's faith by using a form of sign language to communicate what was about to happen. Jesus looked at the man and stuck his fingers in his ears. His ears were about to be opened. Still looking at the man, He touched His own tongue and spit. Something was about to leave the afflicted man. Then He spoke the words: "Ephphatha, Be Opened!" The man then heard and spoke plainly. There are times when you and I cannot hear spiritually. Don't despair. Look around you for the sign language the Lord may be using to signal your healing.

Won't You Dance?

Do you realize what has happened?
God has moved heaven and earth to get you to this shore.

March

> Pick up your instruments of praise,
> And dance before the Lord!

I was as afraid as you were. I thought for sure that we were destroyed this time. I was there, right along with you suffering and dying in hard labor. But we are not there now. Won't you dance?

> Do you realize what has happened?
> God has moved heaven and earth to get you to this shore.
> Pick up your instruments of praise,
> And dance before the Lord!

I was there with you when our babies were being slaughtered. I was there muzzling my mouth right along with the wise old women, the midwives. Giving them a dose of mother wit, letting them struggle to understand how we made it.

> Do you realize what has happened?
> God has moved heaven and earth to get you to this shore.
> Pick up your instruments of praise,
> And dance before the Lord!

I was also there when the whole earth seemed to fall under judgment for their wickedness. We all had bloody water, we all smelled the swollen, rotting frogs, the gnats bit all of us! I held hands with you and watched our knuckles turn ashy white while we held our breath and wondered what God would do next. Though we didn't understand it at the time, He was doing this for us. Won't you dance?

> Do you realize what has happened?
> God has moved heaven and earth to get you to this shore.
> Pick up your instruments of praise,
> And dance before the Lord!

It does not matter if we chose to leave or if they put us out. We are bound for freedom now. Try as they did, they could not hold us. God has opened waters and drowned warriors for our escape. We are bound for freedom now. No one can make us go back there again; we are bound for freedom now.

> Do you realize what has happened?
> God has moved heaven and earth to get you to this shore.
> Pick up your instruments of praise,
> And dance before the Lord!

Knowing Whom to Touch

"What has got into her? The last I heard, she sold her house to buy a ticket to South America. She said that some doctor down there had a cure for bleeding. . . . Sounds like she's lost her mind to me."

"She had endured much under many physicians, and had spent all that she had; and she was no better, but rather grew worse" (Mark 5:26). How often do we whisk past those words to get to the good part where she finally received her healing? Just what had this woman been through before she heard about Jesus? Hope must have been a positive force in her life.

Hope was obviously the one thing that enabled her to try one thing after another. "I hope this one works." "I know my friend, Marcy tried this doctor and he seemed to do fine with her." "Hope that they have found a cure." "Hope I'm one of the lucky ones." "Hope that I don't run out of money before I find the right thing." She was convinced that the right thing was somewhere for her. She was determined not to give up.

Just what might she have tried while enduring under the doctors? Did she try the latest miracle cure-all? Did she taste traditional medicines? Did she go to a psychic? Under similar circumstances, what do we do? Sick people with a hopeful spirit will try anything to get well. The endless search for the right folklore, the right medicine, the right doctor really makes them, or us, ripe for an encounter with God.

This time, she heard about Jesus and His miraculous healings. She was looking for an object of faith. She had tried to apply her faith to every other form of healing known at her time. This time, she applied her faith to the Faithful One. She touched His clothes and was healed.

She touched *Him!* She reached out in faith as she had so many times before to doctors or to anyone offering hope. Can you see those weary, gnarled fingers reaching purposely through the crowd? This time, Hope reached back and touched her!

Have you been reaching out in faith to anything or to anyone who will offer you hope? You are already halfway to your destination. Why not apply your hopeful faith to the Hope of the World, Jesus?

He Went Out of His Way

March 13   *Read Luke 7:11-17.*

What kind of person stops a funeral procession? Only one who could change the procession from a funeral to a celebration would dare do so. Jesus had just been in Capernaum talking to a Roman soldier. Nain was a small village twenty-five miles south. It was no accident that Jesus had come all that distance to stop the funeral.

Though all losses are a tragedy, this particular loss was a great tragedy. Widows were perhaps the most helpless members of that society. Women without husbands were powerless. They often were forced to resort to begging or prostitution unless they had a son who would care for them. The dearly departed was the widow's only son. Who would care for her now? An exceptionally large crowd had gathered to mourn this woman's loss.

Jesus still goes out of His way to change the lives of those who are doomed. For those dying in sin, or those pronounced dead by the large crowds of this world, Jesus continues to go miles out of His way to change the outcome. Whether you are the widow watching your last hope go to the grave, or the dearly departed, expect the unexpected to happen when Jesus arrives.

When He arrived at that funeral in Nain, He spoke to the dead and returned him to his mother. God is still talking to dead folks, and they are still answering. Perhaps you have given up too soon on someone pronounced dead by life's critics. Just as the young man was returned to his mother, look for hope to be restored to you.

Perhaps you might want to dry your handkerchief so you can wave it later as a banner at the celebration party!

A Cup of Cold Water

March 14   *Read Matthew 10:40-42.*

Who are the "little ones" to whom Jesus refers? What does He mean when He says water? Surely Jesus was not only speaking of giving a cup of cold water to the children.

Perhaps the little ones are those who cannot get water for themselves. Open your eyes. See the little ones all around you. Grandmomma may be one of your little ones. Bent over with age, unable to enjoy the process of walking to the water, she needs a cup of water from you when she calls for it.

I wonder if Jesus would add the lady down the street to His list of "little ones?" She is fifty-two and still lives with her mother because she is "just a little slow." Hardly anyone spends any time with her because she has strange notions about most things. Just a little friendly, caring, conversation with you might be a cup of cold water for both her and her weary mother.

Perhaps there's a teenager you know whose mother is on drugs. That girl does the best she can with her hair, and has no one to show her tasteful ways to wear makeup. She cries a lot, and the boys won't date her because her hygiene is, well—different. Doesn't she thirst for a big sister, who will not constantly condemn the mother she loves?

Look at that good brother who lives on the corner. His daughter still cries at night for her mommy who has gone away to live with Jesus. She has no brothers and sisters, and her dad is still in a daze; he's just doing the best he can. Couldn't you quench her need for a playmate? There are plenty of children her age at your house. Come on, break down and let her play in your hair the way little girls do.

If we look around us, there are many little ones in our neighborhood. They wait for a cup of cold water from your hand. Can you see them?

For Abused Women

March 15

We are reminded, Lord, of women whose lives have become prisons. Were they first imprisoned in mind or in flesh? We do not understand what causes them to accept mental or physical pain from their partners. Nor do we understand how they manage to silence what would, for us, become rage.

We petition you for the safety and well being of any woman who has ever been beaten by the man she loves. Have mercy upon them Lord, and spare their lives. We pray for your intervention before these women are physically mutilated. We ask you to prevent their being emotionally crippled for life.

We entreat you, Lord, give our sisters the courage they need to actively resist violence in their lives. Make them aware of the injustice of their circumstances. When they are in physical danger, give them the resolve to place emergency phone calls, and the courage to file formal legal charges against their attackers. Steer their hearts away from the need for retaliation.

We pray, gracious Lord, that you will keep hope alive in those who are in close relationships with abused sisters. Without your help, we female family members and sister-friends often get so disgusted that we refuse to pray for them. Soften our judgmental spirits; help us to respect the choices they make and to support them when they need us.

Finally, Lord, we pray for those who abuse women. Stir their consciences to make them stop. We pray that they may have the capability to abhor the violence that they inflict upon the minds and bodies of the women they say they love. Help them to see the origins of their violence. Set them free from the demons that bind them and prohibit healthy relationships with women.

Only you, Lord, can make it possible for women and men to relate to each other in sacred ways. Heal broken relationships characterized by abuse, in Jesus' name. Amen.

Finding Other Sons to Love

March 16   *Read John 19:26.*

When your child is on a collision course with destiny, whom do you mother? Whom, then, do you love when your child is following a path that no one understands but him and God? Or, worse, when even God does not understand the path that your child takes, who fills your void?

Mary had other children. She had other sons and other daughters to justify her success in motherhood. But, this child was hers too, and He was special. Can you imagine her perplexity when He, at the age of twelve, decided that He needed to stay in the Holy City and teach the elders? Can you imagine the fear that rose in her throat when she heard that His religion had gone to his head? "Boy, if you don't stop this, you're going to end up in jail!" She tried to warn him.

This was even worse than jail. She had to watch Him die. She listened to others taunt and jeer, remembering that He had put her aside and pointed to other mothers and brothers and sisters. She was only trying to talk some sense into His head.

His last familial act of love was to acknowledge what she must have been going through. He turned to the disciple whom He loved (John) and said, in so many words: "Mother, this is your son now!" Jesus seemed to acknowledge that the unknowable had created an unknown emptiness in His mother's heart and He gave her another son to love. Mary had other children, but John was her new firstborn.

Sometimes our sons break our hearts more than lovers. They follow God-given, or God-forsaken, paths that are beyond our understanding. No matter how many other children we have, that child's place becomes empty when we cannot mother him until time to gradually let him go. These are the times when God seems to give us someone else's child to love. Think of the neighbor's child down the street, the one that just likes to hang out in your kitchen. Think of the difficult teenage boy who has no one else to talk to.

Open your heart wide to receive and to nurture these other sons. They are a gift from God, who sees the aching emptiness of your mother's heart. Besides, how do we know that you are not filling in for another mom who aches for that very child? And, perhaps, some other mother is standing in the gap for you.

Jochebed, Nursing Your Dream for Someone Else

March 17   *Read Exodus 2:5-10.*

"How did I get into this condition?" Have you ever asked yourself that question? Think of the questions that Moses' mother must have asked.

Jochebed is a plain old sistah-girl trying to live a good life and protect her child from danger. It would seem that all of society was against her efforts to raise her child. Pharaoh had decreed that all of the boy babies would be thrown into the Nile. Have you ever felt that some invisible evil force was up against your boy-child?

Jochebed speaks to the futility that we often feel when we are trying to get ahead. It goes beyond the feeling that society is against our children. She was called in to nurse a child, her own baby, for someone else. This other woman even reserved the right to name Jochebed's baby! It's like at work when we come up with ideas but others get the credit for them. We devise improvements for humanity, but someone else seems to get the credit for them. Jochebed's injuries are also our injuries. She speaks, silently, for every woman who was ever ignored—only to have her suggestion, through some-one else, save the day! She stands up, invisibly, for every mother, in a school staffing who has been treated as though she did not know what was best for her child. She stands as a monument and memorial to secret victories and those who quietly have the last word. You see, when all was said and done, she did get to see her child live, and she did get to nurse him.

How did Jochebed make sense of her predicament? Did she focus upon her hopelessness as the child's cry became too strong to conceal? Did she look back upon her own sense of powerlessness as she threw the babe into the very river that was supposed to have been his death? Did she fix her eyes upon the palace of the Pharaoh that somehow held her child hostage as a sign of her failure?

Somehow, I would like to think that she chose to remember how God paid her for doing something that she would have gladly done without pay—while proudly beholding the man that Moses became.

Death Gives Way to Life

March 18   *Read Galatians 2:20 (NIV).*

Crucifixion was more than the act that occurred for several hours on Calvary's hill. Crucifixion for Christ was a process; it was a continuous process of self-denial for our benefit. The Cross, the event that we remember and call the Crucifixion, was the culmination; but the cruci-fied life catches my attention today.

There were daily choices to be made. Things that could not be overlooked;

this process of living crucified involved His very being. Jesus could not afford to wait until the day that the Passover Lambs were being slaughtered to offer His life for humankind; by then his life might have been worthless in terms of His ability to redeem humanity. For Him, it started when He was old enough to realize who He was. He lived as one destined to die for others.

When does living the crucified life begin for us? Look around you today. Those women who bear the burden of our history, who live sacrificial lives, when did it begin for them? Did it begin when crisis came or was it much earlier? Look behind you at the women of the past. Were they nursed on the milk of dedication and weaned with self-awareness? Look at your life and ask if God is preparing you for the crucified life.

Before the event that we know as the Crucifixion, Jesus suffered betrayal. He lived with a Judas. He poured energy into a life that would later attempt to benefit financially from His death. Have you been betrayed or wounded in the act of working for someone's good? Perchance the pain of the long, slow death of wounding and betrayal is the hardest part of living a crucified life. Yet, Jesus bore this too.

Believe it or not, there is joy in crucifixion. Self-awareness, purpose, conscientious dedication to a cause, the pain of betrayal and wounding, all these lead, surprisingly, to joy. As surely as the slow death of selfish ambition, and the struggle of living with godly purpose lead to a personal Calvary, new life is certain. There comes a point when we cease to feel personal suffering and begin to experience the joy of eternal life. Death with Christ gives way to resurrection with Him!

You bear the scars of crucifixion upon your soul. Refuse to get depressed when you are betrayed or wounded by those you love. Remember that you are, in actuality, raised with Christ to walk in resurrection life and need not fear death. Why? Because, in some ways you have already died, and survived.

Liberating Praise

Jumping Jehoshaphat, they were in troub-ble! It seemed as if everything and everybody were lined up against them. King Jehoshaphat and Israel were notified that the Ammonites, the Moabites, some of the

Meunites, and the Edomites were ready to make war with them. Jehoshaphat may have felt like the king yesterday, but today he was in the valley of anticipated slaughter and defeat.

He did what you and I would do in such a situation, he prayed, perhaps harder than he had ever prayed in his life. God, true to His nature, did not leave the king out on a limb. He gave him the power to stop the advance of the enemy in his life—praise. When they began to praise the Lord, God set ambushments and the enemy was routed.

The Lord has also given you the power to stop the madness in your life. You have the power to praise God and stop worrying. Why is praise so powerful?

When we praise God in the midst of a terrible trial, we are signaling that we really believe that we will get through it. Praise is the voice of Psalm 23—fearless when going through the valley of the shadow of death. Praise is the contented musing of Daniel when he contemplated the locked lion's jaw. Praise is our affirmation that God will bring us to the other side.

Praise means that we have finally recognized that things are not really in our hands, they are in God's hands. Praise is also a symbol that we have placed the outcome in God's hands. Since God is more powerful than anything in the universe, we need not fear once God is in control.

You have the power to stop the torment in your life. Don't be jumpy; don't allow life to back you into a corner. Throw back your head and praise the Lord!

With All Your Mind

March 20   *Read Matthew 22:34-37.*

I woke up this morning with my mind stayed on Jesus.

I thought I'd love God with my mind today. Made up my mind that every thought and every idea was going to be for His glory.

The devil can't harm you when your mind's stayed on Jesus,
Hallelu, Hallelu, Hallelujah.

Our grandmothers knew how to love the Lord with their minds. They may not have finished elementary school, but they knew, quite early in, their lives, that the Lord wanted us to love Him with our minds. Just what does it mean to love God with our minds in this day and age?

Just as it did for Grandma, it means that we will monitor our thoughts. Some things in the past were just *unthinkable*. Now, we dare to think about anything. If we could just recapture the vision of what it means to love God with our minds! We would learn not to think evil thoughts about the people that we have a hard time loving. We would not dwell so much on the hurts and losses of our lives. Perhaps depression was not the epidemic that it is today, because our grandmothers loved God with their minds.

It would be easier to remember the wonderful works of God in our lives—if we loved God with our minds. If we didn't have idle and evil thoughts to fill up our imagination, what remained would be testimony and praise. Have you ever walked in on an old woman and watched her when she was "caught up" in the Spirit? She may have been standing at the sink with a smile on her face and her head tilted to one side in thought. Or, perhaps she was sitting in her favorite chair in an empty room. No doubt her joyful tears reflected the results of loving God with her memories.

Ain't no harm to keep your mind stayed on Jesus,

Hallelu, Hallelu, Hallelujah!

No Fleas, Please

March 21   *Read Proverbs 6:27-28.*

Whenever the question of corrupt associations became a topic of discussion, our older relatives would inevitably say: "If you lay down with dogs, you'll get up with fleas." There are just some things that we cannot do and remain unaffected. Do you remember how obsessed our parents were with the company we kept? The big taboo in our day was dating boys who smoked or consumed alcohol. As modern parents we also find ourselves concerned with keeping our children away from negative influences. Some of us are trying our best to keep our children from getting fleas.

Have you thought about some of the dogs with whom adults lie?

When we, for example, hear less than complimentary comments about other racial groups, do we laugh or protest? The ethnic person in this week's joke could become an African-American when the joke is retold in our absence. The sexually explicit remark that may amuse us about a coworker could have been about us. Walking on hot coals scorches everyone's feet no matter whom the fire was intended to burn.

Most of us know that buying used televisions from the backseat of an automobile encourages wrongdoing. But, does the company that signs our paycheck dump toxic chemicals in developing countries in Africa? Does the bargain spot, where we can find really exciting items at rock-bottom prices, exploit artisans in the Caribbean? Remember, if we lie down with dogs, we will get up with fleas too. Our backyard could become the next dumping station, or our children could become the next generation of exploited workers.

In the adult world, it is not always so easy to discern negative influences. We often find ourselves standing on live coals wondering how we were burned without recognizing it sooner. Lord, help us to avoid becoming fuel for the fires of injustice, exploitation, and corruption that threaten to consume all of us. Amen.

Standing on the Chair

March 22   *Read Matthew 21:6-9.*

The whole city must have looked different from the back of that donkey on Palm Sunday long ago. Have you ever stood in a chair to change a light bulb and discovered, accidentally, that the whole room looks different from that angle? What would happen if we should purposely change perspective?

What if you could see a certain vexing situation a year from today? What would you see if you could see your problems from a distance? The impossible might appear more possible if we could see things from a different perspective.

Come higher friend and stand on top of something so you can see better. The unbearable becomes bearable when you look from higher ground. The dreaded and miserable is not so bad after all when you begin to look at things from the top of the hill.

When we look from a different perspective we see that every road does indeed have an end; troubles really don't last always; and God really does take care of the bullies and mean people in our lives. When we look at life from a different perspective we'll see that God really does love us; that all was not really lost; and that the thing we thought was the most painful was really the best thing that ever happened to us for it taught us lessons we'll never forget. Perhaps all you need is to stand on the chair and see life from a different angle.

What could Jesus possibly have seen from the donkey's back? Did He see the crowds finally recognize him publicly? Did He see the betrayal that was to come? Perhaps He saw the Crucifixion or the longest three days in the grave. Then again, maybe he saw the birth of the church.

Third Day Morning

March 23   *Read Luke 24:1-8.*

"Third Day Morning" is one of the phrases that causes ears to perk up. It has become a part of the language of the African-American church. One never knows what might happen when those words are spoken in a crowded church on a hot Sunday afternoon. Hands might spontaneously rise up in salute. Feet might move to a rhythm of their own. And you will likely hear a few amens. Preachers often save that phrase to signal the conclusion of a sermon. We've heard "third day morning" time after time, and we all have our own interpretation of what it means.

When the excitement of the preaching moment is past; when the pews have cooled down, the building is closed, and we have all gone to our separate homes, do you remember those words? Third Day Morning! Repeat them. Savor them. Let the words sink into your soul. Ponder their meaning.

On the morning of the third day, people found a surprise! The tomb was empty. Jesus' body was gone and no one had stolen it! Third day morning, God's promises were fulfilled, freedom was purchased, and death lost its sting! You already knew about that.

Did you also know that the morning of the third day was a dress rehearsal for your resurrection as well. One day people are going to find another surprise, your tomb will be empty! You won't be bound any-more! Jesus was the firstborn of the dead (Col. 1:18; Rev. 1:5), and the firstborn of a large family (Rom. 8:29). He carved a pathway through dead places so that we might all follow His example and get up from our graves. You've got a third day morning coming!

Resurrection is all around you. It's more than butterflies coming out of cocoons or dead seeds sprouting into plants. There are situations that looked dead coming alive in your life. God is yet breathing life into dead marriages, and lost children are coming back from the dead. Even if your dreams are dead they can be resurrected when your third day morning comes.

One of the verses of a popular Easter hymn begins: "Death could not keep its prey."

Nor can it keep you—the morning of the third day is coming!

Inherent Weakness

March 24   *Read Mark 14:37-38.*

We are
Like Peter,
coming to the time of prayer,
minds adrift
eyes involuntarily closed in sleep.
Like Judas,
selling our Savior for a
few pieces of silver,
substituting playtime for praytime
woefully perfecting hours of leisure—without God.

If we could only know the Savior's labors,
If we smelled His sweat like blood.

Surely there would be no need to ask
Could you not stay awake one hour?
One would think that

the ceaseless din and clatter of empty stomachs
the rumble of war and death
the pain of worldwide injustice
the tears of incest
the blood of martyrdom
the cries of those abandoned
would keep us awake.

But,
We continue to sleep
as those who have been drugged
with too much wine.
While
The chastising cry
rings through the corridors of
time and
eternity:
Could you not pray one hour?

Today?

See You Sunday!

March 25   *Read Acts 2:46-47.*

Church is the center of our world. We are a spiritual people, and every-thing that we do is connected to our belief systems. We go to church to become whole people. We also go to church to connect with one another and with God.

When we go to church, we expect to touch God. If we don't touch God, how will we make it through the next week? Everything we do from testifying, to singing along with the choir, is aimed at helping us touch the Holy. We sway until we feel His presence, and clap until our souls break out in applause. Limbs leap in ecstatic praise. No matter how many refrains of "Can't Nobody Do Me Like Jesus" it takes, we don't want to leave until God acknowledges our presence.

We come to hear God speak to our intimate needs. The scripture reading becomes a sacred time of listening. Hanging on every word of the preacher, we expect to hear a secret message that calms our secret hurts and fears. Our ears strain to listen between the lines for the confirmation that the Holy Spirit brings. "Girl, I was just reading that very passage last night!" I know God sees me.

The Word confirms that God sees us. Like Hagar at the well, we wait quietly, and sometimes anxiously, for the Lord to break the silence. The Word confirms that God understands. Ancient stories, sacred stories rehearse similar challenges in faraway places from distant times. The Word confirms that relief is on the horizon. We may feel as though we're in the fire today; but tomorrow we won't even remember the flames; smoke won't be in our hair; and we will be transformed from lawbreakers to heroines. Faithful words, holy words, are spoken by the oracle of God in the pulpit.

I need to touch you when I come. I reach out for your reassurance during the "turn to your neighbor" moment. When you squeeze my hand and smile knowingly, I am strengthened by God moving through you. I need to see your eyes laugh again, and feel your acceptance in a land where I am seen as an intrusion or a threat to someone's job.

My children need your hugs; they look for you, too. When they are with you, you don't see them as behavior-disordered, potential shoplifters, or a nuisance to be dismissed—they are your babies. "Baby, come here and let Mama Smith get a good look at you!" Chubby cheeks rise to receive your kisses like leaves receiving morning dew.

I look forward to seeing you all week long—at God's place. Girl, I'll see you Sunday!

It Is Finished!

March 26   *Read John 19:30.*

I wonder if human beings can ever really finish anything? There's always one more thread to be cut, one more nail to be nailed, one more stroke of the artist's brush. Always another sentence that must be written. We never seem to get through everything.

God is the only one who can really finish a thing. Only God can say that creation is finished and declare it, "Good, very good." Only Jesus could forgive His captors and make statements that confirmed Jewish prophecy.

"It is finished." The other Gospel writers do not tell us about this statement. John uses a Greek word that might be used for settling back upon a pillow. The words, "It is finished" were the words of one who had completed an awesome task and was at peace.

What exactly was finished? The earthly work required for our salvation was finished. Jesus had just finished proving that godly living is possible. He had finished preparing His disciples to take over His work. He had finished fulfilling the hundreds of prophecies about him. Jesus' earthly work was finished; nothing remained to be done.

So many things keep our heads from resting on our pillows in peace. Do we ever really finish rearing our children? Is there ironing in the basket or work left to do on the desk? Is the basement, attic, or garage clean? Nothing ever seems finished.

Inside each of us there are so many unresolved issues. Do we ever get over the death of our loved ones? Are we ever going to be satisfied with our present condition? Just when will I stop losing my temper? Can I ever love again?

During this Lenten season, perhaps you have placed some unfinished work of grace before God. Patience may be the answer to your lack of peace. Forgiveness may be giving you trouble. You might be in prayer for more of God's unconditional love. What unfinished business do you have with God? God is truly able to finish what He has begun.

Though human beings have a hard time finishing things, God, who was capable of finishing all of creation, is able to finish His work in you. Philippians 1:6 encourages us with these words: "I am confident of this, that the one who began a good work among you will bring it to completion by the day of Jesus Christ."

Giving Up Your Isaac

March 27   *Read Genesis 22:1, 11-18.*

Have you ever waited a long time for something only to lose it after a short time? Terror must have entered Abraham's heart when God requested Isaac's life. Isaac, whose name means laughter, was longed for. His mother and father had been through more disappointments over this baby. They had been barren until well past childbearing years. When the promised child did not come immediately, they tried to substitute a child with Hagar. What a mess that was! Finally, Sarah did conceive; Isaac was born, and God wanted him back. It almost seemed cruel.

Why did God ask Abraham for Isaac? Perhaps part of the test, to which scripture refers, has to do with Abraham's willingness. Was he willing to give up the thing that he and God knew he cherished most— his only child with Sarah?

If God were to ask you to give up the thing that you love most, what would it be? Would your children be at the top of the list? How about the man of your dreams? Is it a car, a house, a possession that you suffered to obtain? God is a jealous God and we all know the commandments— nothing can become a substitute for God in our lives.

Abraham's test yielded favorable results. Without hesitation, and for all we know without consulting his wife, he made preparations to sacrifice the only child he and Sarah had been given. Surely he was afraid; he was certain to have preferred to do something else; but he didn't offer God a substitute—he offered his beloved son! Read Genesis 22:11-18 and see what happened next.

Once the Lord saw Abraham's willingness to place everything dear before Him; he gave Isaac back to him alive. He also blessed Abraham beyond his wildest wishes.

If God were to test you, what would your Isaac be?

Resurrection!

March 28   *Read John 11:25-26.*

Denise was packing her one suitcase for home. She would be really glad to get back home to her regular clothes. She had forgotten how many variations she had made using the one black pantsuit, three pairs of jeans, and six tops that her husband had purchased once she could wear clothes again. She hadn't decided whether to recycle them or burn them. Either way, they would have to go; they only served as reminders of the last three months.

Among her scant belongings, Denise found hospital slippers, hospital lotion, hospital toothbrush, and a hospital shower cap. How would she ever get the hospital out of her memories? On her way to visit her sister in Detroit, she had hit a patch of ice on the interstate. Her car rolled over several times. She had been critically injured and was near death when the ambulance arrived.

At an unfamiliar hospital, in an unfamiliar city, her family members paced the floor and prayed. For several days the doctors were not sure if she would survive the trauma of the accident. Surgery and bone grafts, transplants and skin grafts, Denise understood them all by the time she prepared to return to Chicago. The danger of infection had passed. With wobbly legs unaccustomed to the weight of her wasted body, Denise was finally leaving rehabilitation and going home.

Denise and Clarence were silent for most of the long ride home. He felt like he was bringing his wife of seven years home for the very first time. Denise felt like a stranger returning to her community. How could she share her near-death experience? She came from a strongly devout church community; they would want to hear her testimony. Her girl-friends had been worried about her state of mind. What would she say to any of them?

Just before they came to the expressway, a gentle voice inside of Denise whispered one word: "Resurrection!"

Emmaus

March 29   *Read Luke 24:13-35.*

Lord,

There are far too many times when you are present, and I don't recognize you. Looking back on the situation, I then see that I walked with you and even told you what you already knew. How could I have been so blind? Was it disappointment that kept me from seeing the many ways that you are present in what often looked like the worst of circumstances?

Perhaps I didn't recognize you when we were walking together because I do not know you as well as I thought. It is so easy to not know a person when one does all the talking. I have been so busy telling you how to solve this problem that I did not take the time to listen for the ways that you wanted this problem solved. Lord, forgive me, I pray.

Perhaps I don't always see you Lord, because I refuse to acknowledge that your will is often fulfilled in ways that I find uncomfortable. I don't look for you to be in those answers to prayers that I disapprove of. I don't expect to encounter you while walking on a road that I dread. When my own unwillingness prevents me from recognizing you Lord, open my eyes. Amen.

Strength in My Hands

March 30   *Read Matthew 12:9-13.*

Sometimes Lord,
When I feel healthy and whole, I forget just how much strength I don't have. Perhaps one of the uncounted blessings of the weak is their constant awareness of need.

Surely the man whose hand was withered had many unrealized plans for the strength that was not in his hands. Maybe he had needed the strength in his hand to steady a load or to point the way for disoriented travelers. Perhaps he had longed to hold his infant grandchild or touch his wife's hair. The man might have harbored noble plans for the hand that had no strength.

The more I think about it, the more I realize that both of my hands are weak. They seem to have no power to pick up the cross that you offer to me daily. There are so many things that my hands need to do. Perhaps, I, too, should think about the things I would do if I just had a little strength in my hands.

Talking to a Dead Man

March 31   *Read John 12:9-11.*

The crisis was past. Mary and Martha had received their brother back from the dead. In the aftermath they are left with Lazarus and his tremendous testimony. People wanted to talk to someone who had been raised from the dead. They came from miles around.

There is something about testimony in the life of the African-American church that fuels the fires of revival and keeps us focused when we are discouraged. When we could not read the Bible, the oral tradition of "telling the story" carried us through. When we did not know all the supposedly "theologically correct" things to say, we simply told the story as we knew it in our hearts. Even now when scholars evaluate those things that tend to cause conversion, they find that personal testimony often carries more weight than hearing scriptural canon. Being able to hear and to see the evidence of a God who is real, alive, not impotent, carries more weight for the unbeliever than mere "holy words on a page." The written tradition is important to strengthen and deepen our faith, but most of us come to faith by hearing the story and by seeing results.

In some churches we are losing the ability to tell our story. At one time you could not stop us from telling our story. Now, only a few of the brave are willing to tell of the activity of God in their own individual lives. When we realized that we were oppressed, we could tell of victories of faith. When we were aware of the day-to-day struggle, simply surviving and being alive to testify were victories in themselves. Now that we have "houses that we didn't build, and land that we didn't plant ourselves," to echo the words of Deuteronomy, we have done the same things that Israel did. We have forgotten, far too quickly, that we are still in bondage, and that even getting to where we are did not happen by our own personal strength. All that we have comes from the Lord.

Well, Lazarus told his story. He must have set the house on fire because today's passage tells us that the crowds were not just coming to see Jesus but also to see Lazarus. The chief priests made plans to kill Lazarus because his testimony was causing many to come to faith.

Lazarus is not the only person raised from the dead. You were once dead, too. Some, who are still dead, need to hear your resurrection story. Others, who are also raised with Christ, need the comfort and strength that come from the story of your personal experience with God. People came from miles around to hear Lazarus' story and believed in Jesus because of it. What might happen if you told your story?

April

I Saw Him

I saw Him this morning.
I saw Him full of splendor and glory.
In the midst of the natural,
        the supernatural occurred.
God appeared.
He filled up the temple of my thoughts
        all else became unimportant.
Nothing else mattered
        I was suddenly there, with Him.

He eclipsed the news of the day:
"King Uzziah dies . . . throne empty . . ."
While others were preoccupied with the empty throne,
the only worthy news was that
                He sits on the throne.
In spite of all that happens on earthly thrones,
the throne of heaven is not empty.
        "Of the increase of his government . . ."
When I saw Him,
        I knew that His government
                could not help increasing because
                        He rules with justice and wisdom.
Who would not want to serve the One who I saw?

The heavenly veil was torn away;
I could see other spiritual beings;
        angels
                seraphim
                        cherubim were there.
I shook with fear as winged creatures
        spoke the words that
                stuck to my throat:

"Holy, holy, holy is the LORD Almighty!"
The impact of their words
      struck the foundations of my soul.

Had I ever really understood holiness?

Holiness developed new dimensions.
Holiness was no longer a concept to be discussed
      in the Woman's class
            on Sunday mornings.
Holiness was not a style of clothing or
      even a human attitude.
Holiness was God's.
We become holy through relationship with Him.
For the first time,
      I understood holiness,
            not with my head,
                  but with my soul.
I knew that He was inherently holy
      and I was not;
            Yet, there I stood in His presence.
There is none like Him!

I was no longer alone.
All of creation applauded in praise.
The clouds circled His head.
Seas roared like drum rolls.
Grass waved
Flowers exuded their fragrant bouquets.
The whole earth is full of His glory!

I saw the Lord today.
My life has been changed.
Somehow all my self-righteousness just went down the drain.
      He is holy
            I am not;
                  Yet, He has allowed me to see Him.
I saw the heavenly creatures that know the right words to say.
They surround Him with the worship that I so often neglect.
They surrounded Him with adoration like a garment.
I saw the Lord,
Higher than your imagination and mine,
Bigger than life.
My life will never be the same.

Have you seen him today?

How's Your Reflection?

In the places where we are employed, there are those established times for employee evaluations. In those places where we are educated, there are periodic assessments of our grades. How often do you perform a physical self-assessment by hopping on the bathroom scales? In this context, it seems quite natural for the Holy Spirit to call each of us to a time of self-evaluation and reflection.

The historic church has often suggested the forty days preceding Easter as a time for prayer, repentance, and reflection. Perhaps this should be a more frequent process and an opportunity for growth.

There are some things that we will only realize about ourselves when we pause to reflect. If we should slow down the treadmill of daily activities, it would become easier to recognize areas of continued spiritual struggle. The old adage says that we cannot see the trees for the forest. When we are overwhelmed by the unpredictable or the unmanageable, it is easy to become blind to that which everyone else can see. Slow down to reflect today on how you are doing.

In the same way, when we are so busy "doing" the faith, we become blind to our own spiritual growth. We often must be distanced from those things that caused us to grow in order to recognize that we have grown. You may need to testify to yourself today.

There are many things that we all need to discover about ourselves. Why not declare today a reflection day?

Wounded for You

Can you remember the pain you felt the very first time you discovered that you had gained something you wanted at another person's expense? Perhaps you got a prom dress when your mother needed a new coat. It could have been as critical as being the only child that your parents could afford to send to school. Most of us would make any number of sacrifices for those we love. However, when we discover that serious sacrifices have been made for us, our faces turn hot with shame.

The sacrifice of Christ is much like this. We, like selfish, undeserving children, are the beneficiaries of great benefits at His expense. Theological controversy has caused a number of churches to avoid the subject of sacrifice, but the truth remains that God, in Christ, gave up something for each of us.

Christ gave up many of His rights. We hardly ever voluntarily give up anything to which we are entitled. Jesus gave up a world of comfort. The comfort of heaven was only a memory for thirty-three years. Instead of loving trust, people regarded Jesus with suspicion. His sojourn with the world was filled with rejection, pain, bruises, and hard work. Instead of the fame and respect He deserved, His life was characterized by controversy and deprivation. He chose the life of a poor carpenter's son. He allowed people to whisper about his mother. Jesus voluntarily suffered injustice through the legal system. These things were done for our ease.

Jesus chose to limit himself on our behalf. Stones could have become bread. The skies should have broken into applause as He rode into Jerusalem on Palm Sunday. Instead of the Crucifixion, things could have been quite different. Thousands of avenging angels might have vindicated His name. He chose to be wounded for you and for me.

Why such a sacrifice? The Bible tells us that Jesus took our pain and paid our penalty. He traded His life for ours. Everything we have ever done wrong, once confessed, is forgiven. Jesus made the ultimate sacrifice so that you and I might exchange a painful past for peace and life's bruises for tranquillity. This one sacrifice has been sufficient for all of humanity's brokenness. We need not bear brokenness any longer. All any one of us needs to do is bring our particular malady to the Lord and leave it with Him.

If you had been the only person on earth, God loves you enough to have made this sacrifice just for you. Are you holding onto despair, pain, or rejection? Give them to God today; God has already been wounded for you.

Testimony from the Tombs

April 4   *Read Matthew 27:51-53.*

How was it when Jesus entered your life? Did it seem like the earth shook as heaven paused to acknowledge your new birth? Perhaps you felt only the tremors within your soul as the grave that held your dead spirit was opened, allowing you to go free.

We are like those saints who were raised from the dead to acknowledge the Christ on that terrible day. The slow death of sin had poisoned and imprisoned us in spiritual tombs. Like those whose bodies are kept alive by machines, we continued our daily routines without knowledge of our condition. We, who were once walking dead, were brought back to life and made holy by the power of the living Christ. In a sense, the fact that we have new life is a testimony from the tombs.

What did people say when they saw you? "Girl, you? In church?" Or did they say, "Girl, church? In you?" Did the old mothers stretch out in praise when you were raised? How did it feel to walk that very first walk? Every place you went became the holy city, for God was with you.

When Jesus gave up His spirit, tombs in Jerusalem opened wide to let those holy ones imprisoned by death go free. Why should this surprise us? Jesus is, after all, the Resurrection and the Life!

It's Not Just You

April 5   *Read 1 Peter 4:12-14.*

When trials come your way, are you tempted to think that something or someone is personally against you? Suffering seems to isolate us; we feel as if no one understands; we think that they do not share our experiences. Isolation often contributes to depression, which causes us to withdraw even further—setting up a vicious cycle. Obviously the group of people to whom Peter wrote were experiencing some of the same feelings.

He reminds us that they, and we, are not the only ones to suffer. Suffering entered the human plane when Adam and Eve disobeyed God. It has been here since they were cast out of the Garden of Eden. Suffering, which is inconsistent with both God's character and God's will for humankind, is just a reality with which we must contend. In this context, why do we behave as though something strange is happening to us when suffering inevitably comes?

Peter reminds us that suffering is not a personal attack. Suffering is the enemy's design to obscure the presence of God in our lives. When we focus upon suffering we cannot sense the grace of God that flows to us continually. It often causes us to miss or to despise blessings. Rather than inspire us to spiritual heights, it often brings out the worst in us. Suffering is a test that we often fail.

Finally, Peter reminds us that certain kinds of suffering are shared. We share similar trials with others. Other mothers have runaway children. Other women have marital problems. Are there really any trials that someone else has not experienced at some time before? We also share in Christ's sufferings. Those who have been re-created in the image of Christ are also heir to His sufferings. Often, we are misunderstood, labeled, or maligned just like Jesus. Strangely, this becomes a cause for rejoicing, Peter says, because of its evidence that the Spirit of God is resting upon us.

Knowing that we do not suffer alone may not relieve all of the pain—but it surely helps!

Where Is the Kingdom?

April 6   *Read Luke 17:20-21.*

I don't often side with the Pharisees, but they asked a question that I often ask myself: "Where is this kingdom of God that we speak of so often?" We pray the Lord's Prayer that affirms: "Thy kingdom come. Thy will be done." Where is this kingdom?

As I look around, it is evident to me that the kingdom of God is not the church. The church is such an imperfect institution. We, in the church, are still trying to figure out what the church is. The church supports the kingdom of God, but the church is not the kingdom of God. If it were, the mission of Christ would be in great danger. So where is the kingdom of God?

Jesus said that this kingdom is different from any other. The kingdom of God is within you. The place over which God extends rule is within you. God is inside of you changing human agendas into godly agendas. God is using you to change the earth into a small glimpse of heaven.

April

Did you know that everyone, unconsciously, is looking for the realization of this kingdom? Parents, disgusted with graphic violence and profanity in the media, are looking for change. They want to see a glimpse of the kingdom of God. Change lies in your hands for the kingdom of God is hidden within you. Businesses are looking for honest employees. We are constantly looking for people of integrity—people we can trust. We are looking for the kingdom of God; and there you have it hidden within you!

How do we share this kingdom with others? Jesus encourages us to just live it out. Romans 14:17 says that the kingdom of God is not a matter of eating and drinking, but of righteousness, peace, and joy in the Holy Spirit. This means that people won't truly recognize God's kingdom coming into their lives through a lot of celebration or through any other material means. Others will see the kingdom of God come when we work for righteousness, peace, and joy. Our communities resemble war-torn areas. They need a little bit of peace and joy. In a land where integrity is so hard to find, we need to see righteousness. We need the kingdom of God.

The kingdom of God is not really hidden after all; it's just been entrusted to you. Long live the King!

Waiting to Crow

April 7   *Read Matthew 26:73-75.*

As Hector scratched around the barnyard, he was feeling that today was going to be special. The bright sun looked special. The sky was especially clear. In fact, he reflected, as the cool breeze blew through his feathers, "I feel special. What is it about this day?"

The special that Hector felt was a nagging kind of thing. He didn't know if it were a "happy special" or a "waiting for the other shoe to drop special." The day was different and excitement rose into his craw as he performed his customary daily duties. He scattered the baby chicks as usual. They needed to know that he was the rooster in charge. He pecked at an unruly hen. He jumped up onto the fence post, ruffled his tail feathers, and he crowed.

Finally, Hector decided to take a walk to find this special thing, or to have it find him. He found himself in a newly plowed field. The soil was loose and moist. "Maybe this is the special thing I am supposed to find" Hector thought. Before long he found two especially long earthworms that he almost gobbled whole. Though they were wonderful, he walked away from the field feeling that he should continue to search out his special destiny.

In the course of the day he found fruit peelings, a handful of grain, and a couple of juicy bugs. The day had been wonderful, but where was "special"? He wandered around until the end of the day looking for his special destiny. By nightfall he found himself in a familiar neighborhood. Yawning, if roosters can appropriately yawn, he strutted over to a familiar spot where chickens were known to roost.

The sounds of the night intruded into his special dreams—the feeling of specialness had not left him at all. Finally, the clamor of the night interrupted his dreams altogether. He leaned forward to hear the conversation.

"You were with him . . ." They were talking to a man Hector thought to be a companion of the Teacher. Hector had seen the Teacher and Hector had seen this man with Him, but the man said "No." By now, Hector was fully awake, wondering why the man disowned his friend.

The question came a second time. "Don't you know him?" Hector's beady eyes were glued to the proceedings. Maybe the man hadn't heard the question clearly. Perhaps he thought they were talking about another Teacher. He found it difficult to suppress the outrage rising in his little rooster bosom when the man again said "No."

The question came yet a third time. Hector had risen to a defensive posture. "Certainly you are also one of them, for your accent betrays you." Hector cocked his head to one side to be sure that he heard the answer. This time the man began to curse and carry on in terrible ways.

Hector was outraged! What a betrayal! Someone must do something he thought. So, without remembering that people did not speak rooster language, he threw back his head, took a deep breath and CROWED! Err-Er Er-Err Oooo!

The people in the courtyard didn't seem to pay Hector, who was still in a defensive posture, much attention. But the man who had been cursing and carrying on seemed to understand what Hector said.

Who knows if you, like Hector, might be waiting for your opportunity to crow? Have a special day today!

April

He Came for You

April 8   *Read Luke 4:18-19.*   •

Imagine what a scene this must have been. Jesus, born in a cloud of suspicion and gossip, grew up right around this neighborhood, and now declaring himself to be something special! The story of Jesus' rejection is much like our story. He indeed was special. He is the beloved only begotten Son of God, now loved and worshiped by millions. He is the Anointed One, come down from heaven to heal the world of its sins and of its rejections. Jesus' story is much like our story as women. Though special, loved, and anointed, He was accused and even rejected by those who should have loved Him most. The message for today is that their rejection did not change His worth. Nor does our rejection change our worth.

Jesus had a mission in life that He understood. He knew why He was here. He came for the poor, the prisoners, the blind, the shattered, and the crushed. He came to declare the year of the Lord's favor.

As a woman, who escapes feeling poor, captured in war, blinded and maimed, shattered or crushed? Jesus, one who also experienced rejection, has triumphed over rejection and comes to us to set us free. He freed a rejected daughter of Abraham who was bent over and could not straighten up for eighteen years (Luke 13:10-17). He freed a woman who had been subject to bleeding for twelve years (Mark 5:25-34). He walked perhaps twenty-one miles out of His way to raise up a dead woman's only son and give him back to his aging mother (Luke 7:11-17). He continues to come to heal us.

Somehow the ministry of Christ becomes more personal in this light. One who was wounded, yet healed, coming to the rescue of others whose hearts are being broken? Maybe this is what it means to be more like Jesus.

Facing Life

April 9   *Read 1 Corinthians 15:50-53.*

Most of us are not ready to die. Yet, each day, death looks over our shoulder. One preacher said that we are marching in endless procession toward the grave. For each one of us, a summons will come, one day. Until Christ returns, all must die.

The words of today's scripture passage are words of comfort. We shall all be changed. We shall be immortal. Knowing not when the day or hour shall come, are you ready, am I ready? How would life be if we lived as those ready to die?

First, we would be sure to start each day with prayer and thanksgiving. Perhaps we would complete more of the tasks that we begin if we thought that this could be our last day. Would we be kinder to the poor? I imagine that we would weigh each word carefully, mindful of the last impressions that we might leave. Our thoughts would frequently drift toward the Lord and the place He has prepared for us.

If this were your last day, would you be more gentle and less quick-tempered with family? Would you look for opportunities to make a memory? Would our friends hear words of appreciation and love that often go unsaid? Would you spend more time with your children and grandchildren? What would you do each time you saw the man of your dreams? Life would be so different if we lived as those prepared to die.

This may sound like Utopia but really it is not; it is just basic Christianity. The Christian is reminded that we are travelers. We are mere pilgrims and strangers passing through an unfamiliar land. We are encouraged to be kindhearted and tender in affection and full of goodwill for all.

If we could live each day as though it were our last! Instead of facing death, we could face LIFE!

I Have Seen the Lord

April 10   *Read John 20:11-18.*

It was the custom, in those days, to visit the tomb of loved ones for three days. Unable to come on the Sabbath, Mary was there early this particular morning. Love and devotion brought her to the grave to perform the service of anointing.

She really did not come to the tomb to find the evidence of a Resurrection, but rather to anoint a body that she believed must surely still be there. She was not focused on His promise to rise again. She was looking at her own physical weakness and worrying about the boulder between her and devotion to a dead body.

Aren't many of our obstacles like that? They are not really obstacles at all because God has reserved a miracle for us to discover. The barriers that we see in our head are only phantoms that mentally block the entrance to faith and discovery. They cause us to look at our failures, our weaknesses, and our inabilities. We see these as though under a microscope, so that they become larger than they actually are. We see pitfalls that hinder us.

When Mary arrived at the empty tomb, she was so convinced that she would find a dead body that she still could not see the miracle. Folded grave clothes only suggested grave robbers. The report of angels was no more consoling. She was so caught up in weeping over a death, she couldn't hear their hints of life.

We are so much like Mary. The everyday things of life loom large in our lives. We expect to see failure; while all along, God wants to show us success. God offers as life, one look for death. Where have you taken his body? We scan the horizons for disappointment; when God really wants us to be alert for windows of opportunity.

Even when Jesus appeared in the flesh, Mary was not quite convinced. She was not looking for Him; she was still looking for his dead body. Today, are you looking for Him or for His dead body? Do you really expect to connect with God or are you looking for ways to verify decay, aborted dreams, and missed opportunities?

Prayer: Jesus, open my eyes that I may recognize the miracles you have placed in my life today. Amen.

If You Had Been Here

April 11   *Read John 11:32-35.*

It was almost an accusation. "Lord, if you had been here, my brother would not have died." How many times have we felt like accusing God when things have gone wrong? Thank God, for Mary's sake and for ours as onlookers, Jesus did not allow the conversation to end there. He loved Mary enough to overlook the irrationality of her grief. He walked out to the tomb with her. He wept.

Things could have been different. Mary could have been so angry with Jesus for not coming sooner that she wouldn't speak to him. Have you ever been that angry or disappointed? There are times, in most of our lives, when it becomes difficult to talk to God because we didn't understand what happened. At times like these, it is important to allow ourselves to just be in God's presence. Look at what happened between Jesus and Mary. Though she was angry, they stayed together during that tender, fragile time of recent bereavement. She stayed with Jesus long enough to see a major change. Lazarus was raised from the dead.

God's ultimate plan for your particular situation may not be as bewildering as it appears today. Have you turned a deaf ear toward heaven? Did you walk away and leave God in mid-conversation? Perhaps the Lord is waiting for you to press through your anger and confusion about something so that you can hear the concluding portions of what he has to say to you. It may be that you have walked away and Jesus is still waiting for you to return to the tomb to see him turn things around.

Returning to the Cross

April 12   *Read Luke 9:23-24.*

I was in the cross selection room early yesterday. I was the first one there. When it came time to pick up my customary cross, the one I'd been struggling with every day, I decided to try out a new one.

LaKeesha's cross had always looked particularly attractive to me. The way she carried it about, I thought that it was hollow inside. Imagine my surprise when I could barely carry it to the door. Before anyone else came into the room, I dragged it back to its place as quickly as I could.

Monica's cross was hand carved out of fine wood like the furniture in her home. Now this was a cross with which I could be seen in public. When I picked it up, there was something very annoying underneath— splinters! How could such a fine piece of wood have splinters? Nevertheless, they were there; gouging pieces of the finest wood, making that cross impossible to bear.

Everywhere I turned, within what seemed to be the longest twenty minutes of my life, were crosses that I had admired from afar. Some looked good from a distance, but up close I could see the termites crawling all over them. Others were impossible to budge. Still others had an odor like that of an open flesh wound.

Finally, I picked up one that was comfortable and manageable. It was old and rugged. It had grooves in the wood underneath that fit my right shoulder perfectly. The cross I finally decided to carry was mine.

> Must Jesus bear the cross alone
> And all the world go free?
> No there's a cross for everyone
> And there's a cross for me.

Nine Times Out of Ten

April 13   *Read Luke 17:11-19.*

Nine times out of ten, it seems, we forget to thank God first. Jesus was just as surprised as we were that only one of the ten lepers returned to thank him for healing. What is on our minds, enabling us to do other things—nine times out of ten?

Those lepers approached Him from a distance because they had been pronounced unclean. Before Jesus healed them, they couldn't be around anyone but themselves. I wonder if they had been thinking about the things they would do if they ever got out of their predicament? Remember how it was when the walls of Jim Crow fell? We were so intent on going places we had not been able to do and doing things that we had not been able to do that we completely forgot to give God thanks for our little corner grocery stores and family restaurants by keeping them open. If it is so easy to forget one another when good times open their doors, how much easier it becomes to forget to put God first—nine times out of ten.

I wonder if those lepers were working on their story. What would they tell the people that had known them when they were rotting and sick? How would they explain Jesus? How many details would they include when they told their story? We can invest a great deal of time and energy in telling people about Jesus and still forget to tell Jesus thank you.

Perhaps, they were concerned about being accepted back into the community. Maybe they were worried about a whole new set of problems that had just emerged. It takes adjustment, on everyone's part, to become whole after chronic illness. Cancer patients have to learn how to be well when cancer is in remission. Recovered addicts have to learn what "normal" people do from day to day. It takes work just to be healthy! What would these newly healed persons do to fit into their world?

Nine times out of ten, it would seem, something else is on our minds when it is time to give thanks. What's on your mind today?

Doxology

> Praise God, from whom all blessings flow;
> Praise him, all creatures here below;
> Praise him above, ye heavenly host;
> Praise Father, Son, and Holy Ghost. Amen

People have been praising God with these words for centuries. They are often our first words of praise. Walking into church for the first time, I was amazed at the way people rose to their feet and began to recite this ascription of praise from memory. The Doxology was designed to be a part of worship in which all could participate.

In my early church days, I did not know how to praise God. After a few visits I learned the Doxology so that I could rise with the people and praise the Lord too! The Doxology became a badge of honor. Through it, I felt a part of the family; and I felt that God understood this strange holy language much better than the fumbled words in my heart.

For me, the old traditional Doxology served as an entry point into worship. It gave me the courage to open my mouth and join in with the household of faith while my personal experiences with God were yet developing. There are many ways to enter worship—many ways for God to call our spirits into praise.

Children, who have learned neither the traditional Doxology, nor the language of the African-American church, hear a different call to worship. They respond spontaneously, with whatever words of faith they have learned. In every culture that honors the Lord there are melodies and phrases that prompt those who love Him to respond in unfettered praise.

Now, there are new doxologies in my heart; new ascriptions of praise that help me to participate in the worship of the family of God. When I hear the words to "I thank you Jesus" my heart chimes in with "Lord, you brought me from a mighty long way." There are new cues that call me to worship. "Can't nobody do me like Jesus—he's my friend." The melody spurs me to misty-eyed reflections about my body, which has also been healed. When I am weary and cannot seem to pray, I need someone to remind me in song to "Call him up and tell him what I want."

Today, may the Holy Spirit whisper the comforting words of your favorite doxology, prompting you to praise.

Giving in the Recession

April 15   *Read 1 Kings 17:8-16.*

Widows in Elijah's day were at the bottom of the socioeconomic scale. They had to depend upon their sons for livelihood at a time when women were rarely financially independent. Elijah's widow lived at a time when her country was in economic recession; they were in the midst of drought. Though this woman had come to the end of her resources, God challenged her to give to a complete stranger in need.

Whether a single parent, never married, widowed, or deserted, today's women struggle in similar ways. It seems both difficult and unfair to ask for people in economic straits to give to the poor and needy. Why don't the bourgeoisie pick up more of their share? Why don't you ask someone with a good job? Don't take my last; ask someone who has more. Have you ever heard yourself think these words?

I find it amazing that the Lord chose to challenge a widow, ready to eat her last morsel and die, in the area of giving; but He did. What lessons are in this story for us today? What example does the widow of Zarephath set for us?

Look around you. The spirit of that woman is still among us. There are a number of women in the African-American community who share whatever they have with whomever it is that needs it. It does not seem to matter that they are considered below the poverty level. It does not matter than the food stamps are almost gone. These women give and give and give. Have you also noticed that these women never completely run out?

While most of us are not on the verge of running out of anything, few of us are known for selfless giving. Some widows and welfare mothers put us to shame. Could it be that they have discovered, even in their own private recession, that it really is more blessed to give than to receive?

Under Deborah's Palm

Imagine what it must have been like to sit under the palm tree with Deborah. The Israelites came for her wisdom. She helped them settle disputes. She provided insights from God. They traveled for miles to sit under a palm tree between Ramah and Bethel.

Wise women are such a necessary part of our culture. They help us to see beyond our noses. They slow us down when we are leaping before looking. They hint at dangers we cannot see. Wise women, like Deborah, are living reminders of God's wisdom. From time to time we all need to talk with Deborah.

The spirit of Deborah is still with us. She lives in your projects. She goes to your church. She works in your office building. She is gentle-spirited and unpretentious. If it were not for the aura of wisdom that surrounds her, you might not realize that she is there, but you need her.

I traveled a few miles last week to sit under Deborah's palm. My Deborah's name was JoAnn. She is just a few years older than I and full of God's wisdom. The Holy Spirit summoned us to lunch together.

Before I knew it, my heart was laid bare before the Lord. I don't know how we got on the subject that I had decided that God and I didn't really need to talk about anymore. In conversation with my Deborah, under her palm, I learned that God wasn't finished speaking to me yet. The

April

tears that rose uncontrollably, and the lump in my throat reminded me that I was still in pain. I sat for several hours, under Deborah's palm.

In Ghana, a council of elders often decide the weightier matters of the village. A group of men meet and deliberate and decide for everyone—after inquiring, "Have you asked an old woman?"

Quicksand

April 17   Read Matthew 13:18-23.

It was a hot dusty day in Louisiana. Waves of heat danced upon the dirt road giving the illusion of water. "This is the street. I saw it on the map." She turned right, slowed down, and began to look for the house number, 1152 Mobile Street. It was Sunday morning and Mona was on her way to pick up a friend for Sunday school.

She was not prepared for the unfamiliar whirring of her rear tires. Slowly, they began to sink into the loose sand—whirrrr, mmmwhirrrr. Mona gave the car more gas, "I must be stuck on something in the road" she thought. It turned out that she was stuck—in the loose sand!

Whirrrrr, mmmwhirrr—the more she tried to get out, the more she got in. Whirrrrrrrrrr stop. Finally, the rear of the car and the front of it was sunk to the axle. Whoever heard of such an odd thing! Mona, who was from the South, had never been stuck on the ice; it was too warm in that part of Louisiana. She had never been stuck in the mud; she was too smart for that. She had prided herself upon being an excellent driver. Now, however, she had to deal with both personal embarrassment and a car that was too big to push out of its predicament.

She was so mad that she didn't even walk to her friend's house, which was several blocks down the street, to call the tow truck. It was going to cost thirty-five dollars for being stuck in the sand! In exasperation, she picked up the Bible that her church had given her a few weeks ago. It opened to the following passage from Matthew 13:22: "As for what was sown among thorns, this is the one who hears the word, but the cares of the world and the lure of wealth choke the word, and it yields nothing."

Suddenly, it occurred to Mona that life was like that dusty old road—full of unexpected surprises. "Those surprises are just diversions

112

designed to take my attention away from God. My being mad is not going to change my being stuck," she thought. "I refuse to let this ruin my day! I may as well make the best of it. I believe that I'll use this extra time to see what else Jesus said about seeds, and roots, and faith."

It was nearly an hour before the tow truck came. An hour was plenty of time for a miraculous transformation. Instead of a ruffled, embarrassed woman on the verge of throwing a tantrum, the driver found a calm woman of growing faith, reading her Bible in the front seat.

Don't let the cares of life choke your faith today.

Lord, Who Do You Think I Am?

April 18   *Read Exodus 3:11.*

We live in a world filled with experts. Rather than feel the blessings of a specialized world, most of us live in the shadow of its curse. Since everyone else seems to be an expert, those of us who are not specialists feel inadequate. Why do our conversations with God and one another go something like this: "I don't have an education. I don't have experience. I don't have training in that area. . . ?" Don't you grieve inside when other women use this excuse: "But I never went to school, I can't speak in front of those people"? Moses seemed to be like we are in that he was not confident in his ability.

Perhaps the biggest obstacle that Moses was attempting to overcome was his own perception. Maybe what he was really saying to God was: "How will they believe that I am in church? After all everybody knows that I killed a man? Who's going to want to follow me, look at the mess that I made of my life! Who would ever believe that you would want me, nobody else does!"

Was Moses really asking: "Lord, who do you think I am?" Do you find yourself asking that question too? The Lord responded to Moses by reminding him of talents and abilities that he already had been given. God drew Moses' attention to the power and ability in his life that only comes from God. When we ask similar questions, God answers us in the same way.

Who does He think we are when He gives us these great opportunities? He thinks that we are like Moses, born for a mission in God's kingdom. He thinks that we are born with a purpose. We have been uniquely prepared and equipped to do something special for God.

We have been supernaturally rescued from death. We have been delivered from the certain death of poverty, oppressions of the past, and present societal pressures. We have a story of deliverance from destruction that parallels the story of Moses. We were not born into slavery—that time was a few years before our birth. Our family and community sacrificed so that we would have a better life.

We've been humbled by life's bumps and bruises. We have learned that God is greater. We have learned to trust. We've been prepared to serve. Now, who does He think we are?

Wherever we see orphans and misfits, God sees children that belong to Him. When we see ourselves impoverished, God sees us seated as queens. God answers our powerlessness with the power that His Spirit brings into our lives.

Today, we are encouraged to recognize who we are, stand on God's promises, and challenge the enemy in His name.

God Bless the Church

April 19   *Read Matthew 16:16-18.*

Lord, to think that you trusted Peter with the church. He was the disciple who I would vote least likely to succeed. He was impetuous, headstrong, hot-tempered. He spoke out of turn and cowered when you were in trouble. Lord, if the church depended upon Peter to survive, we are all in trouble.

The church that you spoke of is formidable and awesome. It stands as a pillar of strength. It advances forcefully so that even the gates of hell cannot resist. It opens its arms to welcome the wounded. It defiantly crosses its arms in the face of your enemies. If only we had a new vision of the church!

To think that you have trusted us with the church. We are no better than Peter—so full of flaws. We bicker and divide. We put people out who should be in and welcome folks in that should be out. We war with unbelievers in the name of the church. God help the church.

To think that you have trusted us with the church. We really don't quite know what a church is. We grope to understand what you had in mind. We miss the mark because we are not even sure where the mark is. Forgive us, Lord, for failing to truly be the church of which you dreamed. How has your church survived?

You dared trust Peter with the church because it was not in his power to make it or to destroy it. He was a mere vessel, a tool, a workman. His mistakes did not change your plans, nor do ours. His so-called successes were yours. The church continues because of You.

You continue to trust us with the church because You are confident that we will not alienate more people than we embrace. You are confident that we cannot pervert its doctrines beyond recognition. You are certain that some seed of truth that belongs to the church will survive and sprout life for the next generation. You have made provisions that the church never die.

God bless the church!

Missionaries

April 20   *Read Matthew 28:18-20.*

I thought I knew what a missionary was until I began missionary training. Suddenly, all previous notions were summoned for reexamination. What is a missionary? Is it some self-sacrificing soul who puts on odd clothes and goes trekking off to places never to be seen again by friends and neighbors? Perhaps a missionary is a person who has all of the answers and rushes off to force-feed strange folk with answers to questions that none of them had bothered to ask.

"I know the way—you didn't even know you were lost."

"Hey! Try it my way, or burn to a crisp in a place that you never dreamed existed!"

What, really, is a missionary?

Today, I discovered that a missionary is a person, chosen by God to cross boundaries. Missionaries are people who make their beds in uncomfortable places because God needs them there to arouse sleepy systems. They cross the street and visit the new people who no one else talks to. They cross town and love the teenagers that everyone else gave up for dead. They cross the state to bring a word of cheer and comfort to remote places. Some cross the rivers and oceans of this world, learning to eat unfamiliar foods, in order to expand God's communion table. Missionaries, sometimes, learn to speak languages that are unfamiliar to their mothers' ears in order to heal the souls of those in need.

Isn't God a missionary? Jesus crossed heaven's boundaries and became uncomfortable in order to bring a word of cheer to us. He criss-crossed the roads and rivers of our earth to embrace us. He ate the bread of affliction and washed in the waters of suffering with us. He learned to speak our language in order to heal our souls.

The Great Commission commands us to cross the boundaries that keep us from people who need us. The fulfillment of your missionary calling may be as simple as crossing the street or as complicated as crossing the ocean.

Today, why not pray to discern where God's missionary calling is leading you.

The Beginning of Wisdom

April 21   *Read Proverbs 9:10.*

Some years ago, right after I accepted Christ, several of us asked a person who was older in the faith to teach us how to repattern our lives. We knew immediately that a confession of faith meant that we were committed to a new way of life and did not know where to begin. None of us knew what to read. I had just bought a Bible and did not begin to know where to start searching for the answers. So we all asked for a shortcut.

Sister Sharon did not hesitate to answer. It only took a moment for her to give us the shortcut that others had offered to her. "Do nothing, nor say nothing that you would not do or say if Jesus were standing here beside you." Her answer was both simple and profound.

From that moment we began to question every action, every conversation, and every thought. We were learning to fear the Lord. Before long, some of us abandoned certain television programs. We jokingly told each other, "I wouldn't dare let Jesus catch me watching this!" Gradually, our nervous jokes were transformed in an understanding that Jesus really does walk beside us, seeing and hearing everything.

That was nearly twenty years ago. As with all new habits, I have since become lax in my understanding of the fear of the Lord. I invite you to renew this covenant with me: Do or say nothing today that we would not do or say if we recognized that Jesus were standing beside us.

Behind Locked Doors

April 22   *Read John 20:19-20.*

Most of us are not known for our courage. We tend to flow with the tides of public opinion. Though our inward convictions may be as different as night from day, there is something within us that fears being different from the crowd. The disciples were no different.

Today's passage finds them hiding in a locked room. The evangelist tells us that the doors were locked because of their fear. They had dared to be somewhat different for the three years that they walked with Jesus. Public opinion, however, is fickle. This fear was not unfounded. It was now more than the reputation of accompanying that unusual prophet. The same man who had been revered publicly as a prophet had recently been crucified as an enemy of the state. Even worse, the disciples who had been identified with his cause could also be executed. What else could they do? What would we have done?

For many of us, this is familiar territory. Quite often we find ourselves on the other side of the proverbial fence siding with an unpopular opinion. Inwardly we struggle with our personal need to stand up for our beliefs. We repeatedly punish ourselves for not being assertive enough. Our painful silence allows us to remain in the comfort of ambiguity. Because of public scrutiny, we remain locked behind closed doors. Those doors often become our private prison.

The beauty of this passage lies in the way that Christ dealt with the disciples' human fears. First, He did not embarrass them further by calling attention to the locked doors. Jesus is acquainted with our personal reasons for fear. Second, He did not chastise them for being fearful, but rather called them to peace. The direct opposite of fear is godly peace, which eventually can give us courage. Finally, He reassured the disciples of His power. The cross still looks like defeat, it still looks like weakness, it still seems to be a sign of powerlessness. For Jesus, and for us, the cross is actually a victory sign. The signs of resurrection, the nailprints in His hands and sides, show how death gave way to life. The very fact that He was publicly disgraced, emotionally wounded, killed, and yet alive was the reassurance that the disciples needed.

This did not mean that they were not still afraid sometimes. It did mean that they were being prepared for greatness and glory in the future. When the time came, these same weak-kneed disciples became bold witnesses of the death, burial, and resurrection of Christ.

Many of us have some area of our lives where we live "behind closed doors." We, like the disciples, hide from the eyes of public scrutiny because of our fears. Take comfort in the fact that Christ will invade our private prisons of fear, not to reprimand, but to comfort and empower.

Shalom.

Taking Too Much Care

April 23   *Read Luke 10:38-42.*

You, too, have seen her. She worked so hard with the details that she remembers nothing of Junior's high school graduation. We all had a wonderful time at the party in her home; we just wish that we had seen more of her that evening. Jesus knew that woman. She may live in your house.

I'm sure, in your history with the church, you've heard the sermon about the profound difference between doing the necessary and being in God's presence. This is a classic illustration of that principle, and Martha is wonderful to study, unless she lives in your house or mine!

What is it that drives us to choose details instead of divine discourse? What still drives us to women's duty when we could have deeper relationships? Somehow, our conscious and unconscious need for acceptance makes it impossible for us to be comfortable with ourselves or comfortable with society's symbols of the self.

Some women see themselves symbolically represented by their children. For them, a child with a problem somehow signals that its mother has a problem. For other women, the most powerful symbol of the self becomes the home. Regardless of our own perceptions about woman's liberation, the home has traditionally been our domain and continues to speak to others about us. By extension, the condition of our homes, our hospitality, and our ability to entertain others, for some, become yard-sticks of self-worth. Both men and women have found it easy to transfer the symbolic self to the workplace as well. When we focus on what we do best, whether at home or in the workplace, we point to the symbols of the self that we find most controlling in our lives.

Returning to today's passage we find Martha complaining: that her sister had left her to be the sole defender of the symbols of womanhood in this household. Jesus' rebuke is stinging. Mary had chosen what was better, and it would not be taken away from her. What was it that Martha struggled to hold onto? Jesus implied that it could be taken away. Perhaps, it was self-esteem derived from what she could do.

What did little sister Mary choose? She chose to not worry about what others thought of her womanhood. She chose to actively pursue the important part of her self—becoming more like Jesus. She chose to take care of her soul! Maybe, the modern lived-in look is merely an indication that something else takes priority in your life.

Today, when it gets down to a choice between dishes and devotion, what will you choose?

Can These Bones Live?

April 24   *Read Ezekiel 37:1-3, 9-14.*

Can these bones live again? Old bones, dry bones, been-dead-a-long-time bones—can they live again? Can your old dead, bones live—I mean really live? Only the Lord knows the things that attempt to prevent your enjoying life. When we look at one another, we find that we are like Ezekiel looking at an enormous pile of bones. No one quite knows how we came to be that way. How did we die, anyway?

Did we die when forced to be the front woman for the bill collector? Or was it when some of us discovered that we were unpaid domestics, or underpaid hood ornaments, begging to be loved, valued, and embraced? Some of us are still little girls inside, did we when we gave our virginity to someone who did not really care about us? Or, was yours taken? Some of us died looking for someone to love both body and soul. Some call us the mules of the world. Others call us abusers and say that we castrate the ones we love. We alternately see ourselves as survivor and victim, loved-one and plaything. When, exactly, did we die? Can we live again?

We are often like the Israelites when they encountered defeat. We say: "Our bones are dried up and our hope is gone"; while God says: "I will open your graves and bring you out!" We say: "They won't let me," while God is saying, "I will open doors that no one can shut." We keep on saying: "I don't have enough money," while God keeps on proving to us that our oil barrel will never be empty. We offer the excuse: "I don't know how," while Jesus reminds us that the Holy Spirit will be our teacher.

Let God's words from Ezekiel 37:14 be the last word today: "I will put my spirit within you, and you shall live, and I will place you on your own soil; then you shall know that I, the LORD, have spoken and will act, says the LORD."

If you still think that you are dead, hear today's encouragement from the valley of dry bones—you will live again!

For Those with a Child in Prison

April 25

Lord, when a son or a daughter goes to jail, it is so hard for us to feel free. Their defilement becomes ours. Their punishment becomes ours. Their failure feels like ours.

Teach us how to support the mothers of the many teenagers in prison.
We pray for the mothers of those who have violated women.
We pray for the mothers of those who have robbed.
We pray for the mothers of those who have shed blood.
Lord have mercy.

Teach us ways to be in solidarity with women who have done their best and yet bear the shame of adult children in jail. Show us how to help our sisters sort through the tangle of emotions that accompanied the courtroom proceedings and the sentencing of one who once shared their heartbeat. Teach us words that bring life instead of death and support instead of judgment.

Show us how to walk with our sisters in humility—knowing that the child in prison could have been ours. Amen.

Mama Ruth

April 26   *Read Ruth 1:15-16.*

When I reread the story of Ruth I am reminded of the tenacity of women of color. She refused to leave her mother-in-law after her husband was dead. I'm sure she knew that among Naomi's people, her people were despised. Home with her family, their traditions, and their gods would have been comfortable and predictable for her. But, being fully persuaded in her heart that she was doing the right thing, she plunged into an unknown future.

In similar ways, I see our sisters plunging into the unknowns of our culture and society as they attempt to follow the still small voice of the Spirit. Following the world's traditions and its gods would be so much more comfortable and predictable. Many find themselves struggling, like a fish swimming upstream, to do the right thing.

Do the right thing. It's a catchy phrase; Spike Lee has forever etched it into African-American consciousness. What does it really mean, to do the right thing? Ruth's story teaches us some lessons about this right thing. If she were alive today, we would probably call her Mama Ruth. Everyone in the neighborhood would understand her or her archetype. Thank God, there are still Mama Ruths in the neighborhood. They say things like: "I ain't lying for nobody, I was looking for a job when I found that one. . . . " They remind us to tell the truth and to stand up for what we believe.

Mama Ruths will put everything else down to do the right thing. Yours may have parted company with her man a long time ago. She is the kind of woman who works in the hardest of jobs to support herself and her loved ones instead of letting some sweet "Uncle" slip her a five under the sheets. If you dared to ask her why, she'd tell you: "Whatever you do, honey, do the right thing."

This particular Mama Ruth believed herself into the genealogy of Jesus Christ. Read Matthew 1:1-5.

In the end, in important ways, God always seems to come through for the Mama Ruths of history; because whatever they do, they try to do the right thing.

Faith to Be Healed

It seemed so cruel at first. The man had never walked, he could not use his feet; he was crippled from birth. Paul was telling that man to do something that he really had never been able to do—stand up! He jumped up like a jack-in-the-box in response. Not only did he stand up, he walked! Was this so cruel after all?

The Lord never tells us to do something that He will not make possible. The instructions given by Paul in this passage, and Peter in another, were patterned after those that Jesus had given on several occasions. He spoke to a paralytic and told him to stand, pick up his bed of affliction, and walk away. Then, He made it possible for the man to do just that! Is there a word of encouragement in this for you today? Jesus, who is the same yesterday, today, and tomorrow, is still telling folks to get up and walk away from misery.

Jesus performed this same kind of miracle several times. Was it to reinforce His point? On another occasion, almost in response to the dares of His detractors, He told a man with a withered hand to stretch out his hand! He no longer had an excuse to assume the posture of one who was injured or deformed. So many times, we are made to feel impaired. Do you feel that being a woman is a disadvantage? Does it seem that being Black is a disadvantage? No more excuses, no reasons to lag along behind—forsake what looks like a disadvantange and stretch out your hand!

It does not matter how long you have felt hindered by life's circumstances. Jesus is able to release you from any malady. One poor man had been laying by a sacred pool waiting for a miracle for years. Others seemed to get miracles, while he just remained in the same condition year after year. Jesus interrupted his self-pity and told him the same thing that others had been told: If you want to be healed, get up and leave this sick place. Furthermore, take your bed away so that you will not ever be tempted to return and lay here again! Are there sick places that you need to abandon?

Perhaps this is the day to realize that God is calling you from misery to health. Get up from there! You can do it, for you have faith to be healed!

Knife Sharpener

"This woman is plucking my last nerve!"
"Doesn't she know that she's a nuisance?"

Two friends shared horror stories concerning a particularly obnoxious person that they both knew. This difficult person was groping in the darkness for her way. That would have been fine except that she was knocking everyone down in the process!

"Iron is supposed to sharpen iron," thought one of the women, "but this woman is dulling my knife!" Or, was the knife already dull before the woman came along to test her?

Maybe none of us is as sharp as we think we are. We could always use a little refinement. We do not have as many opportunities for growth when we surround ourselves with people who are like us. The real, telling moments come when we encounter those who are noticeably different.

For example, there are times when we meet someone who seems as sharp as a knife. Their eyes pierce our souls, their mouths become swords. We alternate between hiding from their piercing gaze and wanting to be around them. Sharp people stretch us; we need them. In their presence, there are fewer choices—either grow or get cut! If we should happen to find a safe place from which to observe them, we might find that their life's experiences, with people who are even sharper, have refined them—as iron sharpens iron.

Then there are others we meet, like the woman who vexed our friends. Refinement for them is still on the to-do list. They need us. We often forget that they too need challenging encounters to sharpen their souls. You or I might just be the sharp person that they have admired from afar.

The process in which iron sharpens iron is a two-way process. Interaction with those sharper than us refines us. In similar fashion we are sharpened by those who need to be with us. In all of our encounters with other people, we learn something. We may even learn that we need more sharpening. Sometimes it's good to have testy people in our lives— they help us recognize when we are losing our edge.

The Hometown Blues

April 29   *Read Luke 4:21-30.*

James Cone, the grandfather of Black theology, wrote *The Spirituals and the Blues*. In this book he examines two musical art forms created by African-Americans. We are all familiar with the spirituals. They affirm our faith and express what we are waiting for. For the early slaves they were a breath of hope and a whispered prayer. "Swing low sweet chariot, coming for to carry me home." I am going to a better place. "Steal away to Jesus, I ain't got long to stay here." Time may be insufferable now, but it's not long. Martin Luther King expressed the same thoughts in his often quoted, "How long? Not long!"

The blues, on the other hand, have often been looked down upon by church folks. In reality, they are as much a part of our experience as the spirituals are. The spirituals look at what we want life to be. The spirituals look at what we hope for. The blues look at life as the singer sees it. The blues explore the tension between the world that we wait for and the world that is right now.

The people in Jesus' hometown gave Him the blues. I'm sure that He could have sung a blues song that B.B. King and Muddy Waters would have cherished. It might have sounded much like "The Hometown Blues," a song written by this author for a sermon.

THE HOMETOWN BLUES

Let me tell you a story,
It's called the Hometown Blues,
The more you trying to win,
The more they try to make you lose.

You get up in the morning
Victory on your mind.
But when you look around you
They pulling you behind.

Refrain:
It's called the hometown blues, they just won't leave me alone.
It's called the hometown blues, I can't get ahead until I'm gone.

Everywhere I turn
They talking about me.
Some talk about my head.
Some talk about my feet.

I can't do nothing right;
They too busy calling wrong.
They bad talk about me
The whole day long.

Refrain:

They just don't understand
What it's all about.
Hometown would be a better place
If we could help one another out.

Moving in the same direction
We can go anyplace.
Lord, will you help us
While we run this race?

Refrain:

Perhaps this song is your song. As we examine today's passage, it becomes quite evident that Jesus could have sung the blues for several reasons. If we return to James Cone's definition of the blues, an attempt to reconcile what ought to be with what is, we discover that we all have a blues song to sing. It's all right to sing your blues sometimes—as long as that is not the only song that you choose to sing!

The Potter's House

Pat saw the size-three woman standing alongside the road selling pottery. She spoke only enough English to invite the travelers to buy her wares. The yellow clay that clung to her ebony hands betrayed the possibility that she was the potter. She was so proud of each line etched into the bottom of the pottery bowls used for grating pepper. They were wet and unfired, yet carefully fashioned by this tiny Ashanti potter woman according to her intent for their use.

The travelers left without buying. Pat's mind lingered there as they drove a few more miles northward toward Kumasi. Then her mind drifted to her own brief encounter with a potter's wheel. For a few seconds she was back at the recreation center in Louisiana kneading water into the dry unpliable clay. She was feeling the light mist that comes when water is poured over the formless lump while the wheel is turning. She was positioning her thumbs in the middle, preparing to throw an earthen pot.

From there, she caught a vision of her own misshapen pot. She felt that life's circumstances had steered her away from God's original intentions for her life. Tears welled up in her eyes as she thought of her current season of spiritual drought. "If only I could feel healing waters poured over my dry, thirsty soul." She forgot to feel conspicuous in the vanful of travelers as she looked out the window and prayed:

> Lord, I am dry and barren
> Water my soul with your Spirit
> Knead the harshness from my heart
> With your own hands
> And mold me anew.

Do you, too, feel that life's circumstances have steered you away from God's original purpose for your life? Perhaps there are many of us yearning to return to the potter's wheel. Today, stand still and allow the Lord to soften your heart, and begin to gently remold your purpose.

May

Faith of Our Mothers

May 1   *Read 2 Timothy 1:3-5.*

Grandmomma's Bible is old and worn. She used to cradle it in her lap in the same way that one cradles a newborn. It was far too big for her wasting arms. Sometimes we had to carry it for her when she went to church. We knew better than to suggest that she use another lighter weight Bible, because that Bible was grandmomma's friend.

She used to read that Bible for hours at bedtime. Sometimes we would notice the light on in her room well into the night. On tiptoes, I would prepare to turn it off, only to find Grandmomma glued to the pages of her Bible looking up at me with eyes that asked, "What are you doing?" Grandmomma could tell you what that Bible said, too. It wasn't just reading; it was learning. It was living. Grandmomma was a real Christian. When she died, we were almost afraid of that Bible—it seemed to have become a living thing.

Momma, as she gets older, is getting the same way. Questions about Nehemiah and Ephesians frequently replace our long distance chitchat about the weather. She's a modern grandma with a computer Bible on her hard drive. Now that she has retired, she has more time to do personal Bible study. Last time I was home, I noticed the pages beginning to age in Momma's old bedside Bible, too.

Because of my momma's and grandmomma's examples, I find it hard to place things on top of any of the many Bibles in our home. In word and in deed, these two women have taught me reverence and have passed on their faith. Whenever I think of my grandmomma, I am reminded to read my Bible. And whenever I talk to my momma, Jesus' name always seems to come up in conversation. Living in the faith has become an expected norm, because of the faith of my foremothers.

I, too, am a mother. I pray that my faith will also rub off on my children in permanent ways. As parents, we can only guess about those aspects of our faith that might impact our children. I often wonder what my sons will think when they see my old beaten-up Bible?

The Truth About Shadows

May 2   *Read Psalm 23:4 (KJV).*

Sometimes, when I am alone at night, I am frightened by the shadows of my own movement. I don't always recognize the reflection on the wall of some activity of which I am a part. How ridiculous to be frightened of my own shadow! Have you ever been frightened by yours?

Shadows are just images; they are not real. Yet, they continue to frighten us. The valley of the shadow of death gives us chills, and we worry about shadows of the things we cannot see.

Actually shadows are poor representations of reality. They are usually much bigger than the object from which they take shape. You can't really touch a shadow because it is not real.

The shadows of life are like that too. The dragons we imagine are always much bigger than the dragons we encounter face-to-face. Sometimes the shape of things is much different than its shadow appears. There are even times when the real danger disappears before we actually see it. Was it ever real?

Perhaps it's time to make certain observations about shadows. Shadows are macabre phantoms that depend upon light for form and intensity. Shadows are not real; they are mere illusions that cannot be touched or felt. The brighter the light, the darker the shadow is. Oh yes, I almost forgot—shadows are also cowards. They can't stand to be too close to light—it causes them to disappear altogether!

"Yea, though I walk through the valley of the shadow of death, I will fear no evil: for thou art with me; thy rod and thy staff they comfort me." Jesus is the light of the world; He chases away all the shadows of our lives.

Sacred Sites

May 3   *Read 1 Samuel 7:10.*

The Bible is filled with sacred sites. These are places to commemorate times when the Lord appeared, delivered, or interacted with men and women in special ways. Moses saw the burning bush and was reminded that he was standing on holy ground. Hagar saw a well of water when perishing and was reminded of God's faithfulness. When Jacob saw the ladder to heaven he knew that God was with him and that place became special. He set up stones and gave the place a name.

Both Abraham and Isaac were known to build altars or dig wells to commemorate their significant moments with God. Here, in 1 Samuel 7, Samuel takes note of God's deliverance and protection from the Philistines. He set up a stone marker and named it Ebenezer, meaning "stone of help." Each time he passed that marker, he was reminded of a point in time, a situation, a particular circumstance, where God had been his helper. After his death others were able, through that same marker, to tell his story and theirs.

I have at least one personal Ebenezer. It is a long illness that began with a kidney infection and ended in antibiotic shock. God's personal intervention saved my life. It is a landmark spiritual event that I return to frequently. It is a testimony that I share with others.

Sisters, we have collectively and individually, many points in time when the Lord has been our help. We have rescue stories, deliverance stories, and close calls that speak of the faithfulness of God in our lives. We have our own Ebenezers. They are points at which our faith is strengthened. They become testimonies that we share at special times with the people we trust as we strengthen one another and celebrate God's presence in our lives.

The second verse of "Come, Thou Fount of Every Blessing" speaks of another kind of Ebenezer experience:

> Here I raise mine Ebenezer;
> Hither by thy help I'm come;
> And I hope, by thy good pleasure,
> Safely to arrive at home.
> Jesus sought me when a stranger,
> Wandering from the fold of God;
> He, to rescue me from danger,
> Interposed his precious blood.

We all have at least one Ebenezer: the story of our rescue from eternal death. Our individual conversion stories stand like monuments in time continually speaking of God's help.

Rhythm Band

Read Psalm 150:1-6.

I've got a tambourine in my bosom. It's beating out praises to God my King. No one else can hear it, but it beats out a rhythm that says, "Praise You. Thank You, Lord!" Its bells shake and accentuate time when I walk through the produce section at the grocery store. Its skin is well worn from praising the Lord.

I've got a trumpet in my heart. It sings with sweet brassy notes. It soars through holy melodies while I'm riding in my car. It flourishes and salutes blue notes and high notes that reach toward the heavens to worship my Lord.

I've got a harp in my hands. Its gentle notes are strummed as I sit at my desk. My hands caress each string each time I think of Him. No one else hears the music as I reach for the harp strings; but its melodious sounds and chords reverberate through my soul. Holy Spirit take control.

The bass drum is in my belly. With each beat of the bass, I bend and sway and reach out in adoration. That drum beats when I walk down the street. It gives me purpose and coaxes my feet to gently pound the pavement. My neck begins to bob in response to its otherwise inaudible beat. I beat the drum down the street.

There is dancing in my feet as I wait for the bus. Left-side-sway-step! Heh! Right-side-sway-step! Just like the choir—along with the choir. There's a rhythm band on the inside of me; there's music in the air; there's dancing in my feet! Praise you, my King. Let everything that has breath praise the Lord.

Deathbed Confession

Read Mark 9:42.

Granddaddy was my male role model. He taught me a great deal about men in general. He was a strong Black man whose parents had been freed from slavery. If Granddaddy didn't have an opinion about it, it wasn't worth talking about. He was a dining room table philosopher. Over dinner, I heard about Malcolm X, the March on Washington, Garveyism, and everything that was going on anywhere. I loved my grand-daddy.

Granddaddy had this one quirk that we never could understand. I never saw him go to church. That doesn't mean that I never saw "church" in him. I mean that I never saw him in the church house.

As a child, some of my fondest memories are of the great hymns of the faith being whistled in the basement of my grandfather's house. He whistled hymns while he hammered and sawed on Saturdays. On Sundays those present in the house heard hymns until the radio wouldn't play them anymore. You see, Sunday was a day for God. We dressed a little nicer, sat quietly, rested, and listened. We listened to the church services on the radio. I heard Billy Graham, the Rosary Hour, and every local preacher on the air. For us the sabbath became holy.

Yet, if you wanted a rip-roaring argument, you got one if you tried to make Granddaddy go to somebody's church. And he didn't want nobody's preacher in the house unless they were kinfolks. I never understood why until just before his death.

Granddaddy died in January of 1982; he was eighty-seven years old. Like many of the old folk, I believe he knew when he was about to die. A few days before his death, he gave me his deathbed confession, which I share with you.

As a young man in rural Oklahoma, he accepted Christ as his Savior. He was excited about Jesus. He joined the church and the choir. One evening, walking home from choir rehearsal, he realized he had forgotten his coat. Churches back then were unlocked, so he returned to get it, only to find that the church was "occupied" by a deacon of the church and a sister in the choir! From that day to his death, church was more than a sour taste in his mouth.

He never returned, not even for his funeral.

How many people have we Christians turned away from the church? Jesus says it would be better for such a person to be thrown into the sea with a millstone around his neck!

Perfume?

May 6   *Read 2 Corinthians 2:14-16.*

What is it that we like so much about perfume, I mean really good perfume? Everywhere we go, the fragrance goes. When heat is applied—I mean we get warm and perspire—the fragrance is intensified! On hot days, during times of stress, or when we want to make a bold psychological statement, we take a bath and apply more fragrance. Good perfume worn properly, is pleasant for everyone close to us.

It's just like that in spiritual things. The apostle Paul reminds us that we spread the fragrance of Christ wherever we go. To those who are being saved, we are reminders of the sweetness and the pleasantness of Christ. To those who are perishing, we are reminders as well. Anyone coming near a Christian should be reminded of the fragrance of Christ. He concludes by asking if any of us is equal to this enormous task. Am I sufficient for such a task?

Some days I feel just like a child. I have so much growing to do. I am spiritually immature. Children don't always know how to wear perfume. Some apply perfume before taking a bath. Do you remember those days? Have you ever been trapped in the car with a youngster wearing generous amounts of both sweat and perfume? Whew! What fragrance, or odor, fills the room when I am there?

I am intimidated when I remember that many people may judge the entire Christian movement by the fragrance that emanates from me. I am not sure that I know how to represent Christ well at all times. Someone has said that you will know the real Christians by noting what happens when life applies a little bit of pressure! I am not sure if my perfume holds under pressure.

When roses are crushed, rubbed, or ground into the pavement they are fragrant. When an onion is crushed, rubbed, or ground into the pavement—oh my! I have good days and bad days like anyone else. What happens when I am crushed? How do I smell?

Thank God that the impression that we make upon others, and the fragrance we leave behind, is not dependent upon our inherent goodness.

What fragrance will you wear today?

Aiming High and Bending Low

May 7   *Read Psalm 121:1-8.*

Lift up your head, you are a child of God! Sorrow and confusion have bowed your head one time too often. Isolation has persuaded you to believe that you are the only sufferer. Don't let any person, problem, or parameter convince you that you are an orphan. God is with you. You are not alone. Help is never more than a whisper away.

Lift up your eyes. Look to the hills. Look higher and higher until you see their gentle slopes and their craggy dimensions. As you peer even closer, you will see the various forms that God will take as help comes your way. Sometimes God will come as the wind and blow your trials away like an open window scatters papers. Other times God comes as the pure, gentle voice of reason. Still other times God comes as a fire, purifying all in us and around us that is not refined. Your help comes from the Lord who made heaven and earth—nothing is difficult for Him.

Bow down before Him alone! Don't bow down to the pharaohs in your life. Heavy taskmasters, like bills and sickness, don't deserve the undivided attention that they often receive, nor do they deserve your inadvertent praise. They were designed to do best what seems to vex you most. Why not give your homage to One who can change things, God and God alone?

Bend low in obeisance to One who never sleeps! He is your protector and your defender. The Lord guards your life. Refuse to allow the challenges of this day or any other to lay your spirit in the dust. Aim your sights high and bend your knees in prayer—your help is in the Lord.

Has Anybody Seen My Child?

May 8   *Read Luke 15:17-24.*

Has anybody seen my child? He walked out of here with all I could give him a long time ago. They say he's standing on the corner, sagging low. Hope he's not up to no good. That boy has a good heart—if only he could get his mind straightened out! Has anybody seen my child?

Have you seen my child? She's been hanging with the wrong crowd. Last week, she came home with things that we could never buy. Haven't seen her since. We're so afraid for her. Has anybody seen my child?

Have you seen my adult son? He works for a corporation somewhere in that city. We sent him to school and he's done well for himself. They say he keeps to himself and will do anything for a dollar. We just never hear from him anymore. I don't even know his address. If you should see him, remind him where we live.

Do you know where my gal is? She don't come around no mo'. I think she's 'shame of us. She git her teeth fixed and her hair did and learned how to talk right. Ain't got no time fo' me—No Mo'! The world done turned her 'roun' and 'roun'. All them brand names done gone to her head! I hear she don't go to nobody's chu'ch neither. Do you know where my gal is?

There are so many ways that we as children become prodigal. We become separated from God and separated from one another. Some of us get lost in riotous living; others of us get lost in corporate America. Lost is lost. God as a faithful father is looking for all lost children. He'd like to celebrate our return.

You Shall Live!

May 9   *Read Psalm 118:12-17.*

There are many forms of death. Hollywood thrives upon unearthing our deepest fears and serving them to us. Blazing flames from which we cannot escape, the slow death of being buried alive, relentless attacks by killer bees; we fear a thousand living deaths. The psalmist recreates the fearful deaths of his day, killer bees and wildfire; in the name of the Lord he lives through them all!

Listen to a paraphrase of his declaration of faith. "I have been surrounded by nations. I have been trapped by what seemed like natural circumstances. None of these were able to prevail against me. God has triumphed over them all. I shall not die, in spite of contrary public opinion; I shall live and tell everyone about the works of the Lord!"

You also shall not die, but live. The worst that could happen is unable to prevail against God's will for your life. No urban nightmare or Hollywood fantasy is able to consume you before your appointed time.

You shall live. There is a vast gap between not dying and learning to live. Some of us live in that gap called existence. Jesus has come into your lives to teach you how to live beyond mere existence. Because the Lord is your strength and your might, you shall live. Strike up those chords of victory within your heart!

When you return from the valley of the shadow of death, remember to tell what the Lord has done. There are so many resurrected souls from whom we have never heard. So many with secret stories of near death experiences from whom we could learn. The fear of death might not be so severe if we just had more witnesses—like you.

You Are Being Watched!

May 10   *Read Job 1:6-12.*

"Somebody must be out to get me!" "What have I ever done to deserve this!" Job must have wondered how on earth he could have merited the misfortune that followed after that conversation between God and Satan.

Our African worldview teaches us to search for the relationship between our deeds and misfortune. You know the things your grand-momma told you like, "If you do good, good things will happen to you; but if you do bad, honey. . . ." Phrases like "what goes around, comes around" cause us to examine our past deeds when trouble comes our way. Though Grandmomma told the truth, her axiom does not always apply to every situation. Sometimes trouble just comes through no fault of our own—from origins we do not see.

There is another reality, to which scripture often refers, where the angels live. We really cannot see what goes on in that realm of the spirit; we only see the effects. The Bible tells us that we are not fighting with flesh and blood, but with powers and principalities that exist in ways that are foreign to us (Eph. 6:12). All of heaven and hell is watching us to see what God is doing in our lives (1 Cor. 4:9).

How fortunate for us that this heavenly conversation about Job was preserved. It begins to answer some questions that likely have plagued you and me. In Job's case, profound trouble had nothing to do with what he had done wrong. As cruel as it may sound, Job was just being tested. In similar ways sometimes you and I are just being tested. As we pass the test others who look on are strengthened; faith in God is confirmed, and God is glorified.

Do not fear the testing that inevitably comes to every life—God is on your side.

New Creation

May 11   *Read Isaiah 65:17-18.*

We stand on the brink of a new creation. Isaiah does not imply that creation is unfinished. He rather seems to be saying that something new, beyond imagination, is going to occur. Creation has been in turmoil since the Garden of Eden. God is about to create new heavens and a new earth. The universe is suspended in a pregnant pause; waiting for this new thing to take place.

Creation has been groaning in anticipation of a second chance (Rom. 8:22). So often when we think of starting over, we can only relate our human experiences like divorce and remarriage. Our starting over is always stained by memories of the past. We are haunted by our complicity with sin; we lament over our failures. God redefines the concept of starting over. The new heaven and new earth will be so awesome that the memory of our previous heaven and earth will be erased.

You and I, along with heaven and earth, are a part of this coming new creation. The realm of this creation extends to Jerusalem, representative of God's kingdom, and to its people. Look at what God is about to do with us!

What an awesome possibility! You and I will be re-created. We will live in a world that is not complicated by racism, selfishness, or power issues. We will gaze at unpolluted heavens; and we won't be tormented by the memory of things as they were.

Can you see us? We will be re-created in His image without character flaws and without stumbling blocks. The painful memories of our failures and foibles will not even be allowed to return and haunt us. We will be a joy and a delight to our God; and at peace within.

Thank God today that this life is not a dead-end street. Something new and wonderful flutters on the horizon.

Lot's Wife

May 12   *Read Genesis 19:17, 26.*

There are many ways to become a pillar of salt. Just like there are many ways to die, there are many ways to become ineffective. Lot's wife looked back and became immobilized. Why did she look back-ward?

Did she look back to the good old days when she had her own home and life was carefree? Proverbial wisdom reminds us that the good old days were really never quite as good as we remember them. We all know this, but it never seems to stop us from looking back and longing. Why do we find it easier to rest on old laurels than to find new ones?

Did she look back to a time in her life when things were not so diffi-cult or so painful? Did her bitterness immobilize her? How many times has our anger and resentment about the past tied us up in rigid knots? How many "thank God" have we forgotten to utter because the comfort of an old wound eclipsed the blessings of the present?

Did her refusal to face the present or the future trap her in a fantasy world? You know what a fantasy world is like don't you? It's a place where we pretend that everything is going our way—whether it really is or not. Why did she, in spite of the warnings, look back? Why do we?

Looking back is a two-sided coin. On one side of the coin we learn from the close calls, deliverances, and victories of our past. We learn to celebrate the progress that God brings into our lives. We learn to appreci-ate life and its blessings.

On the other side of the coin we find danger. Danger lurks behind our twenty-twenty hindsight. Sometimes when we look back all we see is loss, compounded misery, and failure. These are the things that keep us from today's success. Our past often threatens to immobilize us when we look back.

There are many ways to become a pillar of salt. There are many ways to become immobilized and useless. Looking back could be one of them.

Prayer: Lord of my todays and tomorrows, help me to lift my eyes and behold a bright future. Amen.

Understanding Exile

May 13   *Read Psalm 137:1-4.*

Today's psalmist describes days that we all experience at one time or another; days when a song won't come to our hearts or our lips. "How can we sing the LORD's song in a foreign land?" He is feeling isolated, punished, and alone. He is in exile.

You and I know plenty about exile. There is the self-imposed exile of not feeling good about ourselves. There is the exile of alienation, loneliness, or depression. Exile comes when we are rejected. There is the exile of big disappointments. We feel exiled when those closest to us do not understand our pain. There are societal exiles like the divorced or widowed. Perhaps your exile started when you left home for the first time or the tenth time. Did it start when the children left home? Yes, we are also exiles.

But, what really is an exile? Is it a person who has been barred from home or one who has been displaced? Are you displaced? Because our home is in the heart of God, we are never barred from returning. Perhaps those feelings of exile come to remind us where we belong. It could be that those feelings of loneliness and isolation are really signs and markers that God uses to point to our need for Him.

Can anything good come of exile? The exiles in today's passage were happy to go home when the time came. They went home in humility. After being deprived of even the ability to sing, they returned determined to live closer to God. Exile taught Israel to cherish a gift that they had taken for granted—God's presence. In similar ways, exile teaches us to cherish those moments when God is near.

May I invite you to pause and celebrate the teachings of past exiles in your life? Or, if you happen to be an exile, pick up your harp and prepare to sing again. The way home is shorter than you think!

Great Is Thy Faithfulness

May 14   *Read Lamentations 3:21-23.*

Cold tears ran into LaVerne's ears while she lay in bed on her back with her eyes closed. Her life had changed overnight. Only hours ago, her husband had asked for a divorce. She loved him too much to even think of it.

Ugly words and phrases had flown through the air like bullets piercing her heart and rendering her numb. "If I could only tell him that I love him one more time," she thought. After the horrible fight, Larry jumped into his car and drove into the night. LaVerne could not sleep. She just lay in a bed that was wet with tears and numb with the shock of the last few hours.

When we are in shock, sometimes, it seems as if we are suspended in time. We are neither here nor there. It becomes so difficult to grasp life in the face of rejection, betrayal, or disappointment. The writer of Lamentations was afflicted in similar ways. In the midst of a holocaust, he had the disadvantage of having known better days. When we have seen better, happier times, how do we make sense of the contradiction?

Sometimes, it is best to avoid spending too much time in a past that was seemingly better. Lamenting oftentimes creates an environment to revisit pain. Perhaps it is best, in times like this, to live one day, one hour, one minute at a time.

God's mercy comes to us one minute at a time. Each moment holds new opportunities to experience new mercy. When we need more strength, God gives it then. He will never let us be consumed by trials.

What finally happened to LaVerne? The Lord gave her an unusual reminder of the new mercy being offered her. At the regular time, her clock radio played music to awaken her. The local gospel station was airing an old version of "Great Is Thy Faithfulness."

> Great is thy faithfulness!
> Great is thy faithfulness!
> Morning by morning new mercies I see;
> All I have needed thy hand hath provided;
> Great is thy faithfulness,
> Lord, unto me!

For Those Imprisoned by Bad Habits

May 15

Lord, we confess that most of us do not understand the level of despair that causes some women to turn to drugs. We cannot fully empathize with their hopelessness or know their emotional pain; but we can pray for their deliverance. Lord, have mercy upon women imprisoned by bad habits.

We ask you to step into the darkness of despair and bring light.

We ask you to walk into the turmoil of their lives and bring peace.

We ask you Lord, to give hope instead of hopelessness and loosen the chains of bondage.

We ask you to give new friends to the friendless.

We ask you to restore what has been lost or stolen.

Lord have mercy upon women imprisoned by bad habits.

We also pray for ourselves:

Open our eyes

Alert us to helping ways.

Release us from codependency and silence.

Silence our wagging tongues.

Give us compassion.

Show us how to receive spiritually whole women back into the community as one would receive a loved one raised from death. Amen.

Is Your Face Shining?

May 16   *Read 2 Corinthians 3:18.*

Wearing veils may not be in fashion this year; yet most of us occasionally hide behind a veil. Paul Lawrence Dunbar would call it a mask. Whether you call yours a mask or a veil, it's purpose is the same—to hide us from the scrutiny of the world's prying eyes.

Your veil may be an unmovable smile. Some people have mastered the ability to smile even if the entire world should cave in around them. A fixed smile hides pain. It is so much easier to smile than to explain. Others hide behind a harsh exterior. Too many iron maidens are putty inside and fearful that someone will peep underneath and learn that they are as afraid as the rest of us. What exactly, is under your protective veil?

Moses wore a veil. During the Exodus, Moses spent several extended seasons with God on the mountain. They communed together for forty days at a time. After one such extended time, Moses returned to the people not realizing that his appearance had become frightening. He was aglow with God's presence! His face shone like a bright light. The people were terrified. From that time on he wore a veil over his face so the people could bear to look at him. When he was in the Lord's presence he removed the veil and once again communed with the Lord face-to-face. Such was Paul's reference to unveiled faces that reflect the Lord's glory.

Have you noticed that those who frequently experience God's presence seem to glow? They light up the whole room with the freshness of their experience. Spending time with God transforms us. We are changed into His likeness. We become as dazzling as Moses was after his forty days on the mountain with God.

Today you are encouraged to cast off your heavy veil and spend time on the mountain with God. When you return from the encounter don't be ashamed to let your face shine with the light of his glory.

Healthy Space

May 17   *Read Genesis 13:5-13.*

All healthy friendships have boundaries. Power issues, like who gets to boss whom under what circumstances, are decided. We alert one another, in healthy ways, to personal taboos. "I can't talk about this." "I never do that." "This hurts my feelings." The rules of social etiquette are forged with that person. We learn how to speak to one another, when to visit, and where to sit.

Sometimes however, in even the best friendships, the boundaries become blurred. What was formerly mutual respect can turn into bossiness. Playfulness can turn into put-downs. Without healthy boundaries, friendships can easily fall apart.

Abraham and Lot discovered that they needed healthy boundaries in their relationship. They were both friends and family. Lot was a beloved nephew. According to scripture (Acts 7), he was a righteous man. Nothing was wrong with either person, they were both blessed by God. They just needed some healthy space.

When Abraham and Lot decided to take new directions, it was by mutual decision. They did not have to argue. They didn't stop speaking to each other. There was no hint of blaming. In fact, they may even have remained in contact with each other. They just established the healthy boundaries that they both needed.

There may come a time in some of our relationships when we will also need some space. You may need some healthy distance in order to maintain a healthy relationship with someone that has been closer to you than your own skin. You may just need space to think independently or to grow in new directions. Don't despair, boundaries can be a blessing.

Big Foot

May 18   *Read Mark 9:2-9.*

Have you ever been a self-appointed spokesperson clumsily breaking what could have been a wonderful silence? Some of us put at least one of our feet into our mouth so often that the taste of shoe leather is as familiar as that of toothpaste. How do we recover from such moments? How did Simon Peter?

I stand in continual awe as I read the Gospels. Simon Peter is there—and Jesus loves him. That means that there is hope for me. Peter was known to boldly stomp into the most delicate situation, and Jesus consistently used those moments as teaching moments for Peter.

Jesus' reaction to Peter's denial that crucifixion was a necessary part of God's plan continues to teach us that sacrifice is often prerequisite to success.

Peter's reckless boasting, that he would stand to the death with Jesus before any crucifixion took place, was used to teach him an even greater truth about the power of fear in the lives of even well-meaning persons.

The Transfiguration could have been the greatest wordless message ever recorded. Jesus was in heavenly conversation with Moses and Elijah. The Lawgiver, and the Prophet, and the Christ converged—what more needed to be said? Once again, Peter spoke out of turn. Jesus understood that Peter was afraid and did not know what else to do. This passage is another episode in God's long suffering and forgiveness. Heaven spoke, eclipsing the foolish words that Peter had spoken.

There are times that we are afraid and do inappropriate things. God understands those moments and often eclipses them with graciousness. There are times that others around us suffer from the same malady. Do we understand? Perhaps today is a day to gently and discretely help someone, whom God loves, remove a foot from her mouth.

What Do These Things Mean?

In noting the great number of T-shirts, baseball caps, and other wearing apparel sporting an X, one public official asked: "What does the *ten* mean?"

Hardly anyone missed the advertisements for Spike Lee's movie about Malcolm X. Everywhere we turned, there were large advertisements: A Black page with a large letter X—and no other commentary. How many of our children born since 1960 really know what that X means? Both teenagers and young adults are wearing X attire, but do they know how many were in danger of losing their lives by identifying with the man who made the X popular—Malcolm X?

Our school children study a sterile, bloodless version of the life and the ministry of Dr. Martin Luther King Jr. Have we told them our stories? Are they hearing from us or from the media what these things mean?

We stand in danger of rearing a generation of African-Americans who are completely unacquainted with the passion of the struggle. Our ancestors fought too hard and suffered too intensely to let our children fall into the same pit again.

Israelite children were reminded of the powerful way that God Almighty liberated their parents from bondage: Moses was mentioned, as were the ten plagues, the parting of the Red Sea, and the supernatural provision in the wilderness. This was done to strengthen the children's faith in the power and provision of God. Remembering the past provided inspiration in the children's daily life and gave them courage for the challenges that would surely come.

Our children, like the Israelite children, need their faith strengthened. We, like the Israelites, have a story to tell. We have heroes and sheroes like Rosa, Martin, Malcolm, Fanny Lou, Mandela, Medgar, and the four school girls bombed in church during Sunday school. The story we have to tell involves the power of the Almighty God who moved obstacles, caused legislation to pass, and gave our people courage to persevere.

When your children and grandchildren note the Xs all over town and ask us, "What do these things mean?" What will you tell them?

In the Holy Place

It had been a long time since Joy had been able to pray at home by herself. The house always seemed to be filled with people. Today everyone else was busy, and she was alone.

There is a holy stillness that many of us know. It sometimes comes at five or six in the morning when it is yet dark outside, and people are just beginning to stir. Joy recognized that same kind of stillness today, at two o'clock in the afternoon, calling her to pray. Even the air felt charged with God's presence. Joy left her daily chores and went to her favorite place of prayer, a large reclining chair in the sewing room.

Joy sat in that chair and closed her eyes for a few moments. Then she picked up her waiting Bible and turned to the place in Exodus that described Moses' first real meeting with the Almighty God. She began to see that God had created a holy place to meet with Moses right in the midst of ordinary surroundings. What could be more ordinary than a bush?

For a few brief moments, she was there. She watched the familiar scene from a distance. My, how that bush burned! She could almost see the curious look on Moses' face as he left his normal path to see the unusual sight. Then she imagined herself closer, drawn by the sight of dancing flames. She heard the fire. She felt its warmth. Then, she felt God. At this point, her ordinary reclining chair, like Moses' place in the desert, became holy ground, because Joy was in the presence of God.

The presence of God can transform a desert, a bush, or even an old reclining chair into a holy place. Have you set aside an area in your home where you and God can meet in the holy stillness of the day?

Heaven Is Looking for You

Did you know that heaven is looking for you? When you are lost and cannot find a glimpse of heaven, heaven looks for you. That's the message that Jacob's ladder brings to you today.

Jacob was about as low as he could be. He was an absolute stinker and had so wronged his brother that he had to leave home. He was in the wilderness and perhaps away from home for the first time. He did not know if he could ever go home again. Such a man was, in our opinion, unworthy of heaven. But at such a time as this, heaven came looking for Jacob!

Heaven comes looking for us also. When we are pregnant and the father is nowhere in sight—heaven comes looking for us. When we are penniless and the children need new shoes—heaven comes looking for us. When we are on a train, plane, or bus to only God knows where running from the man that everyone warned us about—heaven comes looking for us. When we are in rebellion and don't want anyone's advice, especially if they belong to that church—heaven comes looking for us. When we feel most unworthy of the presence of God—heaven comes looking for us.

God is not just looking for those with it all together. God is also looking for those who are often running in the opposite direction. God is looking for those who are lost and goes to some awfully lost places to find us. While we are looking for heaven in people, possessions, and prestige, heaven is out looking for us.

When Jacob realized that heaven had found him, he built an altar. The cold ground became a churchyard, and the place that symbolized his iniquity became the gateway to heaven. What cold, hard place is waiting to become your churchyard? Are you willing to allow some of the symbols of your past to become your gateways to the presence of God. Why? Because heaven is looking for you right now!

Remembering the Sabbath

May 22   *Read Deuteronomy 5:15.*

So much time has passed since the sabbaths of our youth. They were times to be washed and scrubbed and pressed and still—for God was speaking. So much has happened since we got so sophisticated and learned how to make use of our leisure time, our sabbaths, by playing golf, washing cars, and watching TV shows that would make God blush!

May

We have lost the miracle of regeneration that comes with keeping sabbaths. We have learned instead that we must do something all the time—even on our days of rest. We have forgotten how to be satisfied thinking—and remembering. We forget to remember.

I can recall our sabbaths. I long for them. They were days to read, and pray, and sing, and sit still in the presence of God. When my life is too busy, I wish that I were a little girl again so that someone with good sense could tell me to sit still. They were days to remember the old family histories. As a youth I would cringe at hearing the family stories for the hundredth time. Now, I long to hear those stories just once more. I long to learn the family histories for my children who have no knowledge of them. The tellers of these tales are gone into eternity, and my grandchildren are empty of those memories. The family stories are retreating into the background and with them the ancestors that speak from the past and help to inform our present faith. We have forgotten how many miles Grandpa walked to school, what grade he finished, and how he longed to see just one of us graduate. We have forgotten, sometimes selectively, that Big Mama used to clean houses so we could have enough. We have forgotten how to take in babies from the neighborhood. We have forgotten surviving and loving our neighbors and instead have taken to making God blush on His day off.

Today's scripture teaches us why we should keep a day off. A sabbath is not a day to catch up on the wash; nor is it a day to hear the latest gossip. It is a day to remember that we were once slaves.

People of African descent are well aware of this. We are aware that God heard our cries of agony, just as He heard Israel's. But even we forget that there are many kinds of slavery. Some people are slaves to the pursuit of wealth. Others are slaves to food or drink. We are easily enslaved by unhealthy relationships. We can become slaves to bad lifestyle choices. Before Christ enters our lives, we all are slaves to sin. At least one day each week we need to reflect on and celebrate the miraculous way that Christ sets us free from all forms of slavery.

The sabbath is a day to remember that God remembers our circumstances, even when they appear hopeless. It is a time to remember the mighty deeds of God in the lives of those who prayed for our goodwill before we were ever born. The good news today is that we are not where our ancestors were because they talked to God about us and watered the earth with their tears and supplications.

· Remembering Song
Sing
A Song for my ancestors, little known
A song for Maryann, and Semilen, and Rheta
A song for unknown plantation women in Virginia
A song for modest women who mourned their virginity
A song for women who birthed in the fields with no helper but God
A song for Native women grinding corn with a stick
A song for young girls who grew up too fast
A song for those whose paper dolls were real, and cried at night, and waited to
    be fed at the end of the day.
Sing a song for Mose, and George, and Ben,
Sing a song for unknown papas who could not provide
    for unknown kings who could not dispense wisdom
    for men who bore the lash
    for those whose blood watered the soil.
Sing a song for those who ran,
    and for those who didn't.
Sing a song for my ancestors.

Sing
A song for those who learned to overcome though in chains.
A song for those who heard their names called in brush arbors
A song for those who knew there was another life, another world
A song for those whose songs could not be silenced.
Sing a song for those whose God is Jehovah
    The One who was and is and is to come.

When we are tempted to wallow in self-pity, or to bury ourselves in busyness, we are reminded to remember. That's what sabbaths are for.

Don't Be No Fool!

May 23   *Read Proverbs 26:4.*

"It takes a fool to know a fool!" "One fool does not have to make another one." Which way did your female ancestors quote this proverb to you? No matter how you heard it, the message was the same. Stop participating in foolishness!

Most of us do not intend to be involved in foolish situations. They just seem to happen. Foolish situations are seductive. If we are not vigilant, they lure us into their trap.

Sometimes the bait is this need we have to justify ourselves. I don't know why certain foolish accusations catch our attention. Have you ever tried to clear up your reputation or to set the record straight? No doubt, the more you protested, the more maligned you felt. Of course, the more maligned you felt, the more you felt the need to protest harder—a vicious cycle. The moment we try to answer a foolish accusation, the hook has been set. The more we pursue them, the more foolish we appear. One fool makes another!

I found myself in this vicious cycle some years ago. I was breaking into a new ministerial appointment where the men were extremely opposed to women in the pulpit. I found myself zealously quoting scripture and citing history as my defense. It became a dirty duel. One day, while preaching in the presence of a number of clergywomen, the Lord spoke through me to all of us. "Put away your weapons, stop formulating answers, apologies, and excuses. It is time to stop answering the devil's silly questions!"

That word of wisdom shot through the sanctuary like a bolt of lightning. Suddenly, we were freed of the need to speak up for ourselves. We just closed our ears to what they had to say and ignored them. Eventually, in the absence of fuel, the argument faded into an occasional grumble from our male detractors.

Perhaps this is a word for all of us sisters today. Is the devil constantly shoving some silly question or another in your face? Don't be no fool. Ignore her!

God of the Silence

May 24   *Read 1 Kings 19:9-12.*

It didn't matter how important Elijah had just been in the eyes of the people; it didn't matter how much he had heard from God in the past, the distress was present and urgent. He was at a low point in his life and he needed to hear from God.

Those women whom we call prayer warriors all have times, urgent times, when they need to hear from God—just like the rest of us. Elijah symbolizes the spiritual giant who, like anyone else, fell into spiritual drought. We are human, and there are just going to be days like this. Hearing from God for most of us is difficult; and even the so-called giants will have days of difficulty.

Sometimes we do not hear God because we are listening to the wrong things. There are so many ways to hear God. Elijah's episode on the mountain waiting for God typifies the various ways that we traditionally expect to hear from God. There was first a great rock-splitting wind, which, you might say, represents the spectacular. Though God may have appeared to you this way in times past, He is not limited to the spectacular. Next, there was an earthquake. Perhaps each of us has a story to tell of ways that God's communication has shaken us. We are limiting ourselves and God if we only expect to hear from God in this way. Then, there was a fire. A fiery prophet, a fiery sermon, a fiery prayer session is often a way to hear; but not the only way. Sometimes God speaks in the sound of sheer silence.

When God is attempting to speak to us in the silence, sometimes we cannot hear because of excessive noise. For some of us, the noise of our own fear drowns out that silence. Elijah was afraid, even after having taken part in a major public display of God's power. Fear does not always make sense, but it may come, and it may drown out God's words of comfort. Sometimes, we are unable to hear God because of the noise of our own protest. Maybe we did hear a portion of what God was attempting to say to us and we just didn't like it. How many of us have had to finally sit still and yield to an uncomfortable turn of events, knowing quite well that this too was the will of God? Perhaps we are afraid of God's silence.

God has spoken and will continue to speak in some spectacular ways. God reserves the right to shake us up with His word to us. We are all delighted when a fiery prayer, song, sermon, or prophet is the vehicle of communication. But, God often speaks to us in the silence. Shhhh . . . are you listening?

Growing Up Too Fast

May 25   *Read Exodus 2:1-4.*

You and I may never really know what caused Jochebed to put baby Moses in a basket and place him in the very river that Pharaoh had intended for his grave. We may never understand the desperation that was involved; the sense of hopefulness that, somehow, the river would be a good hiding place. We never hear of Moses' father Amram's grief; but we do see Miriam watching the baby from a distance. Someone shared the pain with Jochebed.

When a family is in an uproar, everyone is affected. We pretend that little babies and small children cannot feel the tension in the air; but we all know they do. Children in a stressful environment are often forced to grow up too quickly. They blame themselves when life is topsy-turvy. They take responsibility for things far beyond their control. Many of them lay awake at night worrying about our problems.

I suspect that Miriam sensed her mother's anguish and silently shared her pain. I can almost see her small fists clenched in defiance when her baby brother was placed in the Nile. Would she try to fight a crocodile? Would she attempt to distract large rodents? Would she act as a decoy if Pharaoh's soldiers came? I suspect that she had made up her mind to do something.

Miriam represents the daughters of the ghetto, who develop ulcers from the stress of urban living. She stands in proxy for the little mothers who help us raise the rest of the children. She is in solidarity with those girls who dream up schemes to stop domestic abusers from battering their mother another time. She is one who picks up our heavy burdens well before her time.

Little woman, can you become a child again? Little mother, will you even want your own children? Sister, tell us about the little girls in your life.

Today, O God, we ask you to restore the childhood of our daughters who have been forced to grow up before their time.

And What About You?

One of the great unanswered questions of the Bible is "Where was the man?" Obviously a man would have had to be present to catch the woman in the very act of adultery. Why was this woman singled out?

Though we have no record of Jesus asking about the man involved, we do see that He was concerned about the sin of hypocrisy. "Let anyone among you who is without sin be the first to throw a stone at her (verse 7)."

Lord, when I am singled out to bear shame that should be shared by others, remind me of this woman.

Lord, when the crowds entice me to join them in persecuting another human being, remind me of the times when I have been persecuted.

Lord, when I am tempted to cast stones at someone who has been publicly humiliated, remind me of my secret sins.

Who knows what Jesus wrote on the ground for all to read. Maybe he exposed the sins of the scribes and the Pharisees!

Baby Boom

May 27   *Read Genesis 29:31.*

Jacob did not love her and everybody knew it. He woke up the morning after the wedding and lost his mind. He fussed at her daddy and complained within earshot of anyone who would listen. He contracted to work another seven years for Rachel her sister, the woman he really loved.

"When the LORD saw that Leah was unloved, he opened her womb." Leah had children to compensate for a husband who didn't love her. How often does that happen in our neighborhood? Her sister was barren, but her sister was loved. Having children, thus irritating her nemesis, seemed to be the only way that Leah could express her opinion.

For Leah, having babies was beyond protest. The names given her children seemed to suggest secret prayers for her husband's love. When Reuben was born, his name meant, "See, a son!" The births of sons, in Leah's day, were supposed to be a father's delight. They were supposed to reflect favorably upon the mother. This baby was, in Leah's eyes, supposed to prove her worth.

Yet, the birth of this son, and the others that followed did not change Jacob's preference for Rachel. Leah's baby prayers continued. Simeon's name meant, "one who hears." Levi's name meant, "attached." Leah was participating in a private, strategic baby boom. None of these children changed the fact that Jacob was obsessed with his love for Rachel.

Modern women do not always have children to persuade their husbands to love them. We choose other means. We often mistakenly rely upon beauty or achievements to buy a man's love. We dupe ourselves into believing that material possessions, new hairstyles, or expensive perfume will persuade a man, who is not interested in us, to discover our virtues. When we do those things, we are like Leah, trying to buy love.

Having children will never buy a husband's love; nor will gourmet cooking, fancy clothes, or a manicured appearance. Where is today's hope? Look at the names of the babies: Reuben, Simeon, Levi, and Judah. The name Judah means, "Now will I praise the Lord." By the birth of her fourth child Judah, Leah had discovered that the presence of God in her life was more important than Jacob's love.

God, present in your life, is able to release you from your private version of the "baby boom."

When the Wind Blows

May 28   *Read Acts 2:1-4.*

Janice was invited to a big church meeting. No one could tell her how long that meeting would last, so she was really unsure about going. She was torn. On the one hand, she really needed to be there; on the other, she had too much business to take care of.

"Knowing these folks," she thought, "I will be able to go downtown, take care of my business, and arrive before church is over. That way I can get everything done and *still* go to church." She was satisfied with her solution as she got into the car.

Have you ever tried to get something necessary done on your way to a big church meeting? It never seems to work out right. Roads detour on that day. Traffic stalls, or the baby throws his bottle out an open window! It seems like the forces of hell line up against you when God needs you to be somewhere.

So it was with Janice. Long lines at vehicle registration, long grocery lines, heavy traffic, and a cranky child that must stop at McDonald's delayed her. She, however, was determined to go to the big church meeting anyway. Surely there were three choirs there to sing before the evangelist, she hoped.

The last delay was more than any three choirs could compensate for; her beeper rang with a call that must be answered. The telephone call droned on and on with a routine problem at work. Finally, she was able to go to the big church meeting.

As she pulled into the church parking lot, she realized that something extraordinary must be happening. Opening the doors, she immediately sensed the overwhelming presence of the Holy Spirit. It felt as though Pentecost had come—and she almost missed it.

> Where will you be when the winds of Pentecost blow?
> Will you be at home, asleep;
> Will you be outside, completing business;
> Or, will you be waiting in the Upper Room?

Alpha and Omega

May 29   *Read Revelation 21: 5-6a.*

Alpha and Omega, A to Z, beginning and ending—life is a series of beginnings and endings. Life is also a series of transitions. We go from the ending of one thing into the beginning of another. Transitions, of necessity, occupy the spaces between the outermost points. From beginning through the end, and at all points between, God is there. Jesus is the beginning and the end.

Jesus is the beginning of a new point of view. You don't have to look at life or yourself the same way anymore. Jesus comes in to make all things new. Your once horrible job can become a source of joy when you invite the Lord along to work with you. An unbearable relationship can become pleasant, because the Lord does indeed make all things new. Your children can begin anew. The old grudges and present tensions with your teens can fade into history as God begins to transform your family. Why not ask the Lord how to begin?

Jesus is also the end of all things. When Christ walks in, misery's days are numbered; because in the end, the Lord has the last word. The trouble you see now cannot last for ever, for Jesus is the ending point of all things.

Jesus is the beginning and the ending of everything. In order to have beginnings and endings, however, there must be this time of transition. Transitions can be frightening. They make us feel like we are nowhere. As you should look at either end of a transitional period, remember that God is there. Today, if you are facing a terrible time of transition, why not look at the places where Jesus has declared an end to one phase of your life and the beginning of another?

Shake the Snake!

May 30   *Read Acts 28:3-5.*

Have you ever found yourself lamenting life's contradictions? In spite of the precautions we take, we cannot escape danger. No matter how many healthy thoughts we think or vitamins we take, illness still manages to overtake us every now and then. No matter how morally upright we try to live, someone will still talk about us. No matter how hard we work, someone will think it is not enough. Does this sound like your complaint?

Paul could have been tempted to sing this song of complaint with a few extra verses. He was often misunderstood or misrepresented. He was deprived as often as he was blessed. Yet, Paul was so certain of his mission in life that he did not allow life's contradictions to slow him down. Even when bitten by a poisonous snake, while trying to build a fire, he just shook it off.

Maybe it's time for you and me to shake off some of the things that happen to us. The Bible tells us that troubles will come to disciples. Shake them off! We are warned that people will tell lies about us. Shake them off! We are even aware that some of us will sometimes feel blasted instead of blessed. Shake it off!

When God has a plan for your life, even the most deadly weapon won't destroy you. Shake it off—and go on about your business!

Tree Stump

We had a tree cut down last year. It had been a mighty tree. It shaded the west side of our home. Neighborhood children had once enjoyed climbing that tree, before it got sick and died.

We hated to cut it down. It was an old tree. How long would it take for a new tree to grow to its present stature? All we have left is a stump—an ugly unattractive tree stump.

You know tree stumps. They are only good for playing king of the mountain when you are eight years old. They are an annoyance when mowing the lawn. Tree stumps are dead, disruptive areas in an otherwise attractive meadow. Tree stumps are things upon which to stub your toe and should be pulled up by the roots. We do not expect much from tree stumps.

There are days when my life is like a tree stump. I feel dead, lifeless, and in everyone's way. There are days when I feel that the leafy limbs of my potential have become diseased and destined for death. I often feel cut down. When I stub my toes on the past, life feels like an old tree stump.

When this passage was written, God's people felt like an old tree stump. They were descendants of David, Jesse's son. The kingdom had crumbled; they seemed to stumble through history. Visualize what Isaiah is saying. Look at the deadness of that particular stump and imagine a strong green shoot pointing its finger to the sky. Imagine the branch that sprang, in defiance, from roots presumed to be dead. God promised, through this imagery, that His people would live again!

Is there a tree stump in your life? Are you tormented by something that looks dead and only seems to be in the way? Look again, closely, at the stump that mocks you; reminding you of what once was or of what could be. Do you see faint signs of life? Your dreams, presumed to be dead, may only be dormant waiting for the right conditions.

Isaiah's shoot from the stump of Jesse is yet another picture of the Resurrection. The often familiar sight of a live green shoot springing from the deadness of a once noble tree is a visual reminder from God. He is the One who brings all kinds of death back to life!

June

What to Wear?

Colorful birds take dirt baths outside my window. I see them through my kitchen window in the heat of the day. Bright yellow birds with black markings flutter their wings in ways that their mothers must have taught them. Crayon-blue birds join this strange dirt-bath dance. Don't they know that they are too dressed up to bathe in the Iowa dust?

It doesn't seem so strange when ordinary birds take dirt baths. It's okay for wrens, or even robins to dust themselves with dry powdery dust—they are dressed for work. They are dressed to make nests and to blend into the scenery—but those other birds? Yellow birds and bluebirds, even red-crested cardinals join the ancient ritual—never seemingly mindful that they are dressed up!

We have much to learn from nature. Birds are beautiful, yet they never worry about what to eat or what to wear; and, they never appear too dressed up to be regular birds! Lilies are perhaps one of the most delicate and intricate flowers; even Solomon, in all his finery, could not compare with their beauty. Nature never worries about apparel. Why then, are we so worried about everything?

I wonder if the often articulated preoccupation with what we will wear is really just a symbol of our common worries about temporal needs? When some of us voice concerns about what to wear, or what to eat, are we really concerned that we will have enough of what we need? At one point in history, that might have been a real question for all of us. Now, the question almost seems rhetorical. Most people have embarrassing quantities of food and clothing, and we continue to worry about what to eat or wear!

The obvious lesson for today is that God will take care of all of our needs. If God clothes the lilies that are here today and withered tomorrow; if He feeds the birds that make no preparation for tomorrow as we do—won't He also take care of our everyday needs?

Each in Her Own Language

"How is it that we hear, each of us in our own native language?" the people asked. They were gathered from at least sixteen different geographical regions for a religious festival in Jerusalem. Some had come from Asia Minor and others from Northern Africa. They had been coming to this festival for ages. It was the expected thing to do. They traveled a great distance in hope of understanding bits and pieces of what was going on in worship.

Are we like that too, sometimes? Traveling from great distances, putting on our best clothes, and hoping to hear something that we can understand? We scrub our children and force some of them to make a weekly appearance at church—hoping that they too will hear a word of encouragement. Our coming is more than fulfilling mere expectations, we need to hear a word from the Lord.

Many of the people from various countries were not able to understand the temple language. Some were new converts to Judaism and others were children of the ancient deportation who did not return to the homeland. They had been away from the temple so long that they no longer understood the dialect that had been reserved for worship. Somehow, they remained encouraged enough in their faith to keep coming. They said the prayers that were allowed in their native tongues and listened, often without understanding, to the prayers and affirmations that were offered in the language of the Jews. They had continued in this manner, for years—when God broke the silence!

They heard people talking about God's deeds of power! No, they really heard the message—in their own language. People who had never visited their lands or studied their languages were speaking words that they could understand, fully! All of a sudden, the Bible made sense. Jesus made sense. Their years of pilgrimage and days of dragging the children along made sense!

There is a message in this passage for us today. All of us were not reared in the church. How often have we struggled with the rituals of the church, only to feel like outsiders? How many times have we wondered if it were all in vain—"why can't I just be a Christian at home?" Or, have you complained that you do not get anything from worship services? If so, continue to have faith, and stay encouraged.

The Lord rewards those who continue in hopefulness. Just as He broke an interminable silence with the devout of Israel on the day of

Pentecost, God will invade the unbearable silences in your life. God knows how to speak to all of us in a language that we can understand.

Measuring Motives

June 3   *Read Matthew 5:20-22.*

Some years back, Spike Lee directed a landmark movie entitled *Do the Right Thing.* It was a commentary on ethical behavior in the African-American community. As viewers, we were invited to think about what the characters should have done in the movie's crisis. Much of modern moral-ethical commentary revolves around what we should or should not do in a given situation.

It was no different for the Jews. The Law told them what not to do if they were to be a righteous people. The scribes and the Pharisees spent a great deal of energy doing those things that the prophets encouraged and not doing those things that the Law prohibited. They measured morality by the use of a list of do's and don'ts. Jesus told them, and tells us, that this approach is no longer sufficient.

Jesus invites the believer to investigate her motives. Where does murder originate? Most murders are not accidental; nor are they usually reaction to provocation. They are most often premeditated. They take place when a person who has made a decision, or engaged in a fantasy, encounters the opportunity. They begin with a motive.

Monitor those things that could lead to murder, Jesus warned. Anger, unresolved and unrestrained, provides motivation for murder. The fact that we continue to harbor seething anger makes us a candidate for murder. This, in itself, is sin. This passage says that if we are angry with a brother or a sister, that we will be liable to judgment.

Measure your motives. "If you insult a brother or sister, you will be liable to the council." One of the most insulting names of their day was fool. One who was angry enough to use that word, given the opportunity, was certainly angry enough to murder! This person was worthy of hell. Are you angry enough to resort to name-calling?

The ethic of Jesus provides a more perfect way to live. It is no longer sufficient to measure morality by the list of things avoided. If we really want to please God, we are challenged to probe into the motives of our hearts.

More, Please

Touch my eyes again, Lord
There are still some things I cannot see.
Open my eyes, make me see clearly
Open my eyes to the things that are near
And grant me a glimpse of things far off.

Touch my eyes again, Lord
I see things that are not there
Trees become men
Men become trees
No matter how hard I stare.

Touch my eyes again, Lord
They've been closed for far too long
New light is disarming
My focus is skewed
All I can see is the sun.

Touch my eyes again, Lord
I still stumble along my way.
I need to walk
As a child of the Light
Through the night and through the day.

Two Cents Worth

She was determined to put in her two cents worth, no matter what others gave. She was not discouraged by her lack. This widow was committed to doing what she could, no matter how little. There is something about the widow's generosity that puts the rest of us to shame. She gave out of her poverty. Jesus tells us that she gave more than the rest of those who gave because she gave all that she had to live on.

Those who study church giving patterns constantly tell us that the people who can least afford it are the ones who really support the church. Older women on pensions and social security often shoulder the load of the church budget. Women on welfare are often known to tithe. These women give proportionally more than the rest of the church because they often give money that they could use to raise their quality of life. Something about their generosity puts many of us to shame.

Their giving is not restricted to what they give in church. They usually live lives that are characterized by giving. These women instinctively zero in on others who suffer from lack. They honestly feel that it is more blessed to give than to receive! Our shame gets in their way. Sometimes we are ashamed to receive gifts from them.

Are you blushing as you recall your own experiences with widows who helped you with money that they really needed for themselves? Perhaps you were a single parent struggling to keep shoes on your young children as I once was. There she came from nowhere, with neither invitation nor explanation, bearing shoes that she had found on sale, or resale, in the right size for my child. "Honey, I know how it is when you are trying to make it with children. . . ." Were you foolish enough to protest or to struggle with her over it—or did you just say thank you?

We know these women. Jesus did too. They teach us that being poor does not necessitate being stingy. God bless their generosity.

This Present Crisis

June 6   *Read 1 Kings 8:37-40.*

O Lord, we have a problem and we need your help. An invisible killer is stealing our strength.

Our ignorance about AIDS enables it to spread.
> We say that we do not understand how it is contracted.
> Yet, AIDS continues to spread.
> We say that AIDS is only for a certain kind of person.
Let us be ignorant no more.
Denial has been our enemy.
> We say that it will never happen to my family.
> We say that it will never happen to me.

AIDS feeds on denial.
Let us claim denial no more.

Our silence breeds shame.
    We have been ashamed of our mothers and fathers who have
        died in silent shame.
    We have abandoned or hidden our babies with AIDS.
    We have lied about our brothers and sisters and said that
        they have died of pneumonia or something else.
Our silence gives AIDS fame.
Let us be silent no more.

Forgive us, Lord. We seem to have forgotten that you delivered Israel from ten plagues equal to this one. We have forgotten how you delivered our great-grandparents from many impossibilities. We have forgotten to ask for your help.

    Help us to face the pain of our present.
    Direct us to future hope,
    Teach us to live responsibly.
    Teach us again how to be our brothers'and sisters' keepers.
    Empower this generation, and those coming, to fight
        back in your Name!   Amen.

To Your Health

June 7   *Read 3 John 2.*

She had just worried herself sick. Carmen had stayed out all night for the umpteenth time and her mother was waiting up for her again. This time, she just stared at the bottle containing the aspirin that had begun to burn her stomach because of frequent use.

"What am I going to do" she thought. "This child is giving me an ulcer. I want to let her go, but I don't know how to stop worrying about her—that's my baby."

Carmen was the baby of the family. Shirley, her mother, and her five brothers had always been protective of her. She felt smothered by her handsome, successful big brothers. They were always asking questions about her dates and checking up on her around town. When she turned seventeen, rebellion hit her heart, and she hit the streets.

"Never a moments trouble out of that girl until now, what am I going to do?" Shirley was so worried that she couldn't even pray. She fell asleep in the big overstuffed chair that had become her favorite "waiting-up" place. When she woke up, she resisted the urge to look out the window. While sitting there numb, she spied her Bible, which was peeking out of the top of her crochet basket. When she picked it up, she could not even read; she just hugged her Bible and cried.

"Lord, help me. . . ." No more words would come. The Holy Spirit touched her body with a speedy reply. A calm peace came over Shirley. Before long, the headache subsided without the customary aspirin. In the stillness that followed, the tune to "It Is Well with My Soul" began to rise up inside of her.

"I have got to stop this worrying; God will show me what to do with my daughter. I believe that I would feel better if I went to bed." This time, Shirley turned out the lights and went to bed before Carmen came home for the night.

There are so many situations that want to trouble our souls and rob us of good health. The Lord knows how to handle each one. Give them to God. Is it well with your soul today?

What Was the Question?

June 8   *Read Mark 8:27-29.*

The late Tom Skinner, noted African-American evangelist, used the following story as an opening illustration in one of his books, *If Christ Is the Answer, What Are the Questions:* A young man was recently converted to the faith. As a way of strengthening this young man, his pastor encouraged him to openly share his faith with others. Well, this young man was quite shy; but, finally he decided that he would use the blackboard in math class before anyone arrived for the first hour. He would write the words "Christ is the Answer" in great big letters, then he would casually come in with the rest of the students, gleefully noting the reactions. He felt that he had done his job. This continued morning after morning. Finally, one morning, another young man, who had been frustrated by the anonymous blackboard messages, wrote in small letters under his statement, "Yeah, but what was the question?"

If we were to look honestly at our faith, many of us would find that Christendom has become a land of clichés. We speak Christianese. We learn ritual answers and ritual responses. Though many of our rituals serve us by teaching renewed thought patterns, they can also be dangerous. The dangers of ritual answers, like: "I'm blessed of the Lord . . . ." is that after a while they become as routine as, "good morning." The declaration that we are blessed loses power. Unchallenged faith becomes stale and routine. We can learn from the wiseacre student who asked: "What was the question?"

What are the questions that we should ask of our faith? So many of us have been taught not to question God and not to question our faith. We've been conditioned to think of honest soul-searching questions as a sign of weakness. Actually, questions can be a source of strength.

The questions of faith are not how to make more money or where to meet good friends. It is not important to God that we know how to control people, land, or resources. Christianity has nothing to do with gathering all the marbles of life into our pile.

The most crucial question of faith is: Who do we say that Jesus is? Do we say as some say, that He is just another good man who went further than any other? Do we say that He was only a prophet? Do we echo what Peter says when he affirms that Jesus is the Christ, the Son of the Living God? What are the questions in your heart?

Perfect People

June 9   *Read Matthew 5:48.*

The Bible says for us to be perfect, as God is perfect. What might it mean to be perfect? Sometimes we spend so much energy policing perfection in ourselves and others, only in the end to be reminded that we have not arrived.

It seems as though our lives are occupied with the quest for perfection. It overwhelms us; it captures our attention. Most of us know that we are not perfect, yet we demand perfection from friends, family, and significant relationships. At the same time, we hide physical imperfections and character flaws from one another, fearing rejection.

Since perfection is so confusing to us, we often substitute illusions of perfection for that which God requires of us. We become preoccupied with things that look perfect: "If I could just get this body together, I could convince them that I am on my way to being perfect," we think. All the while, we know that no manicure, face-lift, or hairdo can make us the kind of perfect that God is talking about.

We can't find a perfect best friend! We have been imprisoned by the quest for a perfect family. Nobody has 2.2 children! The perfect house-keeper does not exist. Perfect children surprise us every time; and even our perfect husbands are only human. Certainly this cannot be what Jesus had in mind! What did He mean when He commanded us to be perfect?

For an answer, look at the people who we consider perfect. In spite of their character flaws and mistakes, we feel that some people have captured God's picture of perfection. Why? Because they mean well and do their best to carry out godly intentions. It could be that Jesus, knowing how imperfect we could be, spoke of perfection as a mind-set. Could perfect people simply be those who pursue godly perfection?

If only we could reframe our expectations about perfection! If you and I could recognize that we are also pursuing godly perfection, maybe we could love ourselves again. If we could recognize this attitude in others, maybe we could stop demanding those illusions of perfection from them that we ourselves have not achieved. The ability to see ourselves and others on the way to godly perfection could begin to break down the barriers that so often characterize our relationships.

Perhaps, for the moment, until Jesus returns, perfection will be found more in our attitudes. Maybe perfection is best embodied by those who earnestly intend to lead godly lives and do their best each day. It could be that this is all that Jesus is asking of you today—to do your best to carry out your good intentions.

Superwoman

June 10   *Read Nehemiah 9:6.*

Look, up in the sky! It's a bird; it's a plane! She is a supernatural creature, endowed with supernatural abilities that benefit everyone around her. Able to stay up night after night, doing all the housework without ever insisting on help. Able to go for days on end without proper nutrition. Able to worry about all of her business, and that of every person that she loves. Able to hold in her emotions, and place her needs on hold, because everyone else is more important. Able to volunteer at church for five nights a week, raise three children—alone, and work a forty to fifty hour week, fifty-two weeks of the year! Are you really?

The myth of the Black superwoman is perhaps one of the last deadly dragons waiting to be slain. How many times have you felt as if everyone around you expected you to be a Superwoman? It seems as if the entire nation has always relied upon Black women for something. Everyone leans on us. When church pulpits are vacant, we are the spiritual force that helps the church stay open. We are most often the single parent who glues the home together and tries to make a decent place for our children to grow up. We are the underpaid worker, trudging along, because jobs aren't always easy to find. We are the group least likely to seek preventive health care or to receive health care until we become ill. We are the stereotypical "overcomer." No one bothers to worry about us, because "a Black woman will always figure out how to make it"

Who sees the silent tears or hears the unspoken fears of the Black Superwoman? When voiced, they are rarely taken seriously. "Come on girl, you're strong. Be strong. Don't get weak on me now!"

We are not guiltless. That myth would eventually dry up and die if we would stop flying through the air. We participate in a conspiracy against ourselves. Black women continue to bend over backwards to save the day. When last I heard, there is only one legitimate Savior.

In today's passage, Ezra and Nehemiah are helping a once captive people to regain their spirituality. They are reminded, in a sentence, of the created order, heaven, earth, and all the inhabitants of both. Not once is there mention of Superwoman! Perhaps this is the time to put our capes in mothballs and turn in our superpowers.

Walking Upright, Anyway

June 11   *Read Luke 13:10-16.*

I'm sure that no one understood your old point of view, Woman-Once-Bent-Over. Though some choose to look at the ground in despair and say, "I don't care," for you, looking up was indeed difficult. How narrow your options had become over eighteen long years.

Did you compare prisons with the prostitutes? They are in prison too. They, too, are captured by a spirit that holds them and forbids that they walk like the rest of us. Perhaps you compared prisons with the workaholics and the alcoholics who also are bound by things unseen. Or, were you alone in your suffering, in your own private cell, left to contemplate how you would spend the rest of your life in that condition?

What does it feel like, to finally be free from a prison that held you so long, Woman-Once-Bent-Over? Did you sigh with relief or rise in disbelief? How did it feel to stand once again? What were your thoughts? Did you prepare to run with glee? Surely all who had seen you before Jesus touched your life and celebrated your good fortune. Or did they?

More likely you had to take time to come up with a story that would satisfy those who preferred seeing you bent over.

The Badge of Your Affliction

June 12   *Read Mark 10:46-52.*

The cloak, in Jesus' day, signaled to all that this man was blind. It was much like the white-tipped cane that causes us to recognize the blind. The blind man in today's passage was accustomed to having his cloak nearby. If strangers saw his cloak, perhaps they would have pity and give him a few pennies. If he should happen to stumble into someone, when they saw his cloak, he would be forgiven. After all, he was blind. The cape was a symbol of his affliction.

One day, however, Jesus called his name. The blind man wanted to be healed; Jesus heard him calling and called for him in return. The blind man responded by throwing away the one thing that had explained his condition to others—his cloak. This was a sign of faith. He intended to get well, because he threw away the badge of his affliction.

Though all of us are not blind, we do have afflictions. Some of us have bodily conditions, and some of us have mental conditions. Most of us have character flaws and have learned how to use our own version of the blind man's cloak.

We cloak ourselves behind excuses. We explain why we are late—again. We explain why we make so many mistakes with our children. It's hard to tell whether the excuses we make to others or the excuses we make to ourselves are the most damaging. Either can imprison us.

Jesus is passing by today. He's calling for you. Don't take that cloak with you to the altar of healing. Throw it away, lest in a weak moment you are tempted to use it again. Do you have the courage to throw away the badge of your affliction and be permanently healed?

It Doesn't Have to Be That Hard

June 13   *Read 2 Kings 5:9-14.*

Naaman, the Syrian, was in trouble. His servants recommended that he see Elisha, the notable man of God. Elisha was known for spectacular things. The sick had been healed and the dead had been raised. The laws of nature were often overturned. As far as Naaman was concerned, his diseased body was sick enough to require a dramatic remedy. Imagine his disappointment when he did not even see Elisha; he only received instructions to go and wash in a muddy river outside his national borders.

When I am in trouble, I don't know what disturbs me most; when God does not seem to give personal attention to my prayers, or when the answers that I do get seem to be too easy. Is it the little girl in me that insists upon being petted when I am hurt? There are days when I know that what I really want is for God to listen to my whining and cajole me back into adulthood.

I struggle between the need to be a carefree small girl again and the need to have my sense of importance acknowledged. I have dedicated my life to the Lord's work. I find myself unconsciously expecting special favors in return. "After all, Lord, isn't my trial severe enough to warrant a house call?" Do you also find yourself expecting special favors from God because of what you have done for Him?

Does it insult us when God does not seem to pay personal attention to some of our needs? Perhaps this is where Naaman felt the greatest affront. He had, in a sense, humbled himself to go and visit a foreign prophet. The prophet, in return, treated him as a servant and not as a ruler. In our self-important eyes, we are the most important agenda. Yet, it seems quite natural that God would treat us as children or as servants because He is the ruler.

Finally, are we really disturbed when the answer seems too easy? There were no consultants to see, no potions to drink, no salve to rub with. Naaman was just told to take a bath! I am always disturbed to see myself in this passage. Many times my healing has been delayed because I refused to believe that God was giving such simple instructions. Could it be that God is telling all of us that solutions to our problems don't have to be that hard?

Explain That Again?

June 14   *Read Matthew 25:24-29.*

"I just didn't understand," she protested later. "I didn't have that much to start with, what did you expect me to do? The directions were not clear, and I didn't want to mess up. So I put that money in a safe place until you came back to tell me what to do with it!"

We rarely look at the dilemma of the one-talent person. No one asked her if she wanted that talent! She demonstrates the chief problem of a servant with an absent master. No one was there to tell her what to do, so when in doubt, she did what looked safe.

She really didn't know her master that well. Subsequently, she could not second guess him. She wasn't motivated by loyalty; she was really influenced more by fear. "I know how you are about your money. . . ." She misunderstood the nature of God. To her God was punitive, and in the end she felt that God was not fair.

We join this one-talent servant. We are all challenged by the tension of risk-taking. "I have so little, everyone else has so much. What if they laugh at my little bit?" We are hesitant to volunteer what seems so meager by comparison. "What if in the course of humiliation I lose the little I have?" We retreat to safe courses of action in times of uncertainty. We enshrine our gift and hold it close to our hearts or we regard it as worthless. Either way, we keep our one little gift to ourselves!

The tension of risk taking increases when we don't see how we will ever have anything else. In times of drought do we eat the last bag of corn, or do we plant it? That tension increases when the master is absent, when we don't understand what he wants, when we didn't ask for the talent in the first place, and when we are afraid of God.

As unfair as it may seem, this parable is still about risks. The one-talent servant is severely chastised for not taking a risk—for not making an investment. What then must we do? Many of us are like the one-talent servant. We are convinced that we don't have any gifts and we are afraid to use the ones that we have. We are paralyzed by our fear of others and imprisoned by our misunderstandings about God.

At the very least, God expects us to make an investment in His work. Today, you are encouraged to find a place where you can feel comfortable doing whatever you can for the kingdom of God.

For Those Waiting to Be Married

June 15

Lord, as liberated as we think we have become, we still feel pressure from without and from within to be married. You created women and men to complement and to complete each other. Though many of us have learned how to experience contentment in singleness, many more of us feel both compelled and called to spend our lives with someone created just for us.

The older we get, the more we are driven. We are driven by the bouquet that flies through the air at weddings. We are driven by a culture that scrutinizes single women. We are driven by questions about our femininity. We are driven by our own inner need to be appreciated and loved. We are driven by biological urges that were designed to be fulfilled in the context of holy matrimony.

Replace, O Lord, drive with patience. Help us to be patient enough to stop sharing men with one another. Teach us to wait for your best. Help us to be unruffled by those who do not understand your timing.

Teach us, Lord, to celebrate singleness while it is here, and to celebrate marriage should it come. Amen.

Falsely Accused?

His name appeared in the newspapers with the common criminals. He made the headline news: "Hanging between two thieves. . . ." When history recorded the event, the names of the criminals were lost. The name of the innocent Christ prevailed. Have you ever noticed how accusations against a good person, whether or not they are true, overshadow those of criminals? Jesus was not the first victim of false accusation, nor was he the last. I have been there and you probably have too.

False accusations have a sting that defies description. Our good reputations that we have worked so hard to build often suffer irreparable damage. The pluses of self-esteem turn instantly to minuses when justice flies through the loophole of falsely planted suspicion. Which distress is greatest, that our names are tarnished or that we are numbered with people that represent the opposite of our values?

Enemies seem to have a heyday. "See, I told you that she was no better than the rest of us!" They take the liberty of reconstructing our otherwise unstained past by planting seeds of doubt about every aspect of our character. Where is justice? Where is God?

God is mindful of the injury of false accusation. God sees our pain through the lenses of experience. Jesus could have made the sacrifice of the ages alone. Our memories of the passion would have been no less precious had He suffered quietly, obscurely, or alone. Instead, righteousness was mocked. He was a public spectacle. His name was listed with those of criminals. His enemies had been watching His steps, waiting for Him to fall. Now, it seemed as though they prevailed. The most innocent person in human history was ridiculed—publicly! This, too, He did for our benefit. God even understands the pain of false accusation.

Not only does God understand, He prevails! Though enemies recorded Jesus' death with those of common criminals, those who love Him know the truth. We note the injustice and cry out against the outrage. Jesus' popularity did not suffer because of false accusation. He has not been diminished in our eyes—in fact, His fame may have grown because of it!

God has a way of bringing out the truth in defense of those who love Him. Those who love you will also know the truth. They will rally to your defense. Falsely accused? Take courage from the story of the Resurrection. You, too, will live again!

Who Do You See?

June 17   *Read Matthew 17:1-8.*

They were in a privileged position. Part of the inner circle, Peter, James, and John were privy to information that the other disciples never received. They came and went with Jesus into places of healing, places of deliverance, and places of revelation. Now, here they were on the mountaintop.

Jesus appeared to them as he had appeared to no one else. His clothes were dazzling, and his face shone like the sun. He was not alone. Two of the greatest Old Testament personalities appeared with Him. That's when the confusion started. Peter, who walked boldly where angels feared to tread, revealed its source. He thought he had it figured out. Jesus must be as great as Elijah, or even as great as Moses. Let's build three tabernacles!

Peter's response sounds crazy and inappropriate, but how many people are tempted to build additional tabernacles today? It seems like a common human temptation to build monuments to God's prophets and to see them on an equal footing with Jesus. Practically every cult leader began as a man or a woman who did not refuse elevation to divinity by people who were confused.

Modern prophets dwell in the narrow region between two major contradictions. On one side of the chasm they are mere mortals chosen by God to speak or to act in ways that change human history. On the other side they are special, they are God's woman or man of the hour. They are deliverers or martyrs. Why wouldn't we regard them highly?

How high? Return to Peter's vision. Suddenly a bright cloud overshadowed the prophets. A voice from heaven called attention to the Son of God. "And when they looked up, they saw no one except Jesus himself alone" (17:8).

June

Jesus and the Fishing Business

June 18   *Read Luke 5:5-7.*

"I can't go home until my drawer balances, and I am $200 short!" My heart thumped loudly, and I had that sick feeling in my stomach. It was two hours past closing, my husband and children were waiting for dinner, and I couldn't find the mistake. It had to be a mistake; surely I hadn't given out that kind of change!

Then, a voice whispered softly in my spirit. "Have you checked the charge receipts?" I almost ignored it. I thought I had gone over every receipt—again and again. I checked them again for what felt like the tenth time, and there it was. A $200 charge slip was stuck to another slip. "Thank you, Jesus!" I didn't know that God knew accounting.

Simon Peter didn't know that Jesus knew about fishing either. You can almost hear the sarcasm in his voice. It was akin to, "I know you don't know anything about what I'm doing, but I respect you so I will humor you." In sheer obedience to the voice on the shore, Peter let down his nets on the other side of the boat, only to pull in the largest catch he had ever seen.

In Peter's case, and in mine, Jesus had to invite Himself into our business dealings. Of course, I had prayed about the unbalanced cashiers drawer, but it was more of a rhetorical prayer. It was one of those prayers you pray because your mother taught you to call on Jesus when in trouble, but you don't really expect an answer. Imagine my surprise when the Holy Spirit led me to the missing receipts!

Simon Peter learned that walking with Jesus involved every aspect of his life, even the fishing business. Some years ago, I learned that He was also interested in balancing my books at night. Have you invited the Lord into your professional endeavors? He knows music, medicine, math, and all kinds of surprising things.

Broken Chains

June 19   *Read John 8:36.*

In one of the major marketplaces of Barbados, there is a statue of a strong, muscular Black man breaking the chains of bondage from his shackled arms. It stands as a visual reminder of the past from which the Bejan people have been delivered. The people of Barbados are proud of the fact that they are free and have vowed that they will never again be enslaved.

Is there a lesson in this for us, ladies? Before Christ entered our lives, we had some obstacle, some barrier, some chains that bound us to sin. The polite tendency is to keep those things secret. We rarely share the mistakes of our past with our children, and we certainly don't reminisce with our neighbors or with our friends in church. Maybe there are some very practical reasons that we don't share with others, but we also forget to remind ourselves of the chains that have been broken.

There is great power in having mental monuments to our freedom. If we could remember the areas in our own lives from which we have been set free, they might help us remain humble. It is so hard to point a finger at another sinner with the same hand that beats the breast in penitence.

If we just had a mental monument to the chains that the Lord has broken in our lives, it would be harder to make some of the same mistakes repeatedly. Could it be that we behave like gerbils on an exercise wheel because we really cannot remember how horrible it was the last time we made that same mistake?

If there were more mental monuments, perhaps our scope of our reach for others in trouble would be wider. It would be easier to care about and reach out to those that we tend to marginalize. Mental monuments are excellent reminders that we too are recipients of the grace of God.

We each have a story of broken chains. Sometimes we forget that we did not break those chains ourselves. True freedom comes from Christ and Christ alone. "So if the Son makes you free, you will be free indeed" (8:36).

Backside

June 20   *Read Proverbs 10:13.*

"That woman thinks she owns me!" Tracy was tired of her mother, who leaned toward being overly protective. Tracy wanted a more relaxed curfew. Her mother, who had once been a reckless teen, was all too acquainted with the temptation of too much unsupervised time.

"That was then, Mom, this is now." Tracy did not realize how loud her voice had become. "You all were not as smart as we are—no offense intended." Tracy thought that she was too smart to be tempted. She just wanted the freedom to be out.

"All right, gal," her mother's speech patterns had reverted. "A hard head makes a soft behind!" By nightfall they were not speaking to each other.

Tracy phoned some girls she had met one evening when she and her boyfriend sneaked into a club. She thought these girls were cool. Actually, they were dropouts whose parents had kicked them out of their homes. They shoplifted, smoked, and relied upon various boyfriends to pay their rent. Tracy was invited to move in with them that night.

What followed was a nightmare. The girls expected Tracy to beg, borrow, or steal her portion of their living expenses. Tracy had never stolen anything in her life. She was unfamiliar with alcohol and so-called soft drugs. Even worse, she learned that the young men around town had certain expectations about the women who lived in that house. She never dreamed that she could do such horrible things. At that point, she realized that she was being whipped by life as a result of her bad choices. She could almost hear her mother's voice saying, "A hard head makes a soft behind."

Just as quietly as she had slipped into that house, she slipped out of it. As she stood on her mother's doorstop, she wondered, "Will life at home ever be the same again?"

Teenage girls are not the only ones who make rash mistakes. Are there days when you knowingly cast caution to the wind in favor of having your own way? Stop right now. Think about your choices, and consider what might happen down the road.

Remember, a hard head does make a soft behind!

Beyond Survival

June 21   *Read Psalm 19:12-14.*

There is a place, in the Christian faith, that is beyond mere survival. So much of life with Christ has been painted as a picture of just staying alive. There is, however, a place beyond that horizon where the real issues are different.

In that place, the chief worry is not about what to eat or where to sleep. The inhabitants of that place are not even obsessed with making it to heaven. Policing the saints is last on the agenda. The order of the day is, "Lord, how can I please you?"

In the Scripture there are glimpses of its inhabitants. Those women and men were captured by God's love. They let their love overflow at the throne of God as did the woman with the alabaster jar of perfume. They filled the air with worship and caused others to hunger and yearn for more.

I have only been there a few times. Each time I have been there, however, I rose from the encounter vowing to do or say nothing that would prevent my return. And each time, stray thoughts, idle words, or malicious deeds eventually returned, chaining me to the gates of mere survival. Lord, make me more vigilant so that I might live with you.

Cleanse my heart of willful transgression. Purge my mouth of words that you hate. Expel those thoughts that take me away from you, Lord. "Let the words of my mouth and the meditation of my heart be acceptable to you, O LORD, my rock and my redeemer" (19:14).

Loving Your Neighbor, Loving Yourself

June 22   *Read Matthew 22:34-40.*

In the complexity of our modern society, one of the problems that we encounter with increasing frequency is self-hatred. Anorexia and bulimia, symptoms of self-hatred, are diseases that were not dreamed of a century ago. Why? Because human beings who are pressured by society to be thin, in order to be acceptable, have found an answer in pathological starvation. Reasons for drug abuse are similar. Often, the abuser is one who feels worthless and needs the extra crutch of a mind-altering drug to feel worthwhile. Violent people also have poor self-images and rely upon a show of strength or violent acts to command the respect they feel would not otherwise be given.

There are so many ways we express self-hatred. Psychologists have long noted that the person who is especially critical of others does so because of self-hatred. There is a human tendency to measure others by self-imposed standards. The words of Christ in Matthew make more sense when seen in this light. How can we possibly love others when we do not love ourselves? I would even dare to say that most of our problems stem from the fact that we are loving our neighbors as we love ourselves. The problem is that we do not love ourselves!

What does it mean to love yourself? Many of us are afraid that loving ourselves will lead to an inflated ego. In actuality, being able to love yourself is a sign of health. It does not mean that we are not striving for godly ideals. It does not mean we think less of others. Loving ourselves means that we are able to accept ourselves and to forgive ourselves as God accepts and forgives us—faults and all! It means that we learn to appreciate our own God-given uniqueness as a special gift and a special treasure to be cared for just as we would care for the uniqueness in others.

Loving ourselves means an end to neglect—like overeating, undereating, or sleep deprivation. Loving ourselves means recognizing that we are created in the image of God as is every other human being. Because of this you and I are special!

Excuses, Excuses

June 23   *Read Luke 14:16-24.*

"I would pray more if my family would just slow down a little. The older ones are in all kinds of activities and need to be driven all over town. My little ones are not quite ready for school yet and really need my time. Hubby works such long hard hours that I always get up early to put a hot breakfast on the table for him. If life would just slow down a little bit, I really would enjoy spending more time in prayer."

"I would attend church more if church were a better place for me. Why can't my church start a singles ministry? So many of us are single. It seems like church is just for old married couples or single *parents*. I feel odd going by myself. Nobody there understands me and my needs. I would attend more often if they would notice me."

"I would volunteer to help if I thought that they really needed me. Those other women come all the time and they already seem to know how to do everything. I will be in the way if they have to teach me what to do. Besides, I'm not that important. Who will miss me if I don't volunteer?"

"Jesus, I really am coming to you when I get it together. When I can stop cursing I will come. Right now, I am afraid that something will jump out of my mouth in front of those holy people without my knowing it. I don't have the right clothes; I wear mostly pants to work. When my money gets right, I will buy a skirt and come—I promise!"

The excuses in today's parable are about as superficial as these. One had to see property. Another had new work equipment. Still another felt that he needed to invest in a new relationship. The reasons that modern people give for not going to church or for not getting to know God more intimately are quite similar. Some need to catch up at work. Others have family or friends in for the weekend. Another group needs to take advantage of the summer sun and go to a theme park.

None of their excuses seemed to satisfy Jesus, nor do ours. He sent for the poor, crippled, lame, and blind. The obvious message was that people in dire situations know that they need God and will welcome the opportunity to come in our stead. We are invited to experience something special with God. The parable called it a great dinner. God is merely asking us to spend some time with Him to be blessed. What is your excuse?

Slowing Down the Pace

June 24   *Read Mark 2:27.*

As pastor of sometimes as many as three churches, I had mastered the art of juggling time. I borrowed time from myself and from my family to work in God's kingdom. Sunday was never a rest day. Monday always held a new crisis. Before I knew it, Sunday had come again, with no day off in between. In retrospect, I now wonder if those things might not have all been accomplished with much less stress had I learned that life has a rhythm.

Look at nature. Nature has a rhythm. Certain animals hibernate during the winter. Others shed their skins or renew their pelts during certain seasons. They rest. Even plants have observed the rhythm that God has given to life. They don't bloom all the time and they don't rest all the time either. They bloom some, and then they rest some.

Slow down and observe the rhythms of life! Maybe it is time for us to stop blooming all the time. We need to discover our rest cycle. The sabbath principle is to labor for a while and then rest for at least a brief time. This rest will give you strength to labor more effectively again.

Don't worry; somehow you will finish what you need to get done!

Weighty Matters

June 25   *Read Hebrews 12:1-2.*

How many times did we sort through our household goods before shipping them to Ghana? We started throwing things away a year before we actually moved. We were allotted 250 cubic feet, which is really not that much. Major decisions had to be made.

Genuine junk was easy. It was easy to get rid of the old jelly jars and the plastic containers. Then came the hard part—deciding, piece by piece, what was important enough to fit into that small shipping allowance.

I learned that I had at least a healthy respect for the god of materialism when my angel collection accidentally found its way to the city dump. Prior to this move, I had always thought that I wasn't materialistic. As I tried to analyze the tears that flowed uncontrollably, I discovered that things had become a weight in my life. Once I recovered from losing the angels, it was easier to voluntarily give things away.

There are lessons to be learned from moving. I really thought that I knew how to move—I was a Methodist pastor. Before each move, I sorted and threw things away that were no longer useful. I had yet to learn that one cannot hold onto everything that is useful. We moved them from house to house as they multiplied and compounded with interest! Everywhere we moved in preparation for the big move to Ghana, we wagged an entourage of unnecessary things. We had so many boxes of usable things that we were weighed down.

I wonder if this is one of the weights to which the writer of Hebrews refers when he encouraged us to lay aside weight and sin. As the day approached to prepare our household goods for shipping, we gave away more and more of the possessions we once thought precious. After a while, it felt good to have less. And of course for the moment, we have vowed never to accumulate again!

Now, I am convinced that everyone should pretend that they are making a major move at least once every few years. It would be an excellent time to discover if we hold things, or if they hold us.

It's What You Say That Counts

June 26   *Read Matthew 16:13-17.*

Identity problems are fascinating. We love twins, doubles, look-alikes, and people born on our birthday. At the same time we use credentials like Social Security numbers and picture identification cards, as ways of asserting our uniqueness. I wonder if we secretly feel that someone else would really want to impersonate us?

Simon Peter was presented with an identity issue. Jesus asked him what others thought about him. We remember the traditional answers. The Jews of the day were confused; they thought Jesus must at least be one of the prophets. Finally, Jesus cut through all the speculation and asked Peter what *he* thought. Peter's answer continues to reverberate through the corridors of holy history: "You are the Messiah, the Son of the living God."

This passage conveniently presents a paradigm for modern believers. Jesus did not plead or present holy credentials in an attempt to convince us of His divine origins. Jesus chose another way to prove His identity. The answer that He gives to Peter and to us is this: "It's what you say about me that really counts!"

Some theologians say that Christianity is a revealed religion. They imply that Christ is known through personal revelation. Our mothers understood theology, too. They just said that God was a mystery. They knew that the mystery of God in Christ, reconciling the world to Himself, could not be completely understood or explained to others, only discerned. For our mothers, it was not necessary to provide proof or to plead—their personal discernment was sufficient evidence. They knew Jesus, and that was enough.

It does not matter what other people say about Christianity. They can neither prove nor disprove your faith. It's what you say that counts. It does not matter what other people say about your Jesus. They may question His authenticity or his ethnicity; but they were not there with you when Jesus revealed the glory of God in your heart. No one can presume to deny, define, or discredit what God, through Christ, has done in your life. Ultimately, it's what you say that counts.

The Two Dollar Bill

June 27   *Read Luke 15:8-10.*

Sheila was not prepared for what she found at Aunt Bertha's house that day. Aunt Bertha was almost ninety and still lived alone. She and Uncle Freeman had been married for sixty-five years before his death ten years ago. Since that time, Aunt Bertha had managed quite well alone—with a little help from her nieces Sheila, LaVerne, and Precious, who all took turns helping Auntie with the housework.

Usually, Auntie was remarkably neat for a woman her age. LaVerne and Precious helped with the cooking and did some of the other chores on their day. Sheila cleaned her refrigerator once a week, wiped down the bathroom, and changed her bed. Sheila always looked forward to the long cheerful conversations that she would have with Auntie after she had done these few chores. From the look of things today, there would be no time for talk.

Bertha's house looked like a burglar had been there! Every drawer was out of the dresser. Clothes were strewn all over the sofa. Even the buffet was a mess. Panic struck Sheila's heart. Was Auntie okay? Where is she?

Sheila ran through the house calling out for her aunt who was not the least bit hard of hearing.

"Auntie! Auntie!"

She found Aunt Bertha in the bedroom, bent over, almost upside down in an old steamer trunk. All that yelling startled her. She stood up and almost lost her balance.

"Sheila! What is wrong with you?"

"Auntie, your house—what happened?"

Oh, that? I was looking for this two dollar bill that your Uncle Freeman gave me for my sixtieth birthday. I just found it in this trunk.

Sheila didn't know whether to breathe a sigh of relief or grit her teeth. She decided to grit her teeth when she figured out who would help clean up the mess.

Can you imagine the way that God looked for each one of us when we were lost?

Need a Miracle?

June 28   *Read Exodus 14:9-16.*

How many times have you known that you needed a miracle to survive? The children of Israel were between the proverbial rock and a hard place. Pharaoh was pursuing them from one direction and there they were camped by the Red Sea. They were trapped!

After the ten plagues that God sent to free the Israelites from the bondage of Egypt, it would seem that they would expect another miracle in the face of this danger. But, alas, how quickly we all forget. We forget that God paid the car note for last month, when the rent is due for this month. We forget how sick we were last year, when God sent healing into our lives. Sometimes we even believe that last year's or yesterday's miracles were circumstantial, or accidental happenings. The truth is, however, that miracles are planned and deliberate. They are designed to bolster our faith.

It is evident that our faith needs a booster shot when we find ourselves terrified about present challenges. How often terror leads to complaint. The Israelites were terrified complainers. They behaved as though they had been freed against their will. For similar reasons, the same woman who prays to be free from a bad marriage today can be tempted to complain tomorrow about having to be alone. Thank God for His patience when we have short memories.

Where, today, will we find faith? Let us reach into the storehouse of our memories to find faith for today's journey. "Jesus Christ is the same yesterday and today and forever" (Heb. 13:8). God's intentions for us have not changed, nor has His power to carry out those intentions. Miracles often come to remind us of the glory of God.

So, today, if you find yourself thinking that things can't possibly go well without a miracle—relax, stranger things have happened!

A Word for the Battle Weary

June 29   *Read Isaiah 43:1-7.*

By the writing of this passage, Isaiah had seen much misery. Some think that as a youth he was relocated by the Assyrian invasion of Israel. He saw his people devastated and taken away from their homes. He joined his nation in prayer when wicked King Ahaz made comfortable alliances with Israel's enemies—alliances that backfired. He encouraged the new king, Hezekiah, to do what was right in the eyes of the Lord. Hezekiah heard God and resisted their enemies. By this time, several wars had broken out and the Israelites had gained the courage to fight back. They were beginning to see God's deliverance. Isaiah 43 was written by a man familiar with battle weariness.

How often I have embraced Isaiah's words to an oppressed people and called them my own. These are words that cradle the reader in loving arms. These are words for the shell-shocked and the fatigued. These words bring comfort and promise hope. Isaiah's passage also holds promises for our youth. I won't bother to quote statistics on drug use, gang membership, or prison populations. We all know that our children are in trouble. They are no less victims of war than children in visibly war-torn countries. They look like refugees on the street corners of our major cities. Their eyes, without animation, scan the neighborhoods for hope. Their efforts are futile, and to them, hope seems elusive. We have been so weary for such a long time that we have not cradled them in our bosoms and given them an anchor. Surely the children of Israel, living in uncertainty, were also the group most affected by such a long struggle.

God's promise is definite. Our children are scattered but He will bring them back from the four corners of the earth. "Give them up! Do not hold them back!" Nothing will be able to keep them away. Let your tears turn into laughter, mothers in Zion; one day our children are coming home.

Insiders

June 30   *Read Acts 19:1-5.*

The people of Ephesus knew John's baptism. John was the forerunner who announced the coming of the Christ. He preached repentance and baptized the people who came to hear him. "Someone else is coming," he proclaimed.

The people faithfully did all that John asked of them. After having completed the religious requirements of that hour, they proceeded with life as they knew it. Surely weddings and funerals continued in regular and customary ways. Boys came to manhood, and young girls learned to cook just as their parents had done before them, while the people were waiting for further instructions.

One day, while those who followed John were continuing in their daily routines, Paul discovered disciples. It seems as though he recognized in them people who were doing their best with what they knew at the moment! As true disciples usually are, these were teachable. They gladly received the news about Jesus the Christ and were baptized immediately.

How many people in this world have heard something from God and are just waiting for further instructions? Scholars are just beginning to acknowledge that all of Africa had already heard something from God. Africa, with knowledge of the Supreme God, was merely waiting for further instructions when colonial missionaries arrived.

The organized church is notorious for defining insiders and outsiders. Unfortunately, we tend to count disciples by the numbers on our church roles. It appears, from this passage in Acts, that we might have to consider some other ways of recognizing those who belong to God. How many of those we have called outsiders might actually be God's insiders waiting for further instruction?

July

Bread of Heaven

> Guide me, O thou great Jehovah,
> Pilgrim through this barren land.

Cousin Viola could line out the long hymns just like the deacons. Her rich alto voice filled the entire room when she threw back her head and closed her eyes to sing. We chimed in automatically, the way our ancestors had for generations and generations in the backwoods of Oklahoma.

I felt the words vibrating in my belly. The walls shook, and I knew that Jesus was near. We are pilgrims and strangers in more ways than one. Pilgrims in this sinful world, and strangers in this country though we were here before many others. Guide us, Lord; guide me, for I don't know the way.

> I am weak, but thou art mighty;
> Hold me with thy powerful hand.

In spite of who I thought I was prior to that moment, that part of the song reminded me of shared human weakness. Power is not found in the places we have been, the subjects we have studied, or the people we have known. Power comes from God, all else is a weak imitation. I found my head thrown back, and my eyes closed along with cousin Viola as she continued to line out the long hymn—just like the deacons.

> Bread of heaven, bread of heaven,
> Feed me till I want no more.

By this time, the Bread of Heaven was filling our very souls. I could feel Him bringing satisfaction to the hunger of our hearts. We responded in raptured praise, and bathed the moment in hosannas. "Thank yuh!"

Cousin Viola's voice rang out. Momma reached for her eyes, as though to stop the tears. Grandmomma waved her hands, while her older sister stretched out her once-feeble legs and reached toward heaven with clenched fists. By this time, the power of God had brought me to my knees. Glory to God! His presence engulfed all of us—Momma, Grandmomma, my hundred-year-old aunt, and Cousin Viola, who could line out the hymns just like the deacons.

Peace Be Still

July 2   *Read Mark 4:37-41.*

They were absolutely stressed out! The storm had come from nowhere. They felt as if they were in the middle and they were certain that they were going to die. They knew that Jesus was with them, but He seemed to be unaffected by the terror. He did nothing. He was asleep. Did you feel like Jesus was asleep when your storm rose from nowhere?

What happens during a storm? Winds blow and waves rise. It seems like even nature is out of control. Only things that are strong and solid are able to endure a terrible storm.

For many people, the storms of life are proving grounds. Without a storm, we have no idea of the inner strength that God has given us. Even weight lifters do not know how many pounds they can lift until their limits are tested. Storms come and push us to the limit—they prove us. We learn more about ourselves in the storm.

Storms are also an excellent time to learn more about God. As in today's reading, He really is present in the storm. Like the fearful disciples, we wait impatiently for Him to wake up to our danger and calm things down. Just why was Jesus asleep in the boat while that storm raged?

Jesus frequently used the regular occurrences of life to teach the disciples. A storm provided an excellent opportunity to teach them faith. Did you hear His questioning rebuke? "Why were you afraid?" We never heard their answer. When the storms of life arise, why are we so afraid? What is the worst thing that really could happen? Wouldn't it be eye-opening to learn that our wildest fears are usually exaggerations, and the worst things that could happen are really not that bad?

"Have you still no faith?" He was speaking to seasoned sailors. Hadn't they survived other storms? We have been in storms before this one. Haven't we survived? No doubt sister, you have a storm story that would hold our attention. And without question, you have a story of divine deliverance from a storm.

So why are we so afraid? Jesus is in the boat with us. He is not indifferent and He is not asleep. He has the power to calm the winds and the waves with a word. He's just waiting for the perfect time to stop them.

Gone Fishing?

July 3   *Read John 21:3-6.*

When our thoughts turn to summer, they often turn to fishing. For most of us, fishing is a fun way to pass the time away. We plan to fish to relax or to share time with friends or family.

For Peter, fishing was his livelihood. This was the way that Peter had formerly earned his living. He put down his fishing nets and forsook all to follow Jesus. Now, however, Christ was no longer visibly with Peter and the other disciples in the same way. They could no longer predict His pattern of movement. They were unable to spend time together as before. Christ was no longer there to bail them out of sudden storms on the Sea of Galilee. To put it in our terms, things had changed and Peter was not sure how to adapt to the change. In an attempt to cope with his own grief, Peter went back to what he knew—fishing.

Peter's suggestion was the temporary answer that several of the disciples thought they needed. They felt that life was never going to be the same again. So Peter and a few of the disciples returned to their former professions.

On the surface, this looked like a good and a practical idea. Often, in our lives, when faced with uncertainty, we instinctively return to the comfort of what we know well. We move back to our hometowns, return to old jobs, and look up old friends from the past. In the routine things of our lives, this often is the band-aid that we need to get us through a crisis. However, when it comes to spiritual things, we must always remember that the Risen Christ, though not always visibly with us, is really there.

Our motivation and direction for life come from God, who has promised to be with us always. We may walk through hailstorms or valleys in our lives, unable to physically see God, but we are reminded by this passage that He is always with us.

Just how did Peter and the others finally come to this realization? Having returned to fishing, these disciples were no longer living to spread the good news. Somehow, they allowed grief and misunderstanding to side track them.. They felt, as we often do, that being unable to see God in their immediate surroundings must mean that they were in the wrong places, doing the wrong things. Jesus, how-ever, came to them on the banks of the sea, prepared a meal for them, and gave Peter further directions for ministry. There was nothing wrong with fishing, but the greater call was to witness to the truth of the Resurrection.

In spite of the continuing truth of the Resurrection, may of us are tempted to "go fishing" by returning to what is comfortable. May we see the Christ of the Resurrection coming into our lives to give us clarity and direction. Amen.

Pulling Weeds

July 4   *Read Matthew 13:27-30.*

"If I live to be a hundred, I will never understand why Reverend Watson won't put that woman out of church." Annette and Cabrina were discussing *her* again. The woman in question was the town's biggest troublemaker. She would alternate between fury and piety. No one ever knew how she would be on any given day. She had been thrown out of every church in town—except that one. Some even thought that Candi might have some sort of mental illness.

"Do you think that the pastor sees some good in her" Annette wondered out loud. "Just about the time he seems ready to give up on her, she does something that makes sense."

"Candi has done this church a lot more harm than good. She gossips from house to house and tries her best to turn people against one another and against the pastor. Have you forgotten that we lost our last two pastors because of her dirtywork?" Cabrina did not want to consider any virtue in a person who had done so much evil.

July

Reverend Watson, in the privacy of his church office, was also discussing Candi. She, again, was at the top of his list of prayer concerns.

"Lord, show me what to do. I know that this woman is your child. If I throw her out of this church, she has no place left to go. Is it right to shut the door of grace in the face of one who needs it so desperately—I just cannot figure this one out!"

Each one of us, at some time or another, has experienced some person that we would like to exclude from our fellowship. Sometimes, it is obvious that they mean the church and its people no good. Other times, it is nearly impossible to distinguish them from well-meaning Christians who make mistakes. Perhaps, we will just have to let God pull the weeds!

Rahab the Prostitute

July 5   *Read Joshua 2:1-4, 17-21.*

Why do we prioritize sins? We name big ones and little ones as though it made some difference to God. We tragically place the former prostitute and the former crack addict in spiritual never-never land. They are never welcome in our churches or in our homes. We never let them forget. God, thankfully, is not like that.

Human nature seems to have a problem with forgiveness. It is so hard for us to really believe that God forgives us. It is equally as hard for us to forgive ourselves. And, it is harder for us to forgive one another, especially people with a publicized past! It would almost appear that we prefer not to know what folks have overcome—as though our polite ignorance would make them better persons in our own eyes and in God's.

The haunting reality is this: God said something good about at least one former prostitute! When the spies went to Jericho, Rahab, the prostitute, provided a safe place for them to spend the night. She was one who sensed the reality of the Hebrew God. She was the person who dared to go out on a limb for her fragile beliefs. When the invasion did take place, Rahab and her family were the only ones spared from destruction.

Is there a lesson in that for us today? Could it be possible that prostitutes and crack addicts are caring people who, in their confusion, have made unwise lifestyle choices? Does God understand their hearts too?

We are all in a sense like Rahab, or any other prostitute. At some point, our confusion has led to poor lifestyle choices or bad decisions. We all have some areas of regret in our lives. Rahab's sins were public sins. Everyone in town knew about her poor lifestyle choices. The major difference between some of us and Rahab is that we have been allowed the luxury of private conversion and private forgiveness.

Actually, there is an important lesson that we can learn from Rahab. In order to be saved, she had acted upon her convictions about God. In her case, the scarlet cord hanging out the window was a signal of her stand with God's people. The act of hanging the scarlet cord outside the window became an act of faith. God rewarded Rahab's act of faith. Her life was saved. Her household was saved. It is also important to note that her name appears with the respectable. In Matthew 1:5 she is mentioned as an ancestor of David, and ultimately as an ancestor of Christ.

Has God been challenging you to take a stand? Is there a scarlet cord hidden in your closet waiting to be hung outside your window in full view?

Chain, Chain, Change

July 6   *Read Acts 22:12-19.*

Have you ever been in a Sunday school class or Bible study trying to figure out when Saul of Tarsus changed his name to Paul the apostle? It's really hard to pinpoint exactly when this happened. A better question might be why did Saul become Paul?

Among the Jews, Saul had a strong reputation. He was known for upholding the Law. He was known for being intelligent. He was a promising young Jewish leader. But, he was on the wrong track.

Saul persecuted the Christians. He thought they were a blasphemous cult group. He dedicated his life to stopping the growth of what he considered a group in extreme error—until Jesus came into his life.

Saul had gained such a reputation for persecuting Christians that Christians had a hard time believing his conversion was genuine. They were suspicious; they excluded him; they feared him. Somewhere along the line, Saul became Paul. He changed his name to signal that he had become a new man.

Are you familiar with this story? Does the infamy of your past intrude into your present? Perhaps it is time for a change in your life. Saul changed his name, you can change your perspective.

Something as simple as a new hairstyle might change the way that you look at yourself or the way others look at you. A changed attitude might be just what you need to prove that you are truly different since Jesus came into your life. Maybe it's a new job, different friends, or a change in or habits. The key word for today is change.

If a haunting past continues to rattle its chains in your life, perhaps God is using this as a reminder to change.

"Salty Gal"

July 7   *Read Matthew 5:13.*

You are the salt of the earth. You are unique, you are different for a reason. Are there ever times when you feel that you do not fit in? When you look around and see the moral decay, thank God that you do not fit. Salt is there to be a deterrent to decay. Do you remember the stories of the old folks at hog-killing time. The meat was rubbed down with salt. Even the sugar cure has salt in it. The salt is there to stop things from spoiling. And so are you.

In a culture of conformity, we are often tempted to lose sight of that reality. We are here to stop the spoilage and moral decay. We are not there to fit in, but rather to say that some things do not fit, are not fit, and do not befit us. You are the salt of the earth.

On the days that all of life seems tasteless, you are the salt of the earth. There comes a time, for so many, that life is just so many beds to be made, heads to comb, or chickens to fry. Life can easily be reduced to quotas on the machine, successfully avoiding pain, or nobody calling you by your name—or out of your name. After so many heartaches, after so many disappointments, life loses its savor. We need you to be the salt of the earth.

You also help us to hold on to water, salty girl. If you have already gone low salt or even no salt, you know what I mean. When I see you hold on in the quagmire of your world, I know that I have to make it in the shoes-stuck-to-the-floor existence that I live in. You help me to remember. I remember Sojourner, I remember Mahalia, I remember Coretta, I remember Fannie, when I look at you. I remember mamas who are gone, and Big-Mama with swollen ankles and an endless hug, when I look at you. You have to make it, lest I think that I can't. You have to stay salty for me.

Salt is here to teach us to celebrate differentness. Salt is here to keep us from being dull and uninteresting. Salt is here to stop us from decaying. Salt is even here to remind us of where the wounds are. Salt is here to help us hold on to the water we need. Just as the Lord put salt on this earth for these reasons, so are you placed here to be that which brings uniqueness, that which causes us to celebrate, that which helps us to hold on.

If salt loses its saltiness, what will we salt with? If you cease to be you, who will fill your place? You are the salt of the earth.

The Secret Place

July 8   *Read Psalm 91.*

There are times in my life when I need a secret place to be. I have never been one to run from a fight, but there are days when I really need a place to retreat and know that no pursuer can overtake me. Are there days when you need to put away your superwoman suit and be still? Sounds like you need a secret place, too.

There are days when I feel like a dumb little bird, unable to see the big traps and snares that are set for me. I need a place to hide and know that no hunter can catch me. The psalmist in today's psalm knew that feeling. He found in God a place where no trap or snare would work. Thank God for the shadow of the Almighty.

AIDS is a noisy pestilence. I am afraid, aren't you? Both urban cities and small hamlets boast of terrors by night and destruction at noonday. The world has become such a dangerous place. Lord, we need a secret place with you.

Israel knew of this secret place in its wanderings. They were naive and exposed to unknown dangers. God was a cloud to shade them by day and a pillar of fire to light their way by night. King David knew of a secret place in Mount Zion. It was a place where he could find God when public opinion threatened to crush him. Daniel found a secret place in the lions' den. He was hidden from the lion's hunger. God created a safe space for him where others saw danger. The secret place of the Most High is safe, no matter where it may be.

Where is this secret place; how can I find it? The secret place can be wherever God chooses to shelter you. The shadow of the Almighty eclipses any vision of danger and creates a haven of rest on the busiest thoroughfare. To find Christ is to find that secret place of safety.

Scripture teaches us to recognize this place of safety. Paul reminded the Colossians that Christ in us is the hope of glory (Col. 1:27). His Letter to the Ephesians tells us that we are seated with Christ in heavenly places (2:6). What safer place could there be? The Letter to the Galatians reminds us that when our own agendas are crucified with Christ, then Christ lives in us (2:20). Your life is hidden in Christ, and everything connected to it is resting in a secret place!

What Time Is It?

July 9   *Read Ecclesiastes 3:1-8.*

What time is it? This is a relevant question to ask in the morning when the alarm sounds. We are so preoccupied with timeliness. American culture holds us to the clock.

In the New Testament, the writers use at least two different words for time. One is *chronos* from which we get chronometer. It reminds us of the ticking of a watch. Time waits for no one and can never be recaptured. The other word is *kairos*. It is used when referring to the birth of Christ in Galatians 4:4: "But when the fullness of time had come, God sent his Son, born of a woman, born under the law . . . ." The best way to conceptualize this kind of time is to think of the phrase, "the right time."

People of color are said to pay more attention to the right time. When something that blocks our progress has to change we say, "It was time!" When something long overdue gets done, we say: "It was time!" When something happens at the most beneficial and opportune moment, we say: "It was on time!"

As you struggle to watch clocks and keep appointments today, may I encourage you to be sensitive to that other kind of time?

What time is it in your life? Is it time to try it again, or is it time to consider something else? Is it time to break the silence of a long argument with a friend? Is it time to look for new job, new friends? Perhaps for you, it's time to invest yourself in old relationships—while there is still time.

Perhaps, the Holy Spirit may be reminding you that it is time to take a quiet walk on your lunch hour. Maybe it is time to volunteer some of your precious, hard-to-come-by time. It could even be that it is time to slow down your pace.

The writer of Ecclesiastes 3:1-8 says it best:

For everything there is a season, and a time for every matter under heaven:
a time to be born, and a time to die;
a time to plant, and a time to pluck up what is planted;
a time to kill, and a time to heal;
a time to break down, and a time to build up;
a time to weep, and a time to laugh;
a time to mourn, and a time to dance;
a time to throw away stones, and a time to gather stones together;
a time to embrace, and a time to refrain from embracing;
a time to seek, and a time to lose;
a time to keep, and a time to throw away;
a time to tear, and a time to sew;
a time to keep silence, and a time to speak;
a time to love, and a time to hate;
a time for war, and a time for peace.

Now, having said all of that, what time is it for you?

Receiving You Back into My Heart

July 10   *Read Genesis 33:4.*

Where have you been,
Love of my life?
Where have you laid your head
For all of these days?
Where are you now,

Brother of my mother's womb?
When will you come home
Dear little sister?
How can I tell you
We're not angry anymore?

Nightly I pray for you,
Hoping you are still alive.
How can I tell you that God above
Has fixed my heart too?
Who will take the message
That all is forgiven?
Time heals many wounds.
It was partly my fault too.
Won't you come home?

I was so very wrong,
My mother, my brother.
I've cried the whole night long
Regretting that day.
It was not worth it,
My sweetheart, my lover.
I only hurt myself.
Can I come home?

Can I have another chance
To prove my faithfulness?
Believe me, loved one,
I was wrong.
Can I come home?

So many never get
The chance to forgive and let
Pride or shame bar the way
To reconciliation.
God changes, time heals.
People grow up, life goes on.
Child of God, won't you go home?
Chances are,
They have all changed too!

God Will Take Care of You

One of my former students calls her "Cousin Hagar." I have heard people refer to her children when they see at-risk youth. African-American women have been compared to her. Hagar stands as a symbol of things gone wrong. In some ways, many of us African-American women really are daughters of Hagar.

How could one woman have so much go wrong in her life? Have you asked that question of yourself recently? To begin with, Hagar was a slave. Her mistress, Sarah, treated her like a toy. First, she was offered to Sarah's husband, Abraham, for childbearing purposes. The resulting relationship was a mess! Sarah became jealous. Hagar was thrown out of the house. Poor Ishmael, the innocent result of everyone's folly, was caught in the middle.

Hagar's history is so much like ours. We are often used, misused, and stranded. Many times we don't know how we will make it. And a child is almost always in the equation.

The good news is that we have never been alone. The Bible records God's concern for Hagar, just as heaven records God's concern for you! The Lord opened Hagar's eyes to a well of water that had been hidden from her view. She would not die, her child would not die. The Lord took care of her.

You won't die either! Ask the Lord to open your eyes as He did Hagar's. The Lord will make a way—somehow! We've never been promised an obstacle-free life. But, the Lord has promised that He would never leave us. The Lord will also take care of you.

If you should find your eyes clouded with tears today, why not dry them enough to see God's intervention in the not so distant future.

The Popsicle Lady

Children from all over the neighborhood flocked to her backyard in the summertime. Mama Smalls was a literal Pied Piper when it came to young folks. The good ones and the so-called bad ones came to her backyard. Surprisingly, they all got along pretty well when they were there.

Some folks thought that they just came to her for the popsicles that she gave out freely. Maybe some did just come for a free treat. Others, however, used the popsicles as an excuse for free counseling, a listening ear, or for the only smile they would get that day. No doubt about it, Mama Smalls had a way with kids.

When some of her popsicle crew grew up and tried to go for bad, you might see her out at night looking for them. She would ask for Joe Jr. or Walt or whichever child she heard had joined a gang or was getting into trouble. When she found them, she would talk, and they would listen, and sometimes some of them would come home.

When the neighborhood changed, those big ol' boys whom everyone else was afraid of would often walk her to church for night service. Every now and then one of them, or their girlfriends, would go inside with her—just to make her happy. She was never in danger, bumping around at night where most of us have no business, because those same big boys and girls had known her love since they were children—standing in line on hot summer days waiting for a popsicle.

Most of the original popsicle crew is grown now. They eventually stopped hanging out at night; most of them have jobs and families. And they never get too busy to stop by Mama Smalls' place to say hello or to bring her something special. A couple of them, who live out of town, send cards on Mother's Day, remembering that they would have probably been in jail, or on ice, had she not been out at night looking for them.

Nowadays, the Popsicle Lady sits in a chair by the window wishing that she weren't too fragile to greet the children who once graced her backyard. I hear that there is a sign in her window that reads "Wanted: Popsicle Lady, No Experience Necessary."

Love, Poured Out at His Feet

July 13   *Read John 12:3-8.*

"What possessed this woman?" I'm sure that's what the onlookers said. "What got into that girl?" Women weren't even asked into their conversations. "She's just trying to show off!" The perfume was quite expensive. Is she trying to get herself noticed? No, the woman was just in love with Jesus. She was expressing her love when she poured precious perfume on His feet.

Mary, with her alabaster box of precious ointment, gets whisked away far too often. In our theological games of trivial pursuit, we explain her away by saying that she performed the anointing rites for a king. This woman, however, did much more.

She teaches us about extravagant love for God. Mary gave Jesus something extremely precious. The ointment was costly, the Gospel writer reports the cost of a year's wages. Too much? She was only responding to God's extravagant love for her. He gave us the most costly gift in the world, His one and only unique son. A jar of ointment was the least she, or we, could do.

This woman also teaches us about boldness in worship. She responded to the love and extravagance of God in ways that could have merited criticism. She did not care. She had probably decided that she would try to pour this precious perfume on Him even if they dragged her out of the room and called her names! She modeled a faith that responds to God, physically and emotionally, in spite of public opinion. I'm sure she wasn't the kind of woman who would hide tears in church or quench the spirit. To her, Jesus was wonderful, and she wanted the whole world to know!

Mary of Bethany, unknowingly, blessed the entire room. The ointment was costly. How many of you are able to enjoy the most costly perfumes? That day, everyone in the room got a whiff! Everyone was able to savor the fragrance and remember the moment with Jesus. When we really enter into worship, in the company of others, everyone present gets the benefit of our expressions of adoration, and God gets the glory!

Jesus applauded Mary and women like her. He cherishes the sacrificial, heartfelt, and bold responses of faithful women, who, like this woman, don't mind being poured out at His feet.

Childish Ways

July 14   *Read 1 Corinthians 13:11.*

When you and I were teenagers, we received such mixed messages. When we were moving too fast for their liking, adults would say: "Who

you think you are? You ain't grown yet!" When we tried to conceptualize
the way our age should act, we were accused of acting like two-year-olds
or of having the stubbornness of a five-year-old. "Grow up!" Somehow,
we mistakenly thought that growing older was the same as growing up.
We would say: "Can't wait until I'm eighteen." Free and twenty-one! Time
has passed. We have grown older; we have turned eighteen, twenty-five,
forty, and seventy. Who, now, is responsible for reminding us to grow up?

Our generation is not the first to struggle with the difference between
growing older and growing up. Have you overheard the older women in
the kitchen jokingly refer to men as a forty-year-old children. We see the
dysfunction of an economic system that seems to reward people who
have not matured.

Paul was speaking to a group of people in a similar plight. They were
jealous of one another's spiritual gifts. They chose up sides, formed fac-
tions, and fought against one another—in the church! They made distinctions between the important members and the so-called unimportant
members—just like children.

Paul's prescription is simple. Stop pouting; you are all important. Start
taking responsibility for your actions. Learn to appreciate one another.
Learn to love. Put away childish things.

At one time, I glossed over this scripture passage because I just automatically assumed that I was always a mature adult. Now, as I look back
at some of my adult tantrums, I realize that the Holy Spirit was talking
to me, too.

No one reminds us to grow up anymore. Yet, so many adults have
grown older without growing up. Thank God for a gentle reminder from
today's scripture reading. It is time for all of us to put away childish ways.

For the Older Women Who Continue
to Parent

July 15

Lord, we thank you for the older women of our community who continue to parent. Thank you for the mothers who have been there to

mother our children when we were too young, too foolish, or too busy. Thank you for the ways that they continue to give of their time, their homes, and their substance. Without them, many a child would have had no childhood.

Thank you Lord, for the space they created for us to grow. Some of us would never have been in college without them. Others of us would not be good parents today if they had not led us by example. They are the embodiment of godly parental love in our communities.

Thank you for the older women who rock babies on their aging knees, while young couples try to repair broken marriages. Thank you for the older women who provide loving hugs and homes for our children while we go on vacation. Thank you for the older women who parent by day, while we are employed. Thank you for so many extra arms and laps for the babies in church.

> God bless you, Grandmomma, Auntie, Big Momma, and Friend.
> Having retired your womb, you have opened your heart
> to receive yet another
> child in need of a mother.
> May you know that we appreciate the sacrifices
> you make.

May the Lord bless those who are mothers twice!

Sunday Morning

July 16   *Read Psalm 122:1.*

===

> Ready yet? It's almost time to go
> To a place where time becomes unimportant
> Where the mundane and the profane
> Give way to the holy.
> It's time to go to church.
>
> It's time we shouted "troubles over"
> It's time we prayed through our grudge

God's house is the place
Where the Spirit works
On everyone who comes.
It's time to go to church.

Are you glad when someone says, "Girl, come go to church with me. Jesus will set you free. Don't worry about sitting in someone else's seat, we like visitors at my church"? Get ready, Sunday's coming!

There was once a time when everyone thought about going to church, whether they actually did it or not. Church was the center of our community. Church was the center of each person's world. Once there, we were able to settle down inside. The noise of a troubled world ceased in the presence of God and the saints. We were glad to hear folk say, "Let us go into the house of the Lord." Though times have changed and churches have changed, God is the same yesterday, today, and forever. And Sunday still comes every week.

Aren't you glad that Sunday comes every week? It restarts the clock and interrupts weekly nightmares. Sunday charges us up and energizes our souls. God calls it a sabbath, a time to be re-created. Sundays are filled with recreation, cool lemonade, conversation, contemplation, speculation, and sometimes just plain old sleep. Thank God for Sundays every week.

When I am bogged down on Wednesdays, it seems like Friday's time clock will never click "quitting-time." It feels like the moment will never come to see the saints again. Other weeks, it feels as if the days bleed endlessly into one another. Before I know it Sunday comes again, bringing the merry-go-round of my existence to a pleasant pause, and allowing me to catch my breath for another ride. Praise the Lord, Sunday's coming.

Prayer: Lord, rekindle our love for the church. Awaken our sleeping community to its possibilities. Bring us to the house of the Lord again. Amen.

Instant Family!

July 17   *Read John 1:12-13.*

Have you ever visited a church, for the first time, and seen someone who looked like a dear friend? It is amazing how something in the way one lady wears her hat, or another holds her hands, will remind us of someone we love.

All over the world, I see sisters that look like somebody I know. You see them too. Sometimes we forget and call them by name. "Excuse me, are you related to Cora Mae Bryant? Oh, I'm sorry, you could be her twin!" It must be more than coincidence.

How would it be to actually treat the sister, who looks like Cousin Viola, the way you would treat your blood cousin? It would be wonderful to accept her and love her—just like you love Vy! What would we do if we learned that we all really were related in some strange way?

Actually, those in Christ *are* related in some strange way. We share a common bloodline. Whether Black, White, Asian, Hispanic, or Native American, we are all part of the same family. The broken loaf of bread used at communion is a visual reminder that we are one. The symbolic common cup reminds us of unity. Those who believe in Christ are just one big family.

The early church recognized that they were suddenly related. Anyone born of God was a sister or a brother. Anyone bold enough to accept Christ in those days was good enough to dip their hands in the plate with the rest of the family members! They were instant family!

We are God's family; we share the same blood. We are also partakers together in the divine nature as God invites us to be like Him. We are supposed to recognize one another! It's a shame that the world teaches us to fear. As members of the same divine family, we are one loaf, one cup, one blood, it is really not so strange that we should begin to resemble one another.

The next time you are in church and see your cousin's look-alike, why not smile, and perhaps wave at a member of your instant family!

Peacemaker

July 18   *Read Matthew 5:9.*

What is a peacemaker? Most of the time, we relegate our understanding of the peacemaker's role to those who arbitrate wars or labor disputes. The Lord spoke of peacemakers as if we would meet one. How will we recognize the peacemakers in our midst?

Some peacemakers in our communities do their work by telephone. They walk the tightrope between people who are at odds. Remember Margie, who could listen to both sides of a dispute but not take sides? Were you aware of the subtle ways that she challenged you to see the issue from both sides without ever betraying the goal of settling the dispute? Before long, you and the other person were in the same room together fumbling your way to a cease-fire, while trying to save face.

Maybe your peacemaker was a comic. There are times when too many of us speak before we think. Before you know it, we have blurted out something that should have been kept to ourselves. Blurting seems to cause an epidemic of ill-placed words. In a split second, everybody's blurting and somebody gets mad. In the height of this madness, likely you heard a voice—a silly commentary that broke anger's momentum. Laughter, which spoke more of relief than humor, averted what could have been quite ugly.

Will peacemakers make the evening news for the ways in which they bring resolution to great family feuds? Probably not. They will probably be unknown people who work in secret. Peacemakers are insightful people who have the ability to reconcile warring forces without needing credit for what they have done. Ultimately, according to the old adage, it's really more important to just get the job done.

"Blessed are the peacemakers, for they will be called children of God" (5:9).

Something to Work With

July 19   *Read John 6:5-13.*

Some people say that the miracle of feeding five thousand pivots around the point that the little boy shared his lunch. There were five little barley loaves and two fish that he naively offered to help feed the multitude. This passage does not tell us that anyone else shared their food; but it does tell us that the Lord multiplied what was offered. No matter how we look at it, it was a miracle of provision.

Though the Lord can make something from nothing, there are times when He prefers to have something to work with. Could that be why some of us have not received our miracle? Perhaps the Lord is waiting for us to offer the inadequate material that we have. He solves the problem.

Do we hesitate to offer what we know is inadequate because we fear losing what we have? The little boy may have been too young to consider that very real issue. When we don't have much, it's easy to be stingy. The devil divides and subtracts, robs and destroys; but Jesus, who adds and multiplies, came to give us an abundant life. (See John 10:10.)

When we search through our history, we see that Black women have been offering God barley loaves and a few fish for a long time. Mary McLeod Bethune started a college with a handful of pocket change. A multitude of daughters and sons have been sent to college, and even medical school, with the pitiful salaries of maids and washerwomen.

As you wait for a miracle of provision, I encourage you to search your own small storehouse. What do you have to offer to the Lord? Remember, the devil divides, but God multiplies!

Don't Look Back

July 20   *Read Luke 9:62.*

"Don't look back—someone may be gaining on you."
—Satchel Page

It is quite natural to find farming metaphors in the New Testament. Most of Jesus' audience would have been acquainted with the discipline necessary for successful farming. Though riding tractors up and down the rows seems boring or uneventful, plowing still requires reasonable concentration. Some modern farmers, who have missing fingers or even missing hands, would warn us that distractions can lead to tragedy, and carelessness can be costly. Plowing takes a serious commitment to getting the job done.

In Luke 9, it became obvious to Jesus that some would-be disciples were not quite aware of the commitment required to follow Him. The first would-be follower vowed that he would follow Jesus wherever He went. Who would not want to be seen with one who was loved and worshiped everywhere He went? Was this disciple really prepared for the uncertainty that caused Jesus to say that, "Foxes have holes, and birds of the air have nests; but the Son of Man has nowhere to lay his head" (9:58)?

Another man wanted to bury his father. In our misunderstanding of culture, we often miss the point that this person wanted to go home and wait until his elderly father passed on. The custom was that the responsible child in the family placed all on hold to provide for elderly parents until their death. Jesus did not mean to imply that we have no responsibility to our elderly, but rather that even good excuses are meaningless because there is no time to wait.

Still another man wanted to go home and say good-bye. On the surface, that seems so reasonable. But, what does the process of saying good-bye involve? Maybe it would be a time of great indulgence. It could mean somewhere in the process of mourning over changes in lifestyle that we might even get cold feet and back out altogether. Taken in this context, the meaning is clear: Christ is looking for disciples who will not get cold feet, who will not wait for a more convenient time, and who will not long for the past.

Is there anything causing you to look back today?

Said I Wasn't Gonna Tell Nobody

July 21   *Read Jeremiah 20:9.*

Simulated conversation:
   Girl, what?
   No, I won't tell a soul.
   He did what?
   No, I won't tell a soul.
   She said what?
   Of course, I know it's a secret.
   Bye.
Long pause, signs of struggle . . . Ring, Ring
   Girl, guess what?
   "Said I wasn't going to tell nobody but I just couldn't keep it to

myself." Some things are just too hot to hold. In Jeremiah's case, the news that he couldn't keep to himself wasn't necessarily good news. He needed to warn the people of impending destruction even though they didn't want to hear a thing he said.

There is something about some messages that must be delivered. They writhe inside and turn you every way but loose! Jeremiah had a word from God that Israel had to have. They were in trouble and some of them pretended they did not know it. Jeremiah was tormented by the words he refused to speak. He sounded as if he would burst if the warnings were not shared. The words were like fire shut up in his bones! After futile resistance he had to say them—whether Israel liked it or not.

Perhaps there are similar words, similar warnings, bottled up inside you. In spite of your vows to never warn that person again, you may have a word of admonition that will save someone's life. What might have happened to Israel had they not been warned? Though Israel seems to have ignored Jeremiah's warnings, certainly some person within Israel heard him and benefited from a word from the Lord. In similar ways, perhaps one person in the crowd may hear what God has given you to say.

Warnings and rebukes are painful. They obviously bring pain to the recipient. They often can be a source of pain and discomfort for those who must deliver them. In spite of the pain, you are God's messenger. The very words that you are hesitant to speak may be God's instruments of healing.

Speak boldly and lovingly, your message is simply too hot to hold!

Can You Trust God?

July 22   *Read Proverbs 3:5-6.*

As Billie Jean sat on the pew, her thoughts were not in the building. Her mind drifted to her son, who was in a great deal of trouble. Where on earth was she going to get the money to resolve the trouble that he had got into this time? "Lord, where have I gone wrong" she thought. "What more could I have done?"

Justin, her middle child, had always been the topic of much discussion with God. Justin, to put it mildly, was unpredictable. He was independent and often irrational. He was one of those children who showed rather than spoke what was on his mind.

This time he had gone too far. He had been involved in a feud with the wrong kind of boys. Tempers flared and before long he had beaten up one of the boys from the West End. Their way was retaliation. They shot at him and drove away! Later, he lay in wait for one of them, who is now in the morgue. Justin wasn't really a bad child; would anyone ever believe that?

> I will trust in the Lord,
> I will trust in the Lord,
> I will trust in the Lord,
> Until I die.

The choir had pulled out a new arrangement of an old standard. Billie Jean did not want to hear this one—not today when she was struggling to keep her composure. Quickly, she jumped up from her seat, holding up the customary one finger, and scurried to the narthex of the church.

She stood by the side door, which opened into the parking lot, and prayed. "Lord, I am forced to trust you with my child's future. Help us both to get through the worst that has ever happened in our lives."

Can you trust the Lord today? Whether you face the least or the worst of your worries, remember that God is always trustworthy.

> Sister can you trust in the Lord,
> Sister can you trust in the Lord,
> Sister can you trust in the Lord
> Until you die?

Mammy-Made

July 23   *Read 1 Samuel 2:18-21.*

Some Bible indexes refer to her as the ideal mother. She prayed for a son and the Lord gave her Samuel. She gave her son back to the Lord. Hannah sent her longed-for son to live at the temple with the high priest.

Don't you know that boy knew he was loved? He wasn't abandoned, he was given a great opportunity. His mother trudged to see him at the time of the yearly sacrifice, bringing with her a priestly garment especially made for him.

Did your momma used to sew for you? Mine did. Every year, getting ready for school meant garments made especially for me. Momma and Big Momma (Gram) sewed things for me because we were unable to buy ready-made clothes. In my mind's eye, I can still see the old sewing machine on the dining room table surrounded by pattern pieces and scraps of cloth.

It became a yearly ritual. In the summer we would scour the fabric stores for sales. Patterns, buttons, zippers, and thread, all to match my special school clothes, in my size, and just for me. They sewed all summer, and took extra care to try to make these Cinderella clothes look like they came from the racks. You see, they didn't want me to look "mammy-made."

I never could understand the word "mammy-made" while I was young. I was proud of my mother and grandmother for making my things. Like Samuel's ephod, they were visible signs of love reminding me how important school was to my family. Not only did I have one-of-a-kind originals, I had the love that makes you feel good about yourself wrapped around my bony long-legged frame.

It's almost too bad that most of us can afford to buy what we want for our children these days. Some of them will never know the sacrifices that have been made for their education. What visual aids will they have to remind them of how important their education is? Is there something personal and special we can do for the school child in our lives? Maybe even something mammy made?

Mother felt ashamed that she had to make my things, but I felt loved and encouraged. I wish my mother understood how special those mammy-made garments made me feel.

Known from the Womb

July 24   *Read Jeremiah 1:4-8.*

"I don't speak well. I am too young in spiritual things."

How many prophets have used this excuse in protest? Most people are afraid of God's call. Few answer immediately with full confidence. Most of us cannot respond without first looking at our inadequacies. "I'm too fat." "I've only been in church for a few years; I don't know as much as everyone else." Do any of these excuses sound familiar?

How did the Lord respond to Jeremiah's list of excuses? He reminded Jeremiah that He had known him all of his life. Not only had He known Jeremiah since birth, but He had also known him before conception. There was nothing about Jeremiah that God did not already know.

Did you know that the Lord has also known you all of your life? There is nothing about you that He does not already know. He knew, when you were yet formless in the womb, what He had in store for you. He directed your playtime when you played life-games and dreamed great big dreams. He arranged for you to be on program that very first time and helped you calm down. It was training for what is to come. He let you feel what it was like to win, or to lead, knowing that days of leadership or competition would come in your adult life. Stated simply, all your life, God has been preparing you.

The Lord told Jeremiah that he didn't even have to figure out where to go, or what to say, "for you shall go to all to whom I send you, and you shall speak whatever I command you" (1:7). The same is true for you. You don't have to decide what, where, or how; God has taken full responsibility for the success of the mission.

Before you were born, God selected you. God knows your abilities, perhaps better than you know them yourself. God has been preparing you, all of your life, for the great future that lies ahead. Don't be afraid, for the Lord is with you, too.

Hearing God in Unlikely Places

July 25   *Read Matthew 3:1-4.*

John the Baptist came to these people bearing a word from the Lord. They had been waiting to hear from God for a long time. They flocked to strange, unlikely places to hear a strange man share the word of God for their times.

John's message was the most important message ever for humankind. Why did God choose such a strange prophet to prepare the way for the Messiah? God might do the same thing today. Are there strange prophets bearing a message for today's church?

Week after week, we go to church to hear a word from the Lord. If John the Baptist appeared tomorrow, he would probably be escorted out of the church. If he appeared on the streets, he would be arrested or observed for at least an evening in the psychiatric ward. We want to hear from God, but not from the nutty or the eccentric. We want to hear from God, but we do not want God to disrupt our lives too much in the process. While we want to hear from the Lord, we do not really expect anything strange to happen, not today.

The people in John's day frequented their equivalent of church. Yet, God chose to speak to them from the wilderness. God chose a bizarre and unlikely messenger clothed in the most coarse and unappealing clothing. The people of that day were challenged to hear God in unexpected and unlikely places.

Are you waiting on a word from the Lord today? Perhaps God has also chosen to speak to you from the midst of the unexpected. Modern day prophets come in strange packaging. Maybe a conversation with an old woman on the bus will bring illumination to some long-standing question. A greeting at the checkout counter of the grocery store may trigger God's activity within you. God may even speak to you while you play a game with your children or grandchildren.

The important thing is to listen. God both works and speaks in mysterious ways!

Chatterbox

July 26   *Read Proverbs 18:2.*

The entire Sunday school class was excited about Mr. Jones's visit. Mr. Jones was a member of another church who had been to the Holy Land on his vacation. He had agreed to teach one Sunday school class at each of the Methodist churches in his city. This coming Sunday was Wesley Chapel's turn.

Mr. Jones was just as excited about his going as they were about his coming. He had prepared slides. He selected artifacts that would give new understanding to certain Bible passages. He packed all of these into a cardboard box and waited for Sunday to come.

At last, the big day came. People from other classes joined the young adult class that morning. Folks who usually slept in came out—including Sister Chatterbox.

Sister Chatterbox hardly ever came to Sunday school or to Bible classes because she felt that they were a waste of her time. She knew a great deal about the Bible, she thought, because she had studied for years. She often told folks that she should have been a minister, but her family didn't have money for seminary when she was coming along. Today, she hoped to learn something from the man who had been to the Holy Land.

Mr. Jones set up the slide projector and carefully laid his artifacts on the table as the students began to arrive. Sister Chatterbox sat right up front where she could see. Sunday school devotions ended and the fifty minutes allotted for the lesson began. "This," began Mr. Jones, "is Calvary's hill." He was showing the first of twenty-five slides. "It is located outside of the city and is presently. . . ."

"Excuse me, Mr. Jones," Sister Chatterbox interrupted. "The Bible says that Calvary could have also been called Golgotha, which means the skull. Does it still look like a skull—or were you there at a time of the day when the hollow places for the eyes and so forth would have been visible? Or, perhaps," she continued, without breathing, "the hollows have been eroded by the activity of the wind and the elements and are no longer even present, which means that Golgotha would no longer look like a skull. Could you comment on that please?"

That was only the first of several questions presented by the eloquent Sister Chatterbox. By the time that the Sunday school superintendent rang the bell, poor Mr. Jones was still on the first slide!

As some wise person once said, the Lord probably had a good reason for giving us two ears and one mouth.

Knowing When to Go

July 27   *Read Exodus 12:33-34.*

They just had to move quickly! Such was the case of the Israelites leaving Egypt. Where had this relationship turned sour? Originally, the Israelites had come by invitation. Famine was in the land where they previously lived; their kinsman Joseph, now an Egyptian official, had kindly invited them to come to a place of safety. Over the course of time, a new pharaoh came to power that did not know Joseph.

Is this what happens in some marriages? Psychologists have been telling us for years that people change over the course of time. Look at yourself. Are you the same person that you were two years ago, or ten years ago?

If both partners in the marriage covenant are not intentional about maintaining shared interests, they can grow in different directions after marriage. How many marriage partners use abusive language and oppressive behavior to mask the fact that they have changed?

Do women remain in abusive relationships because they are holding on to the man that once was? What else could sustain them through one beating after another? Do they linger because they are hoping for the return of a once workable relationship? "Baby, give me another chance and things will be like they used to be." How does an abused woman abandon what she considers her once true love? Does she remove her children from their father?

Do they stay because they don't know how to leave? In a materialistic society, how does one just leave her things behind? The Israelites had to face these issues when confronted with an opportunity for deliverance. We always assume that women who submit to abuse have simply lost self-esteem. Perhaps the reasons are much deeper.

Abused women and abusing men are tangled in a complicated web. The abuser, often weary of the dysfunction, doesn't know how to stop. The abused person, often unaware of the seriousness or the danger, has a difficult time wading through the tangled swamp of issues. Yet abusive relationships are wrong, and they can be deadly.

The Israelites were in an abusive relationship; they were dehumanized and dying. God made a way of escape for them. They, in response, picked up their unfinished bread bowls and left. Maybe this wasn't as easy as we would think. Perhaps they needed that long span of time to decide that relocation was better than death. Could the ten plagues have been God's way of giving an abused Israel more time to discover that their abusive pharaoh was never going to change?

Pray for the abused women within your circle of relationships. May God give them the courage to know when to go.

Don't Reverse Your Miracles!

July 28   *Read John 2:7-10.*

Each time Jesus appeared, changes took place. This wedding was saved because Jesus came and performed a miracle.

The air around you is charged with change. Miracles do happen, don't they? Why don't we see more of them? What has happened? Sometimes we disturb miracles because we did not see them. Could it be that we are unconsciously occupied with reversing the ones that we have?

What miracles do we have? Are we really capable of reversing them? Clean water is a miracle from God. There was once enough clean water for every person. Our industries dumped garbage into it. With little or no effort, we reversed a miracle. Trees are a miracle. Do you understand?

Our very bodies are a miracle; how they suffer abuse! We take all of their intricate parts for granted until something breaks down. We forget that even miracles must be properly cared for. Healing is a major miracle. Too bad the doctor gets most of the credit!

We overlook miracles every day. When we refuse to acknowledge creation as an act of God, we turn wine into water. When we conveniently call divine intervention a coincidence, we turn wine into water.

There are so many ways that we overlook miracles. They are there. Creation, in spite of our mistakes, is still wonderful! Each newborn is a work of art. The successful union of two individuals from divergent backgrounds, what we call marriage, is a modern day miracle. Perhaps what we really need is an eye for miracles.

Look around you today. What uncommon thing is God doing? Did you overlook the changes that have taken place in one of your loved ones? Wasn't it an answer to prayer? Maybe you didn't notice that the tension on your job has ceased. Have you watched the sun set lately?

Prayer: Lord, grant me the ability to see the miraculous wonders that are around me every day. Amen.

Wash Me, Lord

July 29   *Read John 13:5-11.*

I didn't fully understand this passage until I went to Africa. We spent the summer walking. We walked to the bus stop; we walked to find a taxi. We walked in the marketplace, and our feet got dirty. It didn't matter whether I wore sandals or walking shoes, before long the bottoms of my feet looked muddy and smelled horrible. No amount of talcum powder, deodorant soap, or perfume could stop my feet from responding to their environment.

It was expected that we would remove our shoes when we entered some homes. There I was, embarrassed, with what looked like mud on the bottom of my feet. As I looked around me, no other feet looked like mine. It would have been so nice to wash my feet. Imagine what it must have been like to have Jesus wash their dusty, dirty feet!

Peter protested, I would have also. Who would want to touch my muddy feet? "Unless I wash you, you have no share with me," Jesus replied. The act of foot washing has a deeper meaning than just clean feet.

The Lord knew that life would get us dirty. We walk around in a dirty world. We hear dirty news. Our lives touch dirty circumstances. There is no way to avoid touching our environment in some way. No matter how hard we try, eventually something in our environment will cause us to feel soiled. Our minds need a bath. Our thoughts need to be renewed. Our spirits, wounded by the sinful things we see and hear, need healing. At first, Peter didn't get it. "Lord wash my hands, my head. . . ." No, only the parts that get dirty need another bath.

Wash me, Lord. I heard something just yesterday that haunts my spirit and fills my mind with unwholesome thoughts. Wash me, Lord. I just saw another teenager's body carried to the morgue. Wash me, Lord. The people where I work do things that trouble me. Wash me, Lord, and make me clean again.

Mirror, Mirror on the Wall

July 30   *Read James 1:23-25.*

Remember when the mirror was your friend? The mirror is a faithful friend always waiting to play when we were five or six years old. The girl in the mirror cares about us enough to imitate, or mirror, our every silly move. She will make faces, stick out her tongue, or dance the funky chicken if you tell her to.

When we are fifteen, learning to apply our makeup, the mirror is a kind friend that will not burst our imagined bubble of beauty—even if our makeup is too heavy. Our girlfriend in the mirror will look at our fat thighs in a short dress and cheer us along. "Girl, you look good—no matter what your momma says." Is that why we love the mirror so much when we are fifteen?

By the time that we are forty or so, the mirror friendship thing has become honest enough to show us some harsh realities. Flaws, imperfections, and mistakes begin to come to the forefront. We and our mirror-confidante may practice the fine art of illusion, while still secretly sharing the truth. (A tucked in tummy is still a tummy, isn't it?)

Ironically, developing faith is a little like the relationship we develop with mirrors. At first, we may look at ourselves and feel that everything is in place. After a while, however, as we grow older, the mirror of God's Word helps us to see some areas that need work. The real point of maturity comes when we respond honestly and in faith to what we see in the mirror.

Mirror mirror on the wall—please tell me the truth!

Handwashing Is Not Enough

July 31   *Read Matthew 27:21-26.*

Sometimes we are so obsessed with not taking responsibility for things that we dismiss ourselves from them too quickly. Pilate, perhaps, was in such a position.

He was not Rome's favorite governor. He was often in trouble because of the Jews. Now, here they were again threatening to riot if the innocent Christ were not crucified. Knowingly or unknowingly, they were threatening his job, which was in jeopardy if the Jews caused another notable disturbance. Justice was one thing; his job was another. To satisfy his conscience, Pilate washed his hands in front of the people. Then he let them do wrong when he had the power to enforce right. For him, washing his hands in public was merely a way to refuse personal responsibility.

Our lives are no different. We deal with acceptance and popularity in our homes as well as away from them. There are always people who may not understand or appreciate our sense of justice or righteousness. Can we afford to wash our hands and refuse personal responsibility?

Can we afford to wash our hands of children who are doing wrong under our roofs? Can we afford to wash our hands, in local congregations, when we learn of indiscretion in the pulpit? Can we afford to wash our hands and accept a paycheck from companies that violate human rights or toxify the environment?

It appears that the world has become so filthy because there are too many people out there with clean hands.

August

Aftermath

"Did you see it before all of this happened? I was there a long time ago. It was once so pleasant. The sky was clear, the air was clear, the water was clear. It was once so peaceful."

"Yes, I was there before, too. I can't stand to be there now. I just can't get used to the smells, and all of the confusion drives me up the wall!"

"Do you think that the grass was greener then? You know, it didn't turn in those days. Now I won't even visit in the winter. Winter is so depressing."

"Is that why the people are so mean? I hardly go at all now without my sword."

"Gabriel . . ."

"Yes, Michael . . ."

"I think it's beyond just looks. They act different down there since things went topsy-turvy. Animals never used to bite people. And certainly people never used to bite animals, either.

"Gabriel, the plants bite now too. Some of them stick and bite. Well, even the roses have thorns now!"

We live in a fallen world. Life is not perfect for anyone. You are not alone in noting that thorn in your flesh. Look closely; the thorns are everywhere, until Jesus returns.

Playing Favorites

Esau, the first born, was his daddy's favorite. Isaac loved Esau because they had a common interest. As though by default, Jacob was momma's favorite. Rebekah loved Jacob because he was quiet and plain, and besides, his daddy didn't pay him much attention. Did these two parents unconsciously practice partiality?

Do you recognize this story? Perhaps you were your father's favorite. Did your mother pity you because everyone else thought you were plain and uninteresting? Were you a favorite because you were a sickly baby? Or, perhaps you were the black sheep of the family, feeling like the one always left out when gifts and privileges were being distributed.

You may even be the mother who justifies a little extra love because one child seems to need you more than the others. It seems so natural to protect the child who seems weakest, when the other children look so well adjusted. Sometimes, we unconsciously favor a child to compensate for personal feelings of failure. We may have an older daughter by a high school boyfriend who our wonderful husband never quite seemed to accept. Yet, when our other children by this husband see the extra gifts, the special smile, or the defensiveness, they only see partiality. How many brothers and sisters find it difficult to love one another because they felt the sting of a parent's extra, unmerited love for their sibling? How often have we mothers inadvertently alienated our children from one another, or from their fathers, by our expressions of love?

Most people who practice partiality can state some logical, practical reason for their preferences. This reason is usually centered around what they perceive as the child's need. Partiality, however, still destroys families whether practiced by parents or grandparents. Part of its destructiveness comes from the fact that it forces people to take sides against one another. Partiality takes the roundness of family unity and turns it into a pecking order or a vicious triangle. A family triangle can be as deadly as the proverbial lover's triangle.

Psychologists call this phenomenon *triangulation*: when two sides of a family triangle, composed of any number of people, side against the remaining side. In this case, Rebekah and Jacob sided against Isaac to steal a deathbed blessing. Momma Rebekah thought she was looking out for the best interests of an unappreciated son. Jacob had to leave home, Esau purposely married a Canaanite woman in protest. Both parents were deprived of their favorite children. As a result, all family unity was lost! When a family is caught in a web of partiality and deceit, no one wins.

Prayer: Lord, deliver our broken families from the sin of partiality. Help me to make each child or grandchild in my life to feel special today. Amen.

Lord, I'm Listening . . .

What kind of person hears God? Somehow, as we look at the Old Testament account of Samuel, we tend to think of the person who hears God as better, abnormal, or saintly—certainly not a person like us. Though we may think of these persons as extraordinary, there are really just some basic characteristics that they share.

Many of the people who hear from God are available. Samuel was in the temple, he was in frequent contact with God's people, and he lived in God's house. Therefore, it was not as hard for him to hear God's voice. Though God may pursue us to speak, we are more likely to hear from God when we are available.

Samuel was also in a relationship with God. He was not one who just frequented the house of God; nor was he merely a person who did things for God or for God's people. Samuel was dedicated to God as an infant and lived as one in relationship with God from his youth. It seems that people who hear from God are more likely to be those who know God.

Finally, Samuel appeared eager to hear from God. He was attentive when he heard the voice. At first he thought that Eli, the priest, had called for him. When he received directions from Eli to answer as one who knows he has heard from God, he did so without hesitation. Samuel wanted to hear from God.

What does it take for us, in this day and age, to hear God's voice in our lives? For some of us, God speaks through circumstances. For others, God speaks through obstacles. Some experience an inward knowing that God has spoken. Still others can hear God through their surroundings. God knows how you hear best. However, even God's most spectacular attempts will be futile if we are not listening.

Other Boats

Everybody has troubles. The disciples were not the only ones in trouble that night. There were other boats on the sea. When the storm arose, there were quite a few people in the boat. But Jesus was only visible in one of the boats.

How often have you looked around and seen other people in the same condition? Although there are days when you may feel like the only single mother on earth, there are hundreds of others. Though you may feel as if you are the only person ever diagnosed with a lump in your breast, too many other women share that private nightmare. There were also other boats with him.

"Teacher, don't you care if we drown?" That cry is all too familiar. "Lord, don't you care if I graduate? Don't you care that I have cancer? Lord, don't you care that my husband just died?" When we are sinking, and struggling, and simmering in misery, it is so difficult to believe that Jesus is attentive to our cares. May I suggest today that perhaps some of our individual suffering eventually yields blessings for other sufferers who do not recognize the presence of God in their lives?

We are not alone. We are connected to one another in mysterious ways. For every person who suffers in public, there are many others suffering in similar ways in private. In a sense, many of us are in the same boat. So, what's different for you?

The difference is simple. You and I are aware that Jesus is in the boat with us. We may feel that He is asleep or indifferent. We may even forget that Christ goes with us. But if we can ever come to the realization that Christ is here, and that He cares, we are channels of God's blessings for others in the same condition.

What silent cosufferers do we recognize? Perhaps your testimony of victory over pain will help another mother with a pregnant teenage daughter. Maybe your God-given victory over depression will help to lift a suffering sister from her inner prison. A word from you, a tear, or a victory hug just might help someone to recognize that Jesus is in their storm with them.

Jesus is in the boat with you. There are other ships and other sufferers. Awaken today to discover that Christ is there for you and for those others who share similar distress.

Hard Places

August 5   *Read Philippians 2:3-7.*

I stand between a rock and a hard place; they both rub sorely against the grain of who I am. On one side, pride calls to me. It reminds me that

August

I am a person of sacred worth. Pride helps me remember that I have the right to be treated like a human being. On this side I discover that I have feelings, I get tired, and it is fine to say no to demands.

Pride has many cousins. Self-esteem talks to me about carrying myself as a noble African-American woman. Self-respect reminds me that if I don't love myself others won't either. Self-importance whispers sedition in my ears; while arrogance blows her seductive smoke screen. These two often conspire to get me into trouble. When I am with them, I worry most about my image. I rudely question, "Don't you know who I am?" The fine lines between self-esteem and rude arrogance turn paradise into a thorny place of hard decisions.

On the other side, humility calls to me by name. She, too, has lessons for me to learn. In her classroom, meekness becomes strength under control. Modesty relieves us of the need to announce our own virtues. Her ugly cousins are also there. Subservience is a doormat; while spine-lessness plots to take my voice away.

Jesus becomes our balanced model. He regarded our needs superior to His. In Christ, God became a slave and did the dirty work that must be done. He demonstrated power, strength, and ability, proudly kept under reins to achieve purpose. His excellence precluded the need for haughti-ness. His life carved a tight and narrow way for us to walk—between the rock and the hard place.

Save Me a Seat

August 6   *Read Luke 14:7-10.*

Lord,

Normally, when I think of this parable, I think of those who position themselves for the sake of status. Sometimes history gets in the way of my prayerful decisions about where to sit. Where I sit has become extremely important to everyone. When I want to take a lower seat, there are often others who insist upon correcting the mistakes of the past. When I am invited to a more prestigious chair, I find myself questioning motives.

I have become preoccupied with where I sit. I am offended to sit on the back of the bus. I insist upon sitting in the front of the auditorium where I can see and hear better. I want my own seat in the sanctuary.

I pray Lord, that you will someday rebuild a world where color and status do not have to be considered within every interpersonal relationship. I look forward to a world where the ways in which we value character will outweigh everything else. Until we have the world that we want, teach us to live in the world that we have. Teach me how to select a place to sit. Amen.

Have a Little Patience

August 7   *Read Psalm 40:1.*

Isn't it hard to have patience? Of all the virtuous fruits of the Spirit, patience seems hardest. Patience is one of those words that makes us cringe on the inside. Whenever we think of patience, we think of having to do something that we don't want to do at a pace that we find taxing. Few of us look forward to waiting in grocery lines or pausing at long traffic lights. We just plain hate to wait.

It is so hard to wait on God in the middle of a hard trial. At those times I am most tempted to give up or to take a shorter route. Waiting just does not seem productive. It sounds strange to hear the Lord encourage us to continue in some of the mundane, tedious, and distasteful tasks of life.

Listen to David the psalmist. He waited patiently for the Lord. When he wrote this song, was he waiting for God to change his relationship with Saul? Can you wait patiently for a better relationship with your in-laws?

Perhaps David was waiting to be publicly acknowledged as the legitimate king of Israel. David had reigned in Hebron for years before he was considered the real king with the right to reign from the royal city of Jerusalem. How long have you been performing duties without rightful notice or rightful pay? Can you wait patiently?

King David had some private issues upon which he could have been waiting. Maybe he was in a private wilderness waiting for his sons to stop fighting with one another or with him! Can you and I wait patiently while that irresponsible child grows into adulthood?

David could have been waiting for a sign. Shall we go to war, Lord? When can we bring the Ark of the Covenant home again? We may never know exactly what David was waiting for, but we do know that David waited—patiently.

Be encouraged today in the wait. Wait for the peace that is sure to come into your life. Wait for justice—God knows that you have been mistreated. Just wait awhile; you will eventually adjust to change. Read Psalm 40:2-4 and learn to wait for the promise.

The same Lord that heard David is sure to hear you and me. Solid ground is sure to come. Songs and laughter are sure to return. Blessings are promised for those who wait.

Hearing Ears

August 8   *Read Matthew 15:29-31.*

I was a fairly shy teenager who spent a great deal of time alone. Though I was alone, I was not lonely. Music was a welcome and often invited visitor that brought joy to my world of silence. Late at night, I listened to the radio, which I kept near my pillow. I was always fascinated by the radio stations, which were inaccessible in the daytime, that I could find late at night.

You would be surprised at what I could hear on the radio late at night. From Oklahoma, I could hear broadcasts from Nashville and Atlanta. I heard Chicago, and sometimes even Minnesota, late at night. In the quiet of the daytime, my thoughts often drifted to the invisible radio waves all around me waiting to bear news from these faraway places. "If I only had the right kind of ears," I would think, "I could hear the radio all the time—inside of me."

I have since come to realize that God filled the air with sounds to be heard long before we filled the air with waves. Since the beginning of creation, there have been sights and sounds, on a heavenly frequency, which proclaim the glory of God. Angels declare God's glory day and night. Nature sings of God's perfect design. At any given moment, someone in the world is whispering a word of praise. If only I had the right kind of ears!

Open our ears, Lord, to the praise that surrounds us; we want to echo its melodies. Amen.

I Have Made My Preparations . . .

August 9   *Read 2 Timothy 4:6-8.*

Have you ever wondered what enables some people to face death with such certainty and confidence? The old sisters of the church used to testify: "I have made my preparations and the Lord can come for me now." Later, we would reverently listen as their death notices were announced in church. We knew that their troubles were over and they were with Jesus. How does one get to that point in life? How did Paul?

Perhaps Paul could say these words because he had a sense of fulfilled mission. Before his conversion on the Damascus Road, his chief mission in life was to capture Christians and bring them before the officials. He thought that his actions were a service to the religious community. After conversion, when his eyes were opened, he saw that his new goal in life was to convince as many people as possible that Jesus is alive. He was dedicated to declaring that we could live because Jesus lives.

The Acts of the Apostles testify that Paul spent the remainder of his life attempting to accomplish that goal. He preached to whomever would listen. He offered both Jews and Gentiles opportunities to receive Christ in their lives. He helped multitudes discover how to live the Christian lifestyle.

The Great Commission teaches us to do the same. No matter what careers we embrace, our calling is also to proclaim the good news of the death, burial, and resurrection of Jesus Christ. We are to point the way to salvation and discipleship. We do this when we witness to the truth. Our testimonies help others grasp faith. Responsible lifestyles are a silent witness of the transforming power of the gospel of God.

As Paul was near death he examined his past. He was able to say that he had done his best. He could face death and life on the other side without fear. Christianity's message brings reconciliation and restoration. It gives each believer a new mission in life. When we do our best to fulfill God's dreams for us on earth, we too can say: "I have fought the good fight, I have finished the race, I have kept the faith" (2 Tim. 4:7). Thank God that Christianity is more than fire insurance!

In Training

Read 1 Corinthians 9:24-27.

There was a girl in one of our churches who was well over six feet tall. Actually her entire family was tall—everyone was at least six feet or taller. We grew close to the family, especially the older daughter, over the several years that we pastored that church. The girls were beautiful with fine features—and very long legs. Dad was especially excited about them because they were both basketball stars. Both were serious athletes. I learned to admire the discipline the girls observed in training.

It seemed they were always on a diet. They were aware of what they put in their bodies. On the surface, they looked strong enough to me, but they were always conscious of what they should have been doing before the big games. They practiced a great deal, too. Not just when the team practiced, either; they practiced a lot on their own. They set goals for speed and accuracy, and learned all the latest moves. These girls were great athletes because they always seemed to remember that they were in training.

Interestingly, I also learned that the same kind of intensity spilled over into their observance of the Christian faith. To be such a young woman, the older daughter had a great sense of principle and protocol within the faith. I admired her from afar as she made remarkable observations about practical Christianity. My heart silently applauded with glee as I observed her lifestyle choices—from a distance.

I wonder what would happen if we could all approach the faith as those who are in training? Christians need to be on diets as well. We could all stand to be more observant about what we consume both physically and spiritually. How many of us have real spiritual goals that we work toward? I know that it has become a cliché, but do we practice what we preach?

I wonder what kind of world Christendom would be if all Christians were in training?

Trump Card!

Read John 4:15-19.

Jesus and this Samaritan woman could have spun their wheels forever in fruitless chitchat had Jesus not spoken these words. "Go, call your husband, and come back." They were like a trump card, a surprise move!

It almost seems like a cruel thing for Him to say to a woman with a questionable background. Jesus did many things that we do not immediately understand. He used this question to get to the heart of her misery.

This woman had been married five times. She was the victim of cultural norms. Jewish law granted men an easy method of divorce. "I divorce thee. I divorce thee. I divorce thee." The formula was simple. After three magic words, a woman could find herself without a place to sleep, without resources, without companionship. She might have been able to return to her father after the first divorce. By the fifth time, people would surely have begun to talk. For some reason, this woman had been married, and divorced, five times.

Imagine the emotional scars that she had suffered. Can you write the scripts that must have been playing in the sound booth of her mind? "You can't keep a man, and everyone knows it." "You are no longer the kind of woman a decent man would want!" "Everybody in town is saying nasty things about you."

"Go, call your husband. . . ." Jesus understood her deepest wounds. When He changed the subject from small talk to her deepest disappointment, she understood that only God could have told Him where she hurt. Trump card!

The gospel is known for reaching us through the avenue of our deepest needs. You may suffer the emotional wreckage of several unsuccessful relationships. Maybe you worry about your physical appearance, or success in parenting? It might be that you don't feel worthy of good friends. Whatever your need, God knows all about it.

In prayer today, I encourage you to bypass the small talk. Why not place your trump card on the table and get to the heart of your needs?

Lessons from the Wilderness

August 12   *Read Deuteronomy 8:2-6.*

At first it just looked like butcher paper in the back corner. I could have sworn that there was no more meat in the freezer. I had decided to defrost the freezer and make room for a batch of homemade bread. I always baked and froze bread when we were running low on food to make the kids think that the freezer was full. It was between paychecks; I had my beans ready, and of course, the homemade bread that always helped my two boys forget about meat on meatless days. Then I saw it, in the once icy corner of the freezer when I came back several hours later—a whole fryer! That chicken became Sunday dinner and Monday leftovers.

Had it been there all along? That incident was nearly fifteen years ago. I still pause with tears in my eyes and thank God for the chicken that I don't believe was there before I defrosted the freezer.

The *Case of the Appearing Chicken* in my past helps me understand this passage of scripture. Those of you who fret in the least about what to feed hungry growing children know that even a small dose of poverty is humbling. The Israelites went from once predictable meals to having to wait until God fed them. Even Pharaoh's clothing rations were no longer a certainty.

There is nothing like doing without to prove what is in our hearts. In the land of unmet needs, we learn whether or not we would allow dishonesty to creep into our list of possibilities. In that peculiar state, we learn the real source of our contentment—God or mammon. In the nebulous state of waiting to see how God will provide, we learn to trust God as never before. Every day feels like a miracle; our love for Him deepens. We search the Scripture more fervently, and hang upon His every word.

Isn't it distressing that it often takes a wilderness experience to teach us how to lean on God?

Who Is Holding Whom?

August 13   *Read Genesis 22:1-2.*

I have often wondered if Abraham told Sarah what he was about to do. We rarely think of the agony of some of the decisions that affected the families of the Bible. I wonder if Sarah's potential reactions affected Abraham? Possibly having to explain to his wife why he killed their son adds to my respect for his decision to obey the voice of God.

Abraham was tested to the farthest limits of what he understood to be his faith. He was forced to sort through what he had known before, which may have included human sacrifice, and balance it against what he was learning of God. He learned, through this bizarre request what God really wanted from human beings.

What did God really want? He didn't accept Isaac as a human sacrifice. May I suggest that God wanted to know if Abraham would give Him that which was most precious to him—his son? Isaac was a long-awaited gift from God. He was the menopause baby to an old barren couple. He was laughter when there had been none. Isaac was a symbol of everything Abraham and Sarah had wanted. Though God gave Abraham a son to hold, he was tested at the point of the son's hold upon him. Idolatry, stated simply, is placing anything or anybody before God in our lives. Abraham's willingness to sacrifice Isaac proved that God was first in his life, and that he was no longer an idolater.

Ironically, God gave Abraham a gift as a response to this sacrifice. He returned his offering to him. Abraham was able to continue enjoying the company of his son with a new understanding. This son really belonged to God.

What does God want from us today? God still wants to be first in our lives. Do we hold the things that God blesses us with, or do they hold us? Have we unwittingly become idolaters? God wants our understanding that the car, the job, the man, the baby, or the money that He gave to us are not more important than He is. Sometimes we cannot grasp this until we commit the precious things in our lives back to God.

Allow today's passage to challenge you. If God were to ask for your Isaac, what would it be?

The Deep Freezer

August 14   *Read Luke 12:16-21.*

Ora lived out in the country. She and her neighbors had lived side-by-side for over twenty years. Each fall, she and her neighbors would go in together and dress a cow, meaning that they shared both the expenses and the meat. This arrangement made it possible for the widow down the street to have meat each winter. Mrs. Peoples, the widow, did not have enough money to purchase beef from the local meat locker. Besides, her share was more than adequate for the winter when she went in together with Ora's and Claudia's families.

One day Ora, who liked to be to herself, decided that she was weary of the arrangement. It wasn't that her share was too small. As long as they didn't pig out, Ora's portion was more than adequate for herself and her husband. It wasn't that she didn't like her neighbors. She just wanted her own for a change. So, she devised a secret plan to go the stockyards, purchase her own beef, have it dressed, and quietly fill her deep freezer. (She had an extremely large deep freezer.) Then she thought, "I can have beef as often as I want it. I'm not poor like those other two women." When the fall of the year came, she decided, she would see if she could find somebody else to go in with the rest of them—she was tired of being bothered.

Ora's plan worked like clockwork. She bought a good-sized cow and had it cut and dressed in a way that suited her. She borrowed her daughter's van and smuggled the beef home. There were dozens of packages of beef, all neatly wrapped in white butcher paper and labeled. She moved the old beef to her small freezer upstairs and defrosted the deep freezer to make room for the new; but there still was not enough room—even in her large upright freezer.

Ora had much more than she needed, and she couldn't tell her neighbors. She closed her eyes tight and threw away a couple of gallons of ice cream. There still was not enough room. She winced and threw away a gallon of strawberries from her garden. Three packages remained; she would just have to cook them and eat them!

Ora and her husband had been eating leftover beef for a week before she noticed the smell in the basement. She had forgotten to turn the deep freezer back on after defrosting it! Downstairs, there were hundreds of pounds of disgustingly rotten meat—*all hers!*

How much do you really need?

About Midnight

August 15   *Read Acts 16:23-26.*

Midnight has long been representative of the darkest hour of the night. Paul and Silas were experiencing quite a dark hour. Prior to their arrest, they had just been trying to do what they felt was right. They had cast out a troublesome demon. The city owed them a debt of gratitude; instead, its citizens were angry. That demon was obviously a friend of many. It seemed as if the whole city was against them. Perhaps nothing kills the spirit and traps joy like being mislabeled and unappreciated when we try to do what is right. Beaten and bleeding, they were thrown into prison.

Is it more humiliating to be misunderstood or to be thrown into a category with people that we avoid? Have you ever been there? Were you ever mistakenly branded a troublemaker by those who enjoy the demons that you attempted to drive out of your life?

In such times, it is comforting to know that God is on our side. No matter what things look like at their worst, that is the time to muster up your remaining hope and sing praises to the God of your deliverance.

At midnight, when Paul and Silas sang, the other prisoners were listening. They heard some notes of encouragement that helped faith rise up in their hearts, too. When Paul and Silas sang, at their darkest hour, even the earth trembled in response, as God set all the prisoners free.

Eventually, midnight comes to most of our lives. Spiritual prisons still cannot withstand divine jailbreaks. What might happen when you decide to sing?

Signs of Repentance

August 16   *Read Matthew 3:7-9.*

The Pharisees really had good intentions. They intended to lead holy lives. They invested a great deal of energy into formulating rules and rituals that could legislate holiness. They missed their goal because they did not realize that holy living can never be legislated. We just live it a day at a time.

When they heard of John's baptism, some Pharisees thought of this act of faith as another ritual to be added to their ever-growing list. John rebuked them because he did not feel that they understood the significance of his baptism. His baptism was one of repentance, signaling sorrow for sin and commitment to a changed lifestyle. John's condemnation was scandalous—he called the Pharisees snakes! "Bear fruit worthy of repentance" (Matt. 3:8).

What things are we doing that show that we have turned from our sins? In the midst of a harsh conversation with the Pharisees, John communicates spiritual truth. When we come to Christ, our lives change. John challenged the Pharisees to demonstrate, through a changed lifestyle, that godly change had taken place inside of them.

Perhaps you have heard that there is a bit of Pharisee in most of us. We really intend to do the right things. Often we just don't seem to succeed. We prefer rules, rituals, and formulas to the hard work of having to evaluate our actions, thoughts, and deeds each day. Our rules ensnare us. What may appear to be an excellent formula for spiritual success often robs us of the growth that comes from making daily spiritual choices. Yes, unfortunately, there is a little bit of Pharisee in most of us.

Legislated holiness still does not work. Perhaps the question that we must answer each day is, "What are we doing that demonstrates that we have turned from our sins?" It could be something as simple as refusing to listen to questionable lunchroom conversation. Turning from sin may involve restructuring our leisure activities, removing ourselves from the path of repeated temptation, or devoting ourselves to more wholesome goals.

Today, may I challenge you to examine your daily rituals and habits? Do they show that you have turned away from sin? What decisions are you making, what thoughts are you challenging, what deeds are you doing? Perhaps there is hope for that little bit of Pharisee in most of us!

Rod of Correction

August 17   *Read Psalm 141:5.*

Do you remember the old women of the community of the past? They hung out of their windows or sat on their porches and watched us go by. They corrected us, whether related to us or not. Perhaps some of your most intense spankings came from the unofficial co-mother down the street. She had better not catch you smoking, or see you skip school while your mother was working, or she would get you! We saw her as a curse. Our parents thought she was a kindness.

The psalmist for today's devotional would have agreed with our parents. "Let the righteous strike me; let the faithful correct me. Never let the oil of the wicked anoint my head. . . . "

There are times when I, as an adult, need someone to lovingly slap me in the face with the error of my ways. I cry out for mentoring. Yet, there are few who will rise to the occasion of my need. I need correcting, I need rebuke. I need to hear from someone older and wiser who has gone that way before and know that it leads to a dead end.

I am caught between two worlds. One world says, "mind your own business and leave others alone." It says that I am an adult, consenting, and of age. I have the right to make any mistake I so choose without any haunting advice ruining my autonomous experience. The other world says that we are all family. We are all blood. We are all kin. It says that we are all tied together and your failure is my shame. It says that I have a moral responsibility to warn you when I see you going down a dead-end street, and to correct you in love. It says that correction is so expected that it feels like "oil on my head."

Here I am betwixt and between two worlds, grown enough to do as I please with a dry, itchy, unoiled head! I live in a dry, hostile environment, as the old women of my day sit alone, in nursing homes, or watching the soaps while wishing they could say something. Something is terribly wrong!

Ladies, in order to get what we need, community, we are going to have to give up something that we thought we wanted, autonomy. We cannot have it both ways. We are either alone and on our own, or we are in community being lovingly rebuked by the righteous and the wanna-be righteous.

Shall we join the prayer of the psalmist?

Prayer: Lord, today, we open our arms to welcome loving righteous rebuke from the community of the faithful. Amen.

Take Me to the Water

> Take me to the water
> Take me to the water
> Take me to the water
> Baptize me.

The chill started its quick ascent as soon as warm toes gripped the top step of the pool. Flora was finally being baptized. She was well over forty, and had waited all of her life for the right time.

Flora's parents had neither baptized nor dedicated her as an infant. They were not church-going folk. It was up to her, they thought, to make her own decision. So, she had tottered on the edge of decision for over twenty years. She could not decide if she believed the way the other folks in her church did. She could not decide if she behaved the way the other folks in her church did. So many things had delayed her baptism.

As she stepped into this pool, that seemed to hold the chill of death itself, thoughts of her daughter's baptism darted through Flora's mind. She had followed the family tradition of waiting for the child to decide. Myra, her daughter, seemed so sure. "Yes, I am a Christian and I want everyone to know," her actions seemed to say. Secretly, she had envied her daughter's faith. Now, she had her own.

Stepping down into the pool felt like walking into an open grave. As the waters closed in around her neck, she resisted her secret fear of drowning. "Yes," she decided, "it was a grave she was stepping into." After this, her doubts about salvation belonged to a dead past.

The minister spoke words that blurred in her mind. The only thing she could feel was the cold water surrounding her. Almost unaware, she was plunged underneath the water. Flora experienced an instant transformation in thought. She was no longer a dead person in the grave; she was a baby waiting to emerge from the womb! All of this occurred in the scant second she was underneath the water. Afterwards, she opened eyes that seemed to see for the very first time. She attempted to steady herself on legs that seemed to be learning to stand.

She had finally been baptized! It was like sealing a covenant with God. Today felt like the first day of her life!

None but the righteous
None but the righteous
None but the righteous
Shall see God.

Misunderstood

August 19   *Read John 1:5.*

Today's passage is lifted from John's prologue. The first chapter of the Gospel of John uses poetic language to describe the coming of Christ into the world. In a recurring phrase, He is called Light. He is Light for all of humankind. He is Light for those who cannot see their way. He is Light that darkness does not understand.

Truly, the forces of darkness did not understand this kind of Light. Those forces tried to intimidate Him by threatening His popularity. He knew, before He ever arrived on this earth, that some would not like Him, and that others would die for Him. His message or His mission was not affected by popularity. He was sent to be our Light, and He continued to be all of that. The darkness simply did not understand.

Those same forces tried to call Him crazy. His mother and brothers and family were all stirred up. They felt that either the preaching or the hot sun had taken its toll. Jesus did not care who thought He was crazy. He knew what He was supposed to do and merely kept at it. He was Light and just kept on shining. Once again darkness did not understand.

Darkness even tried to threaten Him with death. Death had been every man's enemy, every man's fear. Certainly this Light-bearer had sense enough to fear death. Jesus eluded death from the edge of the cliff, from the center of angry crowds, from conspiracy. When the time was right, He offered his very life to death. He mocked death by giving up His own ghost. He made death and darkness a public spectacle by extracting their barbs. Light, like the sun, rose again!

To this day, darkness still doesn't understand. It doesn't quite comprehend what happened. It doesn't know where its power goes when Light arrives on the scene. It tries, again and again, to overthrow Light, but to no avail. It cannot even prevail against the Light living in us.

Light continues to shine in the darkness, and darkness continues to grope for understanding.

Too Deep for Words

August 20   *Read Romans 8:26-27.*

"No, not our Geraldine!" The news hit us all like a ton of bricks. "Not our baby girl." This couldn't be happening; she was just getting it together.

Juanita came into the prayer meeting fidgeting. When it came time for us to share the challenges of the week, Juanita just cried silently. None of us knew words to even ask what was wrong.

This jumpy behavior was so unlike Juanita. When Geraldine was pregnant with her first child, Juanita hardly missed a beat. She had already figured out just how much she was going to help her unwed daughter—she had already drawn the lines of responsibility. She seemed to handle anything that life pitched at her; and life had thrown plenty her way. This girl, Geraldine, just kept jumping in and out of bed with anyone who would say,"I love you." She also just kept on having babies, by herself. Each time she would swear it was her last, and later, we would all get mad when she would break her vow. Other mothers would have been devastated, but Juanita was really something else. She kept on loving that girl and praying for her until one day, Mr. Right did come along. Geraldine, and her three girls, finally settled down. We all thought that she was finally finding herself.

All of our eyes were fixed on Juanita's tear-stained face as she forced the words to pierce the air, "Geraldine has AIDS!" We piled into a tearful huddle, not knowing what to say or how to pray. It was just too deep for words! It could have been any one of our children.

Prayer: Lord Jesus, there are times when we cannot articulate prayer because life's challenges are just too overwhelming. Thank you that your Holy Spirit chooses these times to pray for us with groanings that defy words. Today, be with each of our sisters who experience circumstances too deep for words. Amen.

Where Would I Be?

Do you know how you made it through? If it had not been for the Lord on your side, when men attacked you (verse 2), where would you be? In a man's world, it seems that men are always waiting for opportunities to remind us that we have crossed invisible boundaries. If it had not been for the Lord protecting us from their flaring anger—where would some of us be?

The writer of this psalm understood that without the Lord's intervention, he would have been swallowed alive (verse 3). He knew that his enemies had so closed in upon him that the flood of insults and injuries could have taken him under. He recognized that the torrent of pain and disappointment would have swept him away in its raging waters. How often has your life seemed so fast and uncontrollable that it threatened to sweep you away in its flood?

This psalm speaks of situations wherein we knew that things were bad and saw God rescue us. It speaks of the near misses and close calls of our lives. God comes to our rescue when we don't have enough knowledge of the danger to be scared. This psalm speaks of secret plots against us that were foiled and damaging situations we discovered after God had removed us from imminent disaster.

If we could ever get a clear picture of what God has already done in our lives! God sustains us when the waters would drown us. God rescues us from the person, who is a snare to everyone else, when she tries to catch us in her web of deceit. God is on our side when some would just love to shred us or to embarrass us! If we could ever truly recognize how important it is to have the Lord on our side—we would have to join David when he gives praise to the Lord.

> If it had not been for the Lord on my side
> Where would I be?
> Where would I be?

For Women with Careers Outside of the Home

August 22

My Lord, our lives are like juggling too many balls in the air! It has become nearly impossible to establish a set of rules by which to prioritize tasks. Some days the children's school play becomes the most important thing on earth. On other days, the boss's deadline keeps us up until well into the night. Still other days, Mother's feelings of neglect cause us to clear luncheon calendars to take her shopping. We find ourselves fighting for the space that we want and need with husbands who patiently wait in line.

Society is confused about our place. One week we are chided for leaving the home. The next week, home is no place for women like us. Here we are, in the middle, trying to be all things to all people—we are exhausted!

Lord, what is a normal life for a woman with a career? Today, show me the priorities that please You. Grant me both the strength and the wisdom to live in the place in life that You have prepared for me. Amen.

A Glimpse of Glory

August 23   *Read Exodus 33:18-23.*

There was nothing terribly unusual about Moses' request. He wanted to see this God-person who had led a band of Israelites out of the hand of Pharaoh. He wanted to see the One who spoke to him from the burning bush. He wanted to see a visual image of the Lord Almighty whose fame and power had caused them to tremble.

Are there ever times that you would like to see God? Are there times when you wish that you could sit at God's feet? Or just have a comfortable conversation face-to-face? Are there times when you would like to simply gaze into God's understanding eyes in silence? As human beings, we long for One who will break the deafening silence of our prisons called loneliness and despair. We long for One who can show understanding and solidarity. We need to see God—at least we think that we do.

Could it be that we, like Moses, are prisoners of popular thought? We really believe that we miss something important when we cannot see it. We long to see the friendly strangers who we meet on the telephone or the internet. We hope to see famous speakers in order to soak in more from a face-to-face encounter than from their books or videos. Conventional wisdom tells us that sight enhances experience. We also believe that sight unveils mystery. "If I could just see God, maybe I could understand Him . . . ." Yet, God dwells in mystery.

God purposely hides in the cloud so that we can bear His presence. This in essence was His word to Moses. God is greater than humanity can fathom. Our eyes could never take in enough information, our minds could never comprehend Him, our ways of gathering and processing knowledge are inadequate when applied to God Almighty. The ancient prophets said that He is, "So high that you can't get over Him, so wide that you can't get around Him, so low that you can't get under Him." This was their way of describing the Unknowable One.

The Lord, however, did honor Moses' request. He offered Moses a glimpse of glory: "See, there is a place by me where you shall stand on the rock; and while my glory passes by I will put you in a cleft of the rock" (21-22a). In Moses' case, he was hidden. God placed him in the cleft or hole in the rock while His glory passed by.

Have you ever been hidden by God's presence? Moses was hidden in a tight spot—a hole. He was also hidden in a hard place—a rock! The old folks might have called it being between a rock and a hard place. What tight spots and hard places have you experienced? Are you in one now? Have there been times when you should have been vulnerable and exposed, yet only the Glory of the Lord was visible? Perhaps there have been times of profound uncertainty, and God supplied direction. Or maybe there were times when you were literally backed into the corner one moment, only to find yourself miraculously rescued in the next. "And I will cover you with my hand until I have passed by; then I will take away my hand, and you shall see my back" (22b-23a).

Later, when we think about these situations, we see how much God was in them, "and you shall see my back . . . ." Looking at God's back we see just a tiny bit of glory. In these tight spots and hard places, we gain glimpses of the compassion of God. When we look backward at the loving way that God works out our problems, we gain glimpses of the wisdom of God. Maybe we have seen God—at least as much of God as we can handle! When we think about it, God is often seen in the tight places and the hard places of our lives.

It's Only Temporary

August 24   *Read 2 Corinthians 5:1.*

I was cleaning out a junky drawer the other day. I can't tell you how disturbed I was when I found a picture of myself from ten years ago. I was twenty-five pounds thinner! There were no wrinkle lines near my mouth or my eyes. My hair was full and healthy-looking. Disgusting!

After that brief encounter with my previous self, I didn't even want to pass by a mirror. As I began to sort through my feelings, I learned that I was just beginning to confront aging. Adding it up, I am twenty-five pounds, several wrinkles, two surgeries, and ten years older. What will the next ten years bring?

Before I could get lost in the land of self-pity, the Holy Spirit began to whisper in my spirit, "It's only temporary!" Aches and pains are only temporary. Wrinkle lines are only temporary. There are so many things that are only temporary. Youth is only temporary. I rejoiced in that fact as my sons grew up. They were only two years old for a short time. They were only five once. They were only sixteen once. They will only be in their twenties for a short time. They, and we, must adjust to whatever stage we are in, recognizing its fleeting nature.

Youthful beauty is only temporary. After that, beauty changes. We exchange the twenty-two-inch waistline for a body that functions well under pressure. We exchange a flawless complexion for a kind face, a wise face, a friendly smile and an easy-to-talk-to twinkle in our eyes. The measurements and the standards change as we age. To coin a phrase from a once popular advertisement—we don't get older, we get better. We must enjoy the kind of beauty we have today.

This aging body is only temporary. It does not define who I am. It only houses who I am; and this house is temporary. The Bible calls it a tent, which means that I am not even to presume it permanent. My permanent dwelling place is in another place with God.

If you are approaching the age where a mirror is no longer your best friend; if you ache when it rains; or if you find yourself struggling in the morning to get out of bed to jump-start your life; do not despair. It's only temporary.

Stop the Music!

August 25   *Read Revelation 8:1-5.*

Heaven is an exciting place filled with vocal praise and activity. From the very beginning of John's vision, we learn that heaven is full of sights and sounds. We hear the, "Holy, Holy, Holy" of the living creatures, the song of the twenty-four elders, and the voices of thousands of angels in the fifth chapter of Revelation. By the seventh chapter, we hear the singing of multitudes.

We grow so accustomed to hearing praise in John's revelation that we are surprised to hear of this half an hour of silence in heaven. What caused all of heaven to become silent? Incense and prayer.

One of the Old Testament symbols for prayer is incense. Did prayer cause heaven's silence? Prayer is indeed powerful. So often we don't pray because prayer appears nonproductive and useless. Yet, we are encouraged to pray throughout the Bible. Psalm 34 tells us that the eyes of the Lord are upon the righteous and that His ears are open to their cries. First John 5:14-15 reminds us that our prayers are answered if we ask according to the will of God. Psalm 145 tells us that God is near those who fear Him and call upon Him in truth.

This silence when incense is offered teaches us some powerful things about prayer. First, none of our prayers get lost. God hears each one and considers each prayer important. The passage mentions the prayers of all the saints.

Second, the prayers of God's people are in the presence of God. The angel was given much incense to offer with the prayers of all the saints on the golden altar before the throne. Those prayers are mixed with the fire of the altar of God and thrown back to the earth as answers! You cannot answer your own prayers. God alone answers prayer.

Finally, the supernatural character of those answers are witnessed by the prophet's language: thunders, rumblings, flashes of lightning, and an earthquake. The world gets shaken up when some of our prayers are answered!

Our prayers are powerful! Our prayers never get lost. In God's own time we will receive an earth-shaking answer!

What Are You Looking For?

August 26   *Read Matthew 11:16-19.*

Those of us who are victims of long-time emptiness often forget what once filled the longing of our souls. Women who lost the love of their lives too long ago often forget what exactly they miss most. Small wonder we cannot exhale.

Others of us, who long for just enough, lose sight of the top of the glass when pouring. More than enough runs into the saucer, and then to the floor as we struggle to understand that we are already full. What exactly are we looking for?

When we don't know what we are looking for, it becomes impossible to value what we find. Jesus compares us to children in the marketplace, complaining about play. The children around us say, "let's play funeral," and we agree with them. We even echo their suggestion: "Give us religion somber and dole!" When recess comes, and it's time to play, we grumble about the game and in protest, refuse to be a mourner.

Giving the issue more thought, we decide that we really wanted joy, after all. "Give us religion that is full of laughter and celebration," we cry. Yet, we won't dance to its music. We prefer to complain that others are not serious enough.

Our lives are filled with the curse of indecision. We don't know what we want from relationships. We aren't quite sure what we expect of life. We are not even certain about that which pleases God. Satisfaction becomes a near impossibility.

Today, Lord, show us your plan for each of our lives. Help us to discern the many ways You choose to answer prayer so that when You answer our prayers we might recognize your will and give thanks. Teach us how to be satisfied.

Visionary

How's your vision today? Can you see beyond what your eyes see? Habbakuk is reminding you that without a vision, people give up and eventually perish. What do you see?

Is your sight limited to the devastation that continually surrounds us? If you look closer, you might see that Claudia's child is getting out of the projects and going to college on a scholarship. Perhaps you might see that J.J. is an artist and just needs the right materials to really shine. If you look beyond the ordinariness of your surroundings, you might just see a dandelion breaking through the concrete of a sidewalk to prove that little things can survive when dumped on!

What can you see? Mary McLeod Bethune could see African-American girls going to college when there was no place that would accept us. Wilma Rudolph's family could see her running like a normal girl, in spite of the effects of the polio and scarlet fever that left her paralyzed at the age of four. She went on to become the fastest woman in her world. Open your eyes to a new realm of possibilities!

Perhaps you should ask, "What can't I see?" Harriet Tubman could not see why she had to remain in slavery; nor could she see why everyone else had to either. She led as many slaves to freedom as she could. Clara Luper could not see why Oklahoma folks couldn't eat in any restaurant. Your parent-person found no reason why you shouldn't grow up well, no matter what the statistics might say! With hope, you can't see yourself stuck in one of the dead ends of your life by this time next year. Don't see yourself making wages below your abilities!

Vision also entails banishing some things from your sight. Prepare yourself to break a bad habit, to look for a more wholesome lifestyle, or to end a physically abusive relationship. Get ready to stop disliking certain things about yourself. Make plans to stop the rat race masquerading as your schedule!

We need vision to succeed. We need vision beyond what our eyes can see to aim for higher goals. Without some kind of vision, life is destined to stay the same.

Back from the Dead

August 28   *Read John 11:43-44.*

He's calling your name! Can you hear Him in your cold dark tomb? Bend your ear this way child, and realize that your name is being called. You do still recognize your name, don't you?

I know that you have been dead a long time. I know that we don't really expect you to come out of the death that has gripped your soul; but He is calling your name! Stella, come forth!

Mary, come forth! This sickness doesn't have to keep you dead. Why don't you decide NOT to give up! When He calls you by name, you can live again—if you answer Him.

Natalie, come forth! Don't keep the poor man waiting all day. He's been calling your name forever. Why won't you come out and live with us again?

In the far away land where crack imprisons souls, can you hear anybody? Can you hear your mother's uncontrollable sobbing? Can you hear your sister's pleading? Do you see your children hungry, sick, and uncared for? He's the only one that can reach you and He is calling your name now! Don't miss your chance.

Having a family member on drugs is worse than losing them to the grave. The person that you once knew and loved is often replaced by a monster seeking money for a habit. The prisoner who peers through wildly glazed eyes is unable to respond to you. It's just like they are dead.

It takes the Lord to truly break the chains of substance abuse. Just as Jesus called Lazarus from the land of the dead, He calls women back from the land of addictions. There is yet hope for the one you love.

Prayer: Lord, have mercy upon the sisters that are bound in the grave-clothes of substance abuse. Help them to hear your voice and come back to us. Amen.

A Good Word for Bad Times

August 29   *Read Isaiah 40:1-5.*

We live in a world filled with broken promises. Have you heard any of these promises?

"I promise to wait for you. . . ."

"Mama if you buy me this dress, I won't ask for anything else for the rest of the year."

"I promise to do my homework right after I die in this Nintendo game."

"I promise to pay you back next week"

"I promise to love and to cherish from this day. . . ."

"I promise that I'm never going to hit you again. . . ."

"I promise to stop if you don't tell my wife. . . ."

"I promise to put the money back as soon as I can."

"I promise to be the best Christian if you will just bail me out one more time."

In a land of broken promises, God makes promises that are sure and will not fail. God promised that the downtrodden will be lifted up, while the high and mighty will be brought low. God promised that the uneven ground will become level. Racism, classism, and sexism are just a few of the uneven places in our lives. Rough places? We all have them. God promised that they will one day become smooth. And the glory of the Lord, not the glory of human beings, will be seen by all.

God is not like human beings—God always keeps His word. Are you scanning the skies for the first signs of God's promises?

May I encourage you to look for reminders? They are more than rainbows. They often take the form of the first rays of light before the sun rises—it is still dark but you know the sun is coming. They are those little flickers of fire before the log lights—the log isn't lit and you're not warm, but you know the heat is eventually coming.

Reminders often take the form of genuine congratulations from a coworker that you know to be competitive or unkind. Or, it could be something as simple as the words "thank you" from a previously ungrateful teenager. Today, let's stay alert for the many reminders that God keeps His promises. Jesus is coming—I just saw Him pass by.

Hard Times

August 30   *Read Luke 15:14-16.*

"Hard times will make a monkey eat red pepper," Grandma used to say. For the prodigal son, one tragic choice resulted in unbelievable hard times. Here we find the prodigal wanting to do something that never would have entered his mind under normal circumstances—eat with the hogs! Before you mentally comment, remember that Grandma also warned us about saying what we wouldn't do.

Mistakes have a way of reminding us that we all need the Lord. Who hasn't made at least one tragic mistake in life? Who hasn't done at least one thing that they had never expected to do? Tragic mistakes like these remind us to approach our comments about one another with humility. Perhaps it was only God's grace that kept you or me from eating with the hogs.

Today's passage is also a reminder that some of the misfortune that comes to our lives can be avoided. Hasty decisions are notorious for coming back to haunt us. A little more time in the decision-making process might spare any of us a lifetime of heartaches. Unwise choices don't have to make a monkey out of us!

God Bless the Children

August 31   *Read Matthew 19:13-15.*

Lord,

We confess that we do not always share your concern for the children in our midst. We do not look out for their interests. Instead, they are often overlooked and shoved to the side. We silence them, sometimes when You have placed your wisdom within their mouths.

Forgive us for failing to protect their minds while they are young and fragile.

Forgive us for allowing them to be murdered in the streets.

Forgive us for not being more careful about the images to which they are exposed.

Forgive us for leaving them alone.

Forgive us for forcing them to become adults so that we could act like children.

Lord teach us how to surround these little ones with the love and the care that You have desired for them. Teach us how to set consistent godly examples that will encourage them in the faith. Finally, Lord, use them to teach us about your kingdom. Amen.

September

Unexpected Peace

September 1   *Read Proverbs 16:7.*

Who would ever have thought that Andrea would be going to college in Chicago? She was a bright, but naive young woman from the Midwest. No one in her family had ever finished high school. Now, here she was graduating from high school and going on to college—in Chicago!

Just a few years before this, other people were arguing and fighting about where young, bright, Black women and men would go to college. They were fighting in Mississippi; in fact, they were fighting all over the Old South. The dispute was so ugly that it made the six-o'clock news in Kansas City, where Andrea joined her family in watching the precarious progression of the battle for racial equality in the United States.

"Will they fight me?" Andrea had begun to get nervous. As a high school senior leaving home for the first time, she almost wanted to continue her education in one of the state schools instead of at this prestigious school that had offered her a scholarship. She had been to the campus of the state school for a few weeks in the summer. Life there would not be so uncertain. "Perhaps," she thought, "I should go to one of the historic Black colleges where my friends will be?" She wasn't quite sure if she wanted to trade the certainty of Black college life for the uncertain future that lay ahead of her.

She was having great difficulty making up her mind. One day, while joining her family in watching the evening news, she came to terms with a decision. She would go to Chicago. "Dr. King ended up getting killed over the issue; the least I can do is try!" (She wasn't quite sure what she would do if tensions erupted over the issue of her race.)

When September came, Andrea went to Chicago. She gritted her teeth, determined to tough things out as long as she could, no matter how ugly it got. Instead, she found a university van waiting for her at O'Hare Airport. Her room was nicer than any she had ever had. The people she met were consistently friendly. Her professors gave her a chance to demonstrate what she was learning. The enemy of racism was peacefully quiet—at least for the moment!

Have you allowed yourself to miss a blessing that the Lord has reserved for you simply because you were turned off by the presence of known enemies? Try it again! Things may turn out better than you expect. The same Lord knows how to cause your enemies to be at peace with you, too!

Wise Words

September 2   *Read Proverbs 9:1-6.*

In today's reading from Proverbs, the most important thing to remember is that wisdom is waiting for us. She has already set her table and prepared a sumptuous meal for us. She simply waits for us to ask for her wealth. The book of James reminds us of the same principle: "If any of you is lacking in wisdom, ask God, who gives to all generously and ungrudgingly, and it will be given you" (1:5).

How do we share wisdom with one another and with our children? Many of us are often criticized for taking a far too direct approach. We tell people point blank what we think they have done wrong and we dare to tell them how they should have done it! Well, most of us know that this only makes people angry. How have our foremothers been effective in transmitting wisdom and cultural teaching? This has historically been done through the use of proverbs.

Our Bible contains a collection of some of the proverbs of Israel. They were designed to be a standard and an acceptable way to transmit wisdom from one person to another, and from one generation to another. Though they were written to instruct Israel, we use many of them like: "A soft answer turns away wrath, but a harsh word stirs up anger" (Prov. 15:1). The exciting thing that scholars are discovering is that nearly every group of people has traditionally used some proverb to transmit values and cultural teaching.

Even our families have proverbs. Whenever I wanted something that we could not afford or that was not absolutely essential (like when our children say they *need* designer jeans) I had a grandmother who would address my greed with the use of this proverb: "I used to complain that I had no shoes until I met a man who had no feet!" When I heard that proverb, I was not offended. I also knew that no amount of arguing or pleading would change her response. That bit of proverbial wisdom meant: "You have more than many people. Learn to be satisfied with what you have. God has already blessed you . . ." all in just one sentence!

Many of you grew up with family proverbs. May I invite you to pause and thank God for the gentle way that your ancestors used these to communicate teaching in your life? And, may I challenge you to begin to share these, without embarrassment, with your friends, with your neighbors, and especially with your children?

In Love

September 3   *Read Song of Solomon 7:10.*

The love between woman and man defies accurate imagery. How do you feel when you are in love? No words can convey the mosaic of emotions that flood through your heart. How shall we describe the way your heart flutters when you hear his key unlock the door? What makes it possible to need and want one person so intensely?

Intense love affairs can also be holy. How sad that most of us have been conditioned to only think of them as lusty and illicit. Perhaps this love story between Solomon and the dark and lovely maiden, whom some believe to be the Queen of Sheba, has been included to remind us of the sanctity of love. If you ever want to read an intense, but godly, love story, read the Song of Solomon.

The Lord wants us to learn to love intensely and unconditionally. When we learn to love that special person, to work for their good, and to tolerate their differences, it becomes easier to transfer those same principles of love to God. Selfish love perverts the model. Unfaithful love does not reflect God's plans. Israel, when spiritually unfaithful, was often compared to an adulterous wife. Wholesome intimate relationships, however, teach us about God's love.

Imagine being able to make the leap from an all consuming love affair with the man of your dreams to an all consuming love for the God of glory! Loving God can be intense, all consuming, and fulfilling. God's love is also two-way. God wants your love as much as you want God's. "I belong to my lover, and his desire is for me." Our days could be full of anticipation and excitement as we watch for glimpses of God's personal attention. Every minute in the presence of God could become one to cherish and to relive. There would be no bad days if we looked forward to living in God's presence. We would never become bored with or disappointed by God. The honeymoon would never end because God has no faults to discover.

It is both possible and godly to be intensely in love with your spouse and to be intensely in love with God. Just remember that God is first!

United or Untied?

September 4   *Read Matthew 12:25.*

While attending a racial awareness seminar, it became clear to me that instead of being *united*, African-Americans have been *untied*. This is perhaps the first time in our history on this continent that we have been so divided. The faceless system of oppression has done well in teaching us to fear one another. Yet, we are reminded by the words of Christ that every kingdom, city, nation, or family that divides itself into groups is destined to fall.

It is customary to think of racism as a tool that divides us from the majority culture in this country. However, we rarely think of what racism does to us within the African-American community. The same attitudes that separate us from mainstream America separate us from one another.

We have begun to divide ourselves according to educational attainment. Some who have advanced in the educational system dare think of others as ignorant. The controversy over whether Black English is a legitimate dialect is an example of this division. Many of our parents are ashamed to be with our friends because they fear that their dialect would embarrass us.

Within the community, skin color still draws dividing lines. Do you cringe when you hear the terms black, brown-skinned, and bright? Why does it still matter? A community that is divided is destined to fall.

Today, will your actions assist the community in becoming united or untied? Examine the ways that you either contribute to the problem or to the solution. United and untied contain the same letters; one is just a bit confused. In a similar way, we have everything we need and everything we once had, we are just a bit confused. May the Lord clear up our thinking and lead us back to unity.

More than Enough!

September 5   *Read 2 Kings 4:1-4.*

So much talk about prosperity confuses us. We live in a church world that reminds us not to live beneath our privileges. In this country, we tend to look at prosperity as a sign of God's blessings. When we are not literally rolling in abundance and excess, we get terribly confused.

What happens to those of us who faithfully serve the Lord, yet have some basic unmet needs? When you, and your family, serve the Lord with all of your energy and substance, how do you reconcile what seems to be an enormous inconsistency? How do we even answer our friends? What word does God have for us when our sons are being sold into slavery and our daughters are ragged and worn out?

Listen to Elisha's question: "Tell me, what do you have in your house?" She didn't see it at first. Her first thought was "Nothing," but after a while she found a little oil. What are you over looking in your storehouse of blessings? Maybe you need to remind me of some blessings that I have not seen. You know that I am tempted to say "Nothing," if you ask me too!

Remember the story? She took the little she had and began to use it. We have really been taught to hoard that last little bit and to enshrine it because it is the last. How often has the last good perfume gone bad because we were saving it? The old widow was instructed to take the last of the oil and use it. She poured it out and God multiplied it. God always seems to astound us with the manner of provision.

She also did this in the company of her sons. She didn't call in the neighbors to boast. She didn't summon the reporters. This thing was between her and God. Could it be that the story of how we got over is not always meant to be a widely publicized thing? Could it be that the story of your prosperity will be between you and Jesus?

Perhaps prosperity is a function of perception! Maybe what this passage says to those of us who feel less than prosperous, is that we need to take another look at what we have. It may not look like much. You may be even tempted to echo the old widow: "All I have is a little oil. . . ." But, look at how God used that little bit to provide an abundance. If we follow the widow's example, we will have to take that little bit out of its shrine and use it. Dont worry. It will be enough.

A Prayer for Good Intentions

September 6

Hear my confession today, Lord. I want to do what I know is right. Yet I find myself, like Paul, knowing holiness and participating in sin— at least in my mind. Yet, I know that evil thoughts are just as sinful as evil deeds, both defile my heart.

Today, I refuse to allow society to grant me permission to do or think what I know brings Your displeasure. I resist my own human impulses to settle long-standing arguments or set irreconcilable records straight. I ask that You perform the necessary work in my heart that will make me content with righteous living.

> When life is far from peaceful
> When circumstances are far from just
> When those I love have been hurt
> by the same ones that hurt me
> Good Lord, give me a heart filled with mercy.
>
> When revenge would taste sweeter
> When another's shame would vindicate me
> When systems fail to champion my cause
> Good Lord, give me the courage to work for peace.

When I find myself
  watching my enemy's steps
  and hoping for signs of failure
When I lapse into both judge and jury
Good Lord, give me a clean heart.

When the evil all around me gives me an excuse
  to retaliate
  to humiliate
  or to harm
Good Lord, give me good intentions!

Glass Houses

September 7   *Read Matthew 7:3-5.*

People who live in glass houses should never throw stones! If Matthew were writing today, from our perspective, he would probably use similar words. Grandma would mutter these words under her breath when some high-and-mighty person was caught doing the wrong thing. "Those are the kinds of people who throws a rock and hides dey hand." By that point, the sermon was on.

Today, most of us do not find it difficult to identify hypocrites. We all know that we are surrounded by hypocrites in government, in churches, in communities, and on the job. We do, however, find it difficult to talk about the hypocrite within. There is probably a hint of hypocrisy in all of us. Gossip is a form of hypocrisy. A gossiper says things behind a person's back that they would never say to them face-to-face.

Jesus says that fault-finding people are hypocrites too. They look all around them for things that are wrong, large or small, while overlooking glaring problems in their lives. They walk around with tweezers in their hands looking for splinters to pick.

Experience teaches that this is a true principle. The people who complain most about everyone else's children, usually have problems with their own. A closer examination shows us that complainers generally complain about the things they like least about themselves. They imagine that our root problems are identical to theirs. They project their problem areas onto us for scrutiny. The real problem usually has nothing to do with us; it is really trapped inside of them.

Perhaps this is a good day to examine ourselves for the sin of hypocrisy. Remember, people who live in glass houses should never throw stones!

Bite Your Lip!

September 8   *Read Joshua 6: 10.*

It is so hard to keep from responding sometimes. Our pride just will not let us be quiet.

"If they only knew how I felt about it."

"If they only knew my personal circumstances."

"If they only knew what I thought of them! . . ."

In this morning's passage, I hear God encouraging us to bite our lips. This verse, coming from the battle of Jericho, contains an often overlooked point—while the Israelites were circling the wall once daily for six days, and seven times on the seventh day, Joshua had commanded them to be quiet until the Lord commanded them to shout. What might have happened if they had been allowed to talk?

They might have been tempted to complain. We often complain, complain, and complain when we do not understand God's instructions for our lives. The children of Israel had already shown that they were capable of complaining.

"We never should have left Egypt!"

"Where is the water?"

"We don't want manna, we want meat. . . ."

Joshua 6:10 reminds them, and us, to bite our lips until God releases us to speak.

Perhaps they suffered from a lack of confidence. Remember, they were going into their first battle. They had already been sentenced to wander in the wilderness for forty years because of their refusal to fight. They had felt as though they were too small, too weak. They felt that their adversaries were giants and they were grasshoppers by comparison. Is this you? Bite your lip!

They may have been instructed to be quiet because they were cocky. Have you ever been tempted to boast when you knew that you had it together? Our boasting tends to go beyond stating a fact to blowing a horn. The Israelites might have made fun of the inhabitants of Jericho if they had been allowed to talk. It is so easy to verbally abuse others when we feel that we are on top of things. Have you ever been there?

God's remedy for complaints, lack of confidence, or cockiness is silence. Silence gives us time to count our blessings. Silence gives us time to see God at work. Silence gives God time to show us the blessings of humility. When we are waiting, and while we are wondering, silence holds many blessings. In the meantime, when we are tempted to complain, to be cowards, or to be cocky, let us remember to bite our lips!

From Pasture to Princess

September 9 Read 1 Chronicles 17:7-8.

"I won't ever get out of this mailroom." Pam had just graduated from business college. It was her first job and it seemed as if none of her schooling had done her any good. "This is a dead-end job, no one will even consider promoting someone who works in the mailroom. Maybe I should quit!" She had only been there for three days; discouragement was taking over.

When her break came, she talked to her coworkers. "Does anyone ever get promoted from the mailroom?" Of course, they didn't know. She was no better off, she grumbled; why had she gone to college? "Four years down the drain," she snarled inside as she threw away the uneaten half of her doughnut.

For the next six weeks, Pam struggled. She struggled to get to work on time. She struggled to smile. She struggled to be congenial with her supervisor. The nagging thoughts remained in the back of her mind. It was all for nothing. Look at my paycheck at the end of the month. Maybe I should look for another job somewhere else. She had been looking for work for three months before landing this job. She was stuck; and she was miserable.

Pam's mother tried her best to be a cheerleader. "Everyone starts at the bottom, Pam. Pam, you are so good at what you do, someone is bound to notice you. Pam, the Lord loves you." To Pam, these words were merely an irritation.

Then, one Tuesday, a new face appeared in the mailroom. The woman was neat and manicured. Her voice was soft, and her face without stress. "Pam," she said, "I have been reading resumes. . . ." Pam had a promotion—manager's assistant! In the back of her mind, one of her mother's cheers burst in the air: Pam, the Lord loves you. The Lord loves you, too!

Kingdom Talk

September 10   *Read Matthew 13:31-33.*

"I may be small now, but watch out, in a little while I'm gonna be taller than you, taller than Dad, taller than anyone else!"

"Now how can I get Uncle Henry's money? You see he hid it in a can out there in that field. The rest of the family thinks that the farm is worthless. . . . I know, I'll buy the farm, and then just kind of find the can. You see, if it's on my property, then it is mine!"

"I have been collecting diamonds all my life. I have 742 of them. Nothing I have compares to the one I saw yesterday. This diamond is cut so perfectly, and it is so BIG! The only way that I can afford it is to sell all the others. . . . I think this one is worth it!"

Jesus used everyday illustrations to describe the kingdom of heaven. If He were describing it today, He might say that it is like a young boy who outgrows the rest of his family. Or, He might say that it is like the hidden treasure that causes relatives to scheme. It could even be like the biggest gemstone that the world has ever seen. How would you describe God's kingdom today?

We know that Jesus is our king. Yet, it is so hard to understand the nature of His kingdom. At times, it even seems imperceptible. Jesus was speaking to people, like us, who really wanted to know how to detect activity and movement in God's kingdom. Jesus described something both valuable and growing.

How, then, shall we describe the kingdom of heaven? It may appear as small as a mustard seed; but once planted, it will grow. The kingdom of God is pervasive, like a little yeast hidden in flour; eventually you will know it is there. The kingdom's value is not widely publicized; it is more like a hidden treasure worth digging for. The kingdom of heaven is worth all that we have.

Promise Ring

September 11   *Read Luke 15:22.*

How can I ever
Understand your love?
When I was worthy of death
You chose to spare my life.

I would have been
Your grateful slave,
for the rest of my life,
Waiting at your feet,
And hastening to each command.

With strength and love,
You broke my chains
And gave me a promise ring.

The circle of your promise ring
has no end
I cannot list
its details
I am daughter.
I am child.
I am joint-heir.
I am bride!
I am warrior.
I am sheltered.
I am loved!
I am called into fellowship above.
I have a home.

I am your house.
You are the shepherd
I learn to follow.
You are the potter.
I am the clay.
You are the rock in which I hide.

Lord, thank you for this promise ring.

Temptations

Some days I am tempted to stop doing everything for everybody else and concentrate on making myself happy. On those days, I am tempted to cook something that everyone else hates, and eat from the pot—by myself. I am tempted to call in sick, stay home, and watch the soaps because if I don't pamper myself, who will?

Then,
  I am reminded
  of Jesus
Who was hungry
  and tempted
  and refused to turn

Stones into bread
  for personal gain
But rather
  told the tempting devil
  to go away
And
Find something else to do.

Some days, I am tempted by things. I want everything that I see. I want things. I want money. I want power. I want them all. I see everything that I want, stretched out before me—waiting for me to go into debt to possess them all! My appetite is so great that I grow faint from my hunger for things. To myself, I say: "I owe all these things to myself, because if I don't pamper myself now, there will be plenty of regrets later."

> Then,
>   I am reminded
>   of Jesus
> Who owned all things
> And
> Claimed nothing for himself
>   not even a home
>   or a car
>   or a condo in Palm Springs.
>
> My soul
>   is then quieted
> And,
> I learn how to
> Be content
> With what I have.

Some days, I am tempted to try to fly on the wings of fame. I want everyone to know my name and rehearse my good deeds. I am disappointed when the preacher does not call my name in the sermon. I lament that the gym teacher replaced me as a role model in my sons' eyes.

> Then,
>   I am again reminded
>   of Jesus
> Who
> Chose to keep his mind
>   on his business
> And
> I am strengthened
>   to keep my mind
>   on
>   mine!

Able to Come Home?

We rejoice in the happy reunion of the prodigal son and his father. It whispers to us about one of our innermost needs. We need to know we can go home, even when we have made an absolute mess of our lives. This passage reminds us of God's forgiveness. It challenges us to remember the days when we were lost in sin. Thank God, we can always return to Him.

Can your children always return home? If they should stop doing whatever wrong they are doing tomorrow; can they come home? For those who are in the position to forgive, the story of the prodigal son presents another challenge. Can we, as parents, forgive as God forgives?

It is significant that God has chosen parental relationships as a vehicle to reveal His love for us. These relationships are protective. They are as intimate as the relationship between husband and wife. Parents are instructive; they also must use discipline. Parents are also figures of authority in the life of the child. For the African-American parent, the challenge to parental authority is probably the hardest issue we face with our prodigal children. Most of us were reared with the understanding that parental authority was beyond question or challenge. It was and still is a supreme insult to ignore, insult, or dishonor our parents. A prodigal child wounds our pride and disturbs our self-esteem. Their foolishness represents us poorly. They make us ashamed.

Israel's culture shared similar norms. Without doubt, the father of this prodigal was wounded. His pride suffered. His self-worth was called into question. How could this child do such a thing to his father if he really loved him? The father had obviously worked past these issues before the prodigal child ever appeared on the horizon. He must have made a purposeful decision to receive that very child if and when he returned. These are the same decisions that God makes about each one of us. We ignore, insult, and dishonor Him—yet He has already decided to receive us when we return.

We are called upon to make similar decisions. We are challenged to decide how we will react before our prodigal child returns. God is able to heal your wounded pride and renew your self-esteem. If your prodigal child or grandchild should return, will they find you waiting with an open heart?

Counting the Cost

September 14   *Read Luke 14:28-33.*

"I wonder if he will really divorce me if I join the church?" Bev had been married to Maurice for ten years. Not once in that ten years had they gone to church together. He wasn't against God, but he was against organized religion. Hypocrites, he called them. He thought that all preachers were "chicken-eating, woman-chasing, money-grabbing hypocrites!"

With a sense of duty, Bev occasionally took the children to church. They lived in a big city and hardly ever attended the same church twice in a row. Lately, however, she had broken with her own tradition and had attended a certain church every Sunday for well over a month.

As the girls grew older, she began to worry about their faith. They needed to learn enough about God to decide for themselves she thought. She had also begun to worry about herself. She believed in Christ, but just didn't feel that she was growing enough spiritually on her own. It was time to pursue an active relationship with God and the church. This church looked like a good place to start.

The pastor did not seem to fit her husband's description. The people in that church were friendly, and they were interested in doing the kinds of things that she believed in—like feeding the hungry people who lived under the bridges near the river. They got involved in politics and prayer meetings. Youth education appeared to be strong and solid. She wanted to join this church and take her children there regularly—but would her husband understand?

Bev finally made up her mind. "I'm the one that will have to answer God about my faith choices. I am going to do this no matter what." She slipped into the aisle and walked toward the altar. She was determined to be a public Christian no matter what it cost her.

What are you willing to do for your faith development?

Mud Pot

Over the years, I have had a succession of clay pots that have been used as doorstops. You know the kind, they are hand-thrown pots with lumpy insides and rough spots on the outside hidden by bright colored paint. Quite the opposite of fine crystal or china, they are heavy and cumbersome. They are decorative, but not good for much else besides propping uncooperative doors open.

While reading this passage, it occurred to me that I was very much like those pots. Spiritually lumpy and messed up inside, I too, hide the rough spots on the outside with globs of flashy bright paint. Most days, I feel unrefined, not fit for the fancy dinner table, heavy and cumbersome. Yet I am special because God lives in me.

Why would God want to live in a mud pot like me? Today's passage is clear. He chooses to live and to exert His extraordinary powerful presence through our humble clay vessels to prove a point. We are frail and imperfect by design. All may clearly see that this extraordinary power belongs to God and not to us.

We tend to think that we get so much done on our own. We take the credit for so many of God's accomplishments. Money, education, our family name, or even our so-called good looks overshadow our realization of the power of God in our lives. To tell the truth, we really do very little on our own.

Actually, we are like vases that God uses to carry the sweet bouquet of His glory. We are like pipelines, used as channels of blessing. We are vessels, and receptacles, designed to carry something greater than ourselves. The glory is God's, the power is God's, even the beauty is God's, for we are merely houses of clay.

If I were fine china, so to speak, where would the boasting end? I would insist that my perfection and great beauty were the determining factor in my life, not the power of God. If I were together I would feel that I deserved the special treatment that I often receive. Realizing that I am a mere mud pot, covered with flashy bright-colored paint, serves to keep me humble, not only before my sisters, but also before God.

Ultimatum

It was a simple case of ego. King Nebuchadnezzar was in charge of everything, or so he thought. He decided upon the image to worship, he commissioned its design, and he told the people how to worship. "Just as soon as you hear the sound of the instruments, bow down—or die!"

It was an ultimatum. To the king, it made no difference how the people felt about his golden idols. Their loyalties to other gods were not his concern. It certainly made no difference about those three Jewish men, Hananiah, Mishael, and Azariah, having firm belief in the God of the Ages. He had already taken the liberty of renaming these men and now he was intent on dictating when, how, and to whom they would pray!

Ego trips continue. Perhaps there is someone in your world that doesn't quite see life your way and has chosen to rename you and your reality. You know the story, assertive Black women are renamed. Nurturing Black women are stereotyped. Those who choose singleness or celibacy—renamed!

Bible history does not record any protest from Shadrach, Meshach, and Abednego when they were renamed. Perhaps that was not the time for them to protest, not yet. Renaming a person does not change their reality, unless they choose to have it so. No matter what they call the single parent woman, or the assertive woman, or the shy woman, she is still the same woman on the inside—if she knew who she was before others named her. These three men knew who they were because when it got past what others called them or said about them to dictating religious practice, they drew the line.

"King Nebuchadnezzar, we don't even need to discuss this. We already know where we stand." You can go ahead and heat up your furnace; you can go ahead and fire me; you can have your job back; you can elect someone else. We just won't do it! They chose to trust God to carry them through the consequences rather than compromise their core beliefs. They did not presume that God would just get them a better job. They were ready to die, if necessary, to remain true to God's voice inside of them.

King Nebuchadnezzar is not dead. He is still renaming people's realities and still attempting to dictate things that are too close to our hearts.

Today's passage teaches us that things could get ugly, even hot, when we refuse to bow to the golden images of our day. If you should receive an ultimatum, what will you do?

It's Not that Serious

September 17   *Read John 4:20-24.*

Measured by Jewish standards, the Samaritans really did have some bizarre worship practices. They were a peculiar mixture of several worship traditions. They held firmly to their mountain. They used religious imagery that was, at best, disturbing.

The rest of the Jews, by contrast, believed that Jerusalem was the holy city, and that the Temple was the only proper place to worship. They followed the symbols and imagery that Moses had introduced. Theirs, they believed, was the only valid style of worship.

This was the running argument between Jews and Samaritans. Each group was of the opinion that they were absolutely, unquestionably correct in their worship choices. Neither was willing to acknowledge other possibilities.

We live in a world that has similar problems. We are presented with so many alternatives in worship. The older members claim that the worship of the youth is sacrilege. The youth claim that the older members are obsolete. Women and men disagree about imagery and symbolism. Blacks and Whites disagree about the role of emotions. When we focus on the method of worship we often neglect the reasons we have to worship God.

If we had the private audience with Jesus that this woman had, He would probably treat our doctrinal questions the same way. We really do not know, and it really doesn't matter as much as worshiping in Spirit and in truth. God is looking for worshipers who approach Him in heartfelt ways with integrity. Symbolism is not as important as motive. The worship site is not as important as integrity. Though denominations continue to split over every conceivable interpretation of doctrine, Jesus seems to be saying: "It's not that serious."

The Fall Girl

You were not the only one, Eve! Yet, you are the one we remember. You were not the only one. It was a group project, everybody on earth was involved. Adam was with you when it all happened!

Life is funny. Sometimes it does not really matter what actually happened. The way people remember it seems to matter more. That's the way it is with our memories of Adam and Eve. They were both there, they both ate, and Eve continues to receive nearly all the blame for what happened. It just doesn't seem fair, does it?

Later, when they had to give an account to God for their actions, Adam was quick to blame Eve for the entire episode. Eve quickly blamed the serpent. In actuality, they were both to blame. They both chose to disobey God.

Humankind still doesn't like to take responsibility for its actions. We are still looking for others to blame. Prisons are filled with people who say that they were not the only ones involved in crime. We blame society for keeping us down. We blame family members for neglecting us. We blame indifferent spouses for not giving us enough attention. We blame children for holding us back. When all else fails, we go back and blame Eve!

Who is really to blame? Can we really blame anyone else for things that we have failed to do? Can we really blame anyone for missed opportunities? Do we have the right to make anyone else responsible for our decisions?

May I challenge you today, to look at your list of excuses. Don't blame Eve!

Friend at Midnight

It was our first trip to Africa. We were so excited that we did not sleep the night before. Even the actual flight, which has since become tedious, was exciting. The anticipation of going home was overwhelming. Needless to say, after more than thirty-six hours of airplanes and waiting rooms, we were exhausted—and hungry.

Our plane arrived at night. Our stomachs thought that it was lunchtime. It took forever to go through customs, pick up our luggage, ride to our hotel, and check in for the evening. Above the excitement of finally being there, we were reminded by a few intruding growls that it would be a long night if we didn't find a bite to eat.

The street vendors were still out, but we were not quite that brave. We decided to venture downstairs to the hotel bar in hopes of a few potato chips or some other snack to hold us through the night. When we communicated our intentions to the bartender, he disappeared for a few minutes and came back with another person. He woke up the cook!

The kitchen was closed, but they opened it for us. We woke up a new friend at midnight who took our order and fed us a full meal. No food ever tasted as good as that first meal in Africa. We cried as we gave thanks.

In retrospect, I am reminded of many failures to be a friend at midnight. In shame, I recount the many times, over the years, that I have cited convenience as an excuse for not helping someone in need. I have since been inspired to do better.

May the Lord remind us all to get out of our beds of convenience to help someone when they need us.

Not Without Honor

September 20   *Read Mark 6:1-6.*

Hometowns can be both a blessing and a curse. Sometimes they are safe places where you can receive a shero's welcome. They anchor us in time and give us identity. We measure time by changes that take place in our hometown. We identify with soil, geography, and African-American history by looking back at our hometowns. They are often the places that hide us and nurture us when life has taken its cruel toll upon our lives. We need our hometowns, they remind us that we belong somewhere.

Other times they are places of limitation. Everyone thinks they know you. It is hard to get permission to change. You become a part of the hometown history. Stories of your youthful errors are often recycled there. Hometowns never seem to forget.

We find ourselves held hostage by the concrete prison of their opinions. Then we are placed in a dilemma. Should we work hard to prove that they are really wrong? Do we answer the silent accusations? How can we do what we are called to do, trained to do, hired by our employer to do? How do we respond when the gossip gurus say that we can do no right?

Today's passage describes Jesus' struggles with His hometown. Jesus grew up around folks who did not want to believe what God was doing in their midst. He was in a small town and they wanted to chain Him to his family history. "Isn't that Mary's baby?" They could have been referring to the scandal that surrounded His birth. "Isn't He the carpenter's son?" The obvious implication was that carpenters are nobody special, so neither was He.

Jesus gives us a model. First, He recognized the problem. "Prophets are not without honor, except in their hometown" (verse 4). Sometimes we are destroyed by denying the limitations of hometowns. He acknowledged that this was not the war to win. He came to earth to accomplish a mission. He could not let limiting opinions stop Him from doing His Father's work. He did what they allowed Him to do for them, and when He could do no more, He gently moved on.

Is all of your energy wrapped up in proving that you, or your family, can do something good? Perhaps it is time for you to do whatever you can and then gently move on.

Lord, My Mouth

September 21   *Read Psalm 141:3-4.*

I didn't mean to say it! As much as I try, I always seem to say the wrong thing. Is there a center of the brain from whence wrong things proceed? Actually, Jesus said that they proceed from the heart. "But what comes out of the mouth proceeds from the heart, and this is what defiles" (Matt. 15:18). Which of us really knows what is in our heart? Lord, stand watch over my mouth.

I believe that the psalmist understood this relationship between heart and mouth because he prayed these words: "Do not turn my heart to any evil" (verse 4). Our mouths become mirrors reflecting what is really going on inside of us. Slips of the tongue and accidental insults are really reflective of our innermost thoughts. These inappropriate thoughts remind us that grace is a slow, lifelong work in our hearts. They tell us, and others, that we are still under construction.

There is another important reason to guard our speech. Our words are part of a chain reaction of events. Words reflect thoughts, and words also reflect attitudes and intentions. Unrestricted thoughts and unrestricted words can lead to evil deeds (verse 4). Unwholesome words can either attract us to, or make us attractive to, evildoers because they recognize our conversation. The psalmist prays to not be drawn to such temptations. Today, Lord, I do not want to take part in evil deeds, especially with those who are evildoers; please stand guard over my lips while I learn to think and even to believe more appropriately.

Lord, gossip is so delicious, let me not eat of it (verse 4). Lord, if you stand guard over my lips while my heart learns wisdom and truth, I will not become intoxicated by the wine of slander.

As women, we are often conditioned to think that we have no defense except language. As women of color, we often use our mouths as a weapon. The psalmist reminds us that unguarded speech can lead to evil and position us with evil people. Let God become our defense.

If we are realistic about our faith, we must accept the fact that some changes do not happen overnight. While we are waiting for our innermost being to catch up with the best of our intentions, there are plenty of opportunities for others to hear or see what we are still working on. There are plenty of opportunities for sin. Shall we echo the prayer of the psalmist? "Set a guard over my mouth, O LORD; keep watch over the door of my lips."

Po Folks

September 22   *Read Luke 4:18-19.*

Practically every society shuns its poor. We behave as though the poor are some personal embarrassment to us. Jesus said that the poor would be with us always. Yet the poor are quite important. So many pivotal, historical figures came from poor, humble homes. Practically all the heroes and sheroes of African-American history would have been considered poor by today's standards. Each of us has heard a rags-to-riches story about someone who began in poverty and later became rich and famous.

There are certain images of poverty that have become familiar to us. We are all too familiar with the swollen bellies of those starving in Somalia, and the sad eyes of those who live under bridges. Most of us have escaped this kind of poverty.

When speaking of our own personal poverty, we do so jokingly. We speak of certain extravagant behaviors as putting us in the poorhouse. Rarely do we come face-to-face with our actual areas of need. We fear poverty.

We are frightened and speak less of those who were once rich and became poor. It has been said that we are all only a paycheck away from poverty. We whisper about people like Joe Louis and Alex Haley who died owning very little.

What is poverty really? Consider the following definition: not having what you need and want when you think you need it. By this definition, most of us are poor. Our vocabulary reflects this truth. We use phrases like poor thing, poor health, poor condition. When we lack health, well-being, or peace of mind, we become the poor of whom Jesus spoke.

Jesus' words to those in Nazareth continue to speak to us today. He came to see about our poor condition.

Are you one of the poor? Jesus has come just for you.

Riding Out the Storm

September 23   *Read Matthew 8:24-27.*

Everyone on campus loved Dr. Jeri Anderson. She was easy to talk to; not stuffy like other Black professors. She was the author of several easy to comprehend chemistry books. Dr. Anderson was just a brilliant Christian woman. We often wondered if that is what made the other professors in her department so jealous of her.

September

To be honest, everyone on campus knew that the other professors were eager to have her fired—only they couldn't find a good reason. Jeri Anderson knew it too. She would often pray that the Lord would just help her through this storm, which she had always felt would be temporary. No one had a reason to fire her—she really deserved a raise or a promotion. Her student ratings were exceptional. The students who studied chemistry under Dr. Anderson always did exceptionally well on their graduate school exams. Those who worked as lab assistants for her always qualified for exceptional positions in the workplace. Her approach to teaching made chemistry more than tolerable for the nursing students. She was just an exceptional professor!

One day, the other professors devised what they thought was a certain plan to rid themselves of Dr. Anderson. They decided to alter the test scores of the students in her classes. One of the professors was a computer specialist and saw no problem with lowering enough of the scores to make her teaching look questionable. They would just do this as often as was necessary to have her fired. The plan might have worked had it not been for the new director of the computer lab.

The new computer lab director was concerned about reports that students at other universities break into the system and alter their grades. He programmed the mainframe of the university's computer to trace any unauthorized entry into the registrar's records. When the other professors discreetly changed Dr. Anderson's students' grades, Mr. Gregg, the director knew exactly who they were! He gathered his evidence, took it to university security, and heads began to roll! Two professors were dismissed, and Dr. Anderson was promoted to department chair!

For Dr. Anderson, this action was like stilling a storm. Never again did any of the other professors attempt to have her fired!

Do you have any storms in your life that need stilling?

Shoulder to Shoulder

September 24   *Read Psalm 133:1-3.*

I sat between
Two noble ladies today

While we were shoulder to shoulder in church.
The day was hot
        Sweat-rings formed around my neck
While
Two noble ladies shouldered me
    On the Lord's day.

On my left shoulder
    Sat a woman
    About forty-five years old.
The laughter lines etched around her eyes
    Were there from years of practice.
Her eyes laughed a greeting my way
    While we sat there
Shoulder to shoulder.
All through the service, she had
    Happy feet
    Happy hands
    Happy hair
    Happy smile!

Happy rubs off when you sit so close.
    Before long, I was happy too!
    I was happy to be there
    Shouldered with this woman.
    Happy for her laughing eyes
    Glad for the songs which made my feet get happy
    Happy for the words of life
        Flowing out to me.

On the other side
    Sat an old saint
    Barely able to move in response
    To the moving of the Holy Ghost
    Which stirred our very souls.
She shouldered me gently
    I gentled her shoulder
    Which was bowed and stooped with age.
    I gentled her leathery hands
    Which barely gripped mine in greeting.
And reached for her gentle smile
    When she offered it to me.

Her eyes were squinted with age
   And wrinkle-worn from seeing
   Things I had yet to see.
Everything
   About this woman
   Cried experience and wisdom.
I longed to have the wisdom
   That was on my right side
Infect me as did the happiness on my left side,

As we all sat shoulder to shoulder on the Lord's day.

God of Our Mistakes

September 25   *Read Genesis 17:18-21.*

O that Ishmael might live in your sight! I can hear Sarah and Abraham saying: "Lord, if you could just accept the way that I have interpreted your promises to me, it would be all right." I see myself in this situation. Do you? I do not seem to have any problem realizing that God has made numerous promises to bless me. My problem lies in the ways that I feel that God will fulfill those promises. More than once, because of my misguided faith and zealousness, life has been a mess.

How often have I hurt people and circumstances that I truly cared about in my efforts to help God? How often have you jumped ahead of the glory cloud in your eagerness to see the fulfillment of the will of God? Sarah and Abraham were not negligent believers; instead, they were overly eager to see God's will in their lives.

I join other mothers in mourning over the mistakes that we have made with our children. So many of us have wanted to do the very best we could, only to discover that it was the very worst. We post–Civil Rights mothers tried to give our children all the blessings of American life that were denied us during the Jim Crow years. Yet, so many of us forgot to give them the knowledge of a resilient past that would sustain them in the present and propel them into a more certain future. In our zealousness to be truly free of the past, we have confused and imprisoned our daughters and sons.

Ishmael, a product of Abraham and Sarah's zealousness, and Hagar's victimization, would have been an easy to forget casualty. It would be easier to ignore, or to justify the whole disaster. Instead, every time we look at Abraham and Sarah's blessing, we are forced to remember just how costly it was. Some of our blessings are just as costly; they seem to come at the expense of the innocent. What of poor Ishmael and Hagar?

God, who is just, understood why the tragedy occurred and also made promises concerning Ishmael: "I will bless him and make him fruitful and exceedingly numerous; he shall be the father of twelve princes, and I will make him a great nation" (verse 20).

We do not always hear Ishmael's story, but nevertheless, he too, belongs to the Lord. Your children and mine also belong to the Lord. God has written their stories in His heart. Their future is bigger than our blunders. Blessed be the Lord, who even cares about our mistakes!

I'm Here for You

September 26   *Read Ruth 1:16-17.*

We have heard the words from today's passage spoken at weddings, but rarely do we apply them as they were intended, to female friendships. Naomi's daughter-in-law was also her friend. Naomi had left her hometown to go and live near her sons and their wives. Before both of her sons died, Ruth became Naomi's friend. After her husband's death, Ruth chose to leave her hometown, and her gods, to maintain this friendship. Many Bible passages celebrate healthy same-sex friendships. Some of us celebrate the concept, yet fail to cultivate necessary female friends.

Many of us have been taught that it is not possible to have both a husband, and family, and a good female friend. We fear the men in our lives may misunderstand our continued need for best friends. Some of the brothers think that our female friends compete with them for time or loyalty. Sometimes this is true. There are sisters who have not learned to maintain a nonthreatening friendship with their best friend. For others of us, modern time constraints have caused us to abandon and eliminate one of our most important needs.

September

We never outgrow our need for a good friend. Recall the friendships of older women you have known. How different might their lives have been without a good friend to go through the rough times? Allow your mind to return to the friends of your high school or college years. Remember the days of shared secrets and girlish joys? We never outgrow the need for someone who will be there for us.

Men and women, married, single, and widowed, need good friends. Ruth was that kind of friend for Naomi. She was one who chose a future of uncertainty rather than abandon the friendship.

One tribe of Native Americans has an interesting definition of friend: one who carries my sorrows on his back. How often we need someone who will also carry our sorrows on her back. Our prayer today is that God will teach us how to maintain the healthy friendships that we need.

. . . If You Try

September 27   *Read James 1:12.*

There are so many reasons to succumb to temptation. It is not just the temptation to sin; the temptation to give up also dances around in our thoughts from time to time. It would be so easy to let life go by and do nothing. So much of life in the '90s feels like swimming upstream or fighting an uphill battle.

Back in the '50s there was an old blues song that my mother used to listen to. "You can make it if you try." Bobby Blue Bland's voice rang throughout the house convincing us that we could make it. He sang every note he knew, "You can make it. . . ." He sang between the notes, "if you try. . . ." I heard it in the car, on the 78 record at home, and with all of my mother's friends singing along. They knew each note, each inflection, and all of the background music! All of them were committed to making it; they were all determined to try.

Perhaps what we need in the '90s is a simple word of encouragement. We complain to one another more than we encourage. We do autopsies on dead conditions, but rarely speak life into those that are faltering and could be revived. We need a modern day holy blues singer. One who has seen the rougher side of life and has decided that she will overcome. We need a tune, or a tome, that will rally the masses of women to the knowledge that they can succeed in life.

Today, why not try out your tune on a sister who doesn't seem to have a song? Tell her that the rough side of the mountain is not the end of life, but a place where she can grasp a foothold. Let her know that the rough places are there to keep her from making her bed in the land of failure. Give her a good dose of, "You can make it if you try!"

I Know Him for Myself

September 28   *Read John 20:26-29.*

Have there ever been times when you needed to see something for yourself? It may have been test results, final grades, or Aunt Sadie's birth certificate. Some things are so hard to believe that we must see them to believe them. Our faith is really no different.

Poor Thomas, he dared to raise a faith question, yet his name has become a proverb. The title Doubting Thomas has become notorious. Perhaps it's time to clear his name. Maybe he should be called Honest Thomas instead. He was just honest enough to say I don't care what you think you saw. I need to see Him for myself—then I will believe! Thomas simply refused to risk his life for secondhand information. What about you?

In a very real way, our foremothers had Thomas' kind of faith. Those old ladies refused to ride on the shirttails of anyone else's confession of faith. Faith, for them, was a personal and individual experience. Their encounters with God were so powerful that they did not hesitate when there was an allotted time for testimony. Can you remember their words? I know Him for myself!

Most of us are experienced enough to remember the dangers of secondhand information. The Christian faith is far too important; its issues are far too serious to rely upon someone else's experience. Each of us, like Thomas, has a need to encounter the risen Lord. Do you know him for yourself?

Transitions

Stand tall, you are a child of God! There is a big difference between a child and a slave. The Bible teaches us that those who belong to God are no longer slaves, but children and heirs.

It has often been said that one of the major problems in the African-American community is the slave mentality. The Emancipation was signed nearly 130 years ago, but so many of us still think like slaves. I often wonder if the present wave of violence and hopelessness that we are experiencing in the African-American community is a by-product of this mind-set. What happens to a people after hundreds of years of humiliation and enslavement? Perhaps only Africans and Israelis can answer this question.

Sometimes we get so stuck in the quagmire of human slavery issues that we forget about other forms of slavery. We can be enslaved by certain intimate relationships. Economic slavery is possible. In today's reading, Paul refers to spiritual slavery. Paul's contemporaries had to be reminded that they were no longer slaves. They obviously had not made the mental transition from being slaves to being children. Those enslaved spiritually serve their masters because they fear reprisals. Their actions are motivated by fear or duty, but rarely by love. By contrast, children usually know their parents. They demonstrate their love for them by doing those things that please them. Children imitate their parents because they identify with them. Their goal is to become like them. Children who are heirs anticipate their role in the family's enterprises.

Paul's words come to challenge us today. Are we thinking like slaves, or like children of God? Do we fear God as a harsh taskmaster who exacts perfection from His servants; or do we see that God is a loving parent desiring to inspire us to achieve human potential? Are we in a mental tug-of-war, torn between earthly desires and godly examples? Do we serve the Lord because of duty, or because of love?

Lord, help all of us to make the mental transition from slavery to becoming children of God. Amen.

Greens and Cornbread

September 30   *Read Luke 11:5-8.*

Diane and Roger were having a dinner party—their first! They invited everyone they knew. Before they knew it, their guests numbered far beyond the capacity of their modest home. What would they do? After giving it a great deal of consideration, they decided to ask their friends, the Websters, if they could borrow their home—just for the evening.

The Websters were an older couple. They looked at Diane and Roger's enthusiasm and agreed without hesitation. Diane assured them that they would clean before and after the party, and they would cook and furnish all the food.

When the big day came for the party, Diane was a nervous wreck. Nothing seemed to go right that day. The cake, which was late, was vanilla instead of German chocolate. The large coffee urn, which had been borrowed from the Smiths, blew a fuse in the Websters' borrowed basement. To make matters worse, Diane, due to her inexperience with such matters, had not prepared enough food! What would she do?

Without being asked, Mrs. Webster knew exactly what to do. She rolled up her sleeves and started cooking greens. She cooked greens that smelled so good that no one could think of anything else. She cooked a big chittlin' pot of greens with smoked turkey—and a great big pan of buttery cornbread. It goes without saying that Diane and Roger's first dinner party was a great success. There was plenty of everything—after Mrs. Webster's contribution.

The parable for today teaches us that God will never let us down. Jesus compares God to a friend who would loan you three loaves of bread at midnight to feed your guests. I suspect that if Roger and Diane told the story they would use greens and cornbread.

October

Homegirl

It was Fish Day at Elmina, on the coast of Ghana. Boats lined the coast as far as one could see. Women, with baskets on their heads, walked away from the shore carrying large fish by their gills, while others pressed in to barter with the waiting fishermen, who would not be there again until the next Fish Day, a week later. Babies, strapped to their mothers' backs, curiously eyed the fish and the people until lulled back to sleep by the familiar cadence of their mothers' steps.

By this time, I had grown accustomed to the British accent of my new kinsman. Kwame had cradled my husband Kwasi and me like newborns, and was carefully introducing us to the rhythms of life in Africa. People were crowded in everywhere. After all, it was Fish Day. I scanned the unfamiliar crowd for familiar faces. I had already seen faces like those of my cousins in America. Somewhere inside of me, I longed to have them here with me, drinking in the new sights and smells. I longed to hear voices from home.

Almost on cue, I did hear a voice from home. Hey girl! A homegirl! Where was she? I turned around to find that voice. A handsome ebony woman, dressed in traditional garments, was the owner of that voice. "Oh, I thought you were someone I knew back home in New York!" As we struck up a conversation, I remembered just how important it was to hear another person speak my dialect of English. Someone who speaks our language, touches our souls.

Is that how the woman with the hemorrhage touched Jesus? Something about that woman stood out in a crowd. There were too many people to distinguish an ordinary touch from the inevitable jostling that must have come from contact with so many. That woman must have reminded Jesus of home in some strange way.

I also long to touch Jesus in the way a voice from home comforts our souls. I yearn to speak a dialect of faith that is familiar to His ears. Lord, teach our hearts words and phrases in the heavenly language that are most familiar to you. We long to be your homegirls.

Divine Positioning

October 2   *Read Genesis 45:3-8.*

What did Joseph think about while separated from his family? He had gone through a series of hardships because of his brothers' jealousy. They had been separated for so long that they did not even recognize him. How did it now feel to see them struggling, uncertain, and at his mercy?

This would have been an opportune time for revenge. His brothers had sold Joseph into slavery, while the father he loved dearly thought that he was dead. His brothers had been in comfort while he was in prison, falsely accused. Now, Joseph, who had become a prominent leader in Egypt, had the upper hand. Today, they were begging him for food.

Some of us have also been similarly estranged from families we love. Jealousy and misunderstanding have caused some of us to part company. Geography and grudges have distanced too many of us from our brothers and sisters. How can we face them again? How did Joseph?

Perhaps Joseph was only able to face his family once he made certain realizations about the sovereignty of God. Believe it or not, God is in charge of all things. God never allows more to overtake us than we are able to bear. Even the horrible things that God allows are part of a larger plan. In Joseph's case, his being sent to Egypt as a slave was part of God's divine plan to save a nation. Joseph was being divinely positioned.

Joseph started as a slave and a prisoner. God did not allow him to stay there. Eventually, he was a leader in a position to save the children of Israel. Who knows how they would have survived had things been different?

God is yet placing people in position through strange circumstances. You may be in one of them. Are there some positive things in your life that would not have been there were it not for the misfortunes that you have suffered? Perhaps you are still in prison but can see the new horizons toward which you are headed. Why not pause today and thank God for placing you where you really need to be?

In My Right Mind

Kim had been to Texas visiting some family members, and was returning home on the plane. The few weeks she had been away seemed like an eternity ago. She had flown from Brooklyn to her aunt and uncle's home in Dallas to get herself together. Now, she was on the plane, hoping to resolve the mess she had made of her life.

Kim and Mike had moved to New York two years ago. Mike had secured a very promising position with a growing business. After three years of marriage, they had become the parents of beautiful active twin boys. On the surface life looked idyllic; but the pressure of twins, a young marriage, and Mike's long hours at his job proved to be too much for a new mother. Before long, the isolation of big city living and old-fashioned claustrophobia had turned Kim into a monster. On one particular evening, the couple had an awful fight. Something came over her and she viciously attacked Mike. She said horrible things that she would normally never have said, about their marriage, the twins—even about his family! Now several weeks away had given her plenty of time to think, and to pray, about what had happened.

On the long flight home, she began to ask herself what went wrong? Mike was a wonderful person. They had what others would call a wonderful life. It suddenly occurred to her that her Christian life had been left in the background. They were not immoral people, but they had become too busy. They had been too busy to find a local church fellowship. They had become too busy to share in devotions as a couple. They had even become too busy to pray.

That must be the missing ingredient, she thought. We have left God out of the picture entirely. This time, things are going to be different! Then, she smiled on the inside as she remembered the frequent testimony of one of the old women in her aunt and uncle's church. "I woke up this morning in my right mind. . . ."

The Christian faith is not just for times of crisis. We need God's strength every day, for everything, including peaceful rational thoughts.

One-Legged Rainbows

It was early on the first morning of our vacation. The sun was not quite visible, but it was light enough to see a piece of a rainbow on the horizon. In the distance, it only looked a few feet long, about an eighth of an arc with faint colors. Rainbows represent God's promises. Where do rainbows live?

Scientists would give us a curt explanation involving light refraction and such—but I am not a scientist. I tend to think of rainbows as having a secret life waiting to be discovered. Where did this rainbow live?

While we continued in early morning conversation, we continued to look out of the corners of our eyes for more than one leg of this elusive rainbow. Isn't life like that? Do you find yourself looking for the other half of an unfulfilled promise? Our lives are filled with promises that seem to hide behind the clouds.

Within the next hour, we watched our one-legged rainbow grow in size. Little by little, it began to stretch across the sky until it almost reached the other side of the horizon. For a few brief moments, the missing leg of this rainbow appeared. In life, there is something quite comforting about seeing most of a promise fulfilled. It reminds us of the surety of God's promises. It confirms our hopes and dispels our fears. Seeing the better part of a promise come to life helps us to know that we are not crazy for holding on to dreams.

As quickly as it had revealed itself, this rainbow disappeared. The sun now occupied its place. Did the sun chase it away? Of course not. The rainbow only served as a promise until the sun rose. We don't really need a rainbow promise when the sun is shining, do we?

Fixin' To . . .

Something must be wrong with today because we rarely want to live there. We either "used to" do something, or we are "fixin' to" do it.

October

Moments, which bleed into hours, go by with us planning for tomorrow or basking in the stale air of yesterday. What is wrong with this day and this moment? Why are we so afraid of the now?

Have we become so taken with the good old days that we cannot find a comfort zone for today? Has late night advertising duped us into believing that the golden years were in the past and today is merely an eye open nightmare? Today is filled with blessing and opportunities because God is here—today.

Could it be that we have become so focused on the "best that is yet to come" that we have lost our point of reference? Somewhere along the line we must have caught up with the future that we imagined last year, last month, or even yesterday. It is here right now. God has given you a present that will be gone tomorrow—it is called today.

There are some things that you and I are probably not going to do twice! This occurred to me one day when it dawned on me that my life was probably halfway completed. We Black women always seem to focus on a day when our money is better, our children are grown and out of the house, or when we get moved into our new place. How many unused towels and fancy dishes have you inherited from female ancestors who were waiting for the right time to use what they already had? Take a good look at some of those things—they represent our loved ones tomorrows. There are just some things that we will never have an opportunity to do better. Do what you can today, for life is like a vapor.

Before procrastination, the thief of time, blows upon the vapor of your life, why not live it! When was the last time that you watched a sunset, did your nails, or spent time with someone that you wanted to know better? Have you used your good towels, or eaten off your own good china without a special occasion? It is time for all of us to stop living in the land of yesterdays and tomorrows. Today may be your tomorrow in disguise.

God's Permission Slip

October 6   *Read Galatians 5:22-23.*

One morning, many years ago, this passage was the memory verse for our youngest son. He skillfully read all of the words, seemed to recognize most of them, and proceeded to ask about the sentence that read, "There is no law against such things."

Of all the questions that he could have asked, this one seemed most like an eleven-year old's. Adolescents are learning where the boundaries are and want to know what's legal. Yet, it wasn't quite an eleven-year old's question, because as we answered it together, we found that it gave permission—not prohibition.

Most of us grew up with a list of things that are against the law of God. We grew up with the list of restrictions memorized. Thou shalt not kill. Thou shalt not steal. Thou shalt not. . . . How sad that those things that please God get so much less attention.

"There is no law against such things." Does this really mean, to paraphrase, that there is no law against loving? Could it mean that there is no law against having joy? Are we to understand that it is fine to be peaceful, patient, or kind? Yes, goodness and faithfulness are also in vogue this year, and gentleness and self-control never violate God's law either. In essence, Galatians 5:22-23 is God's permission slip!

In God's Word, there is much more permission than prohibition. We are encouraged to be cheerful, to be helpful, and to sing! We are encouraged to come out of depression, to love one another, and to be at peace with God, with ourselves, and with others. This passage is both a picture and a permission slip.

The do's and don'ts of the faith say BEHAVE! And, we all know that they are necessary. But passages like these encourage us to just BE! Isn't that more natural?

What a Fellowship!

October 7　　　　　　　　　　*Read Acts 2:42-47.*

What a time these people called Christians were having! They sound like they knew how to enjoy life. They were a devoted group, for they fellowshipped, took communion, and prayed often. The group was amazed with the power of God in their midst; signs and wonders were a part of their customary experience.

This group was an unselfish group. They shared everything: their bread, their possessions, even their property! They were happy, and they were popular. And many people wanted to be like them.

Modern scholars tell us that these were people of color, perhaps even Northern Africans. They sound a lot like African-Americans. God used their culture as a means of bringing them joy. God also used their culture as a means of bringing others to faith.

Many people look backward, with nostalgia, to the good old days of the church, when everyone was happy and shared with anyone in need. People wanted to be part of it because it was good. In many similar ways, people also look back to the good old days of the African-American community, when God wasn't part of a "cuss word," and we shared and loved in ways that made others want to be like us.

Let us join in prayer that today will mark the beginning of a mighty restoration—for God's people and for our people.

Prayer: Almighty God, we weep and mourn for what was once good and holy in your sight. We pray, together, for the healing of our community. As we examine this passage in Acts, we feel like we have seen a snapshot of a family reunion of our past. We miss that past. Help us to return to your vision of the church and the community. Amen.

Give Me Children, or I Will Die!

October 8   *Read Genesis 30:1.*

How many of us have looked at our own mortality and seen that our future lies in our children? I don't mean a voyeuristic thing where we vicariously live our lives through our children. I speak of a conscious realization that the tasks of this lifetime cannot be finished during this lifetime. Someone we love must share this vision with us and carry the torch into the next generation.

Seen in this light, those who desire motherhood are not simply yearning for someone to take care of; nor are they looking ahead to old age for someone to take care of them. They are looking for lives to influence who will change the whole of human existence. "If my son can just finish his education, he might have a chance to be the one. . . ." "Maybe she will be the principal of a school, or a president one day. . . ." "Perhaps that little one could find a cure for the world's diseases. . . ." Mothers have often been the ones who dream the dreams that change the world.

If we look at this whole issue of motherhood being the extension of the desire for productivity, we learn something new about mothers of color. Mothers of color, not only dream the dreams that change the world for their children, but we also dream those dreams for our time.

We are unsung heroines, bumping up against the world's systems in an old ragged dress. Rarely taken seriously, we shake and disrupt until some measurable comfort zone emerges "for my chile and yours."

Our mothers went without makeup and brassieres while dispensing wisdom like a lifesaving fountain. Everyone wanted to call our mothers Mama or Auntie because they also wanted to be productive. You see, being bumped and bruised by Auntie meant that something productive was going to spring from the encounter. The world has become a better place because of Black motherhood.

Today, modern Black mothers point at mismatched morality with long, sculptured fingernails. We wear Fashion Fair and smell good, and shake up all of creation without so much as disturbing a fingerwave. We go out on all kinds of limbs in the name of productivity.

Even our modern motherhood is a desire to be productive, to change the world, to share a dream with someone we love that will carry it through. Whether you are a biological mother or not, if you strive for the dream that changes the world, God bless you.

Misplaced Memories

October 9   *Read Philippians 3:13-14.*

Baby boomers are accused of reveling in the good old days. Our memories are misplaced. Nighttime advertisements seem to indicate that we prefer the golden years when Smokey was our sweetheart, and Aretha, not Oprah, was Everywoman. Why do we love the past so much?

Perhaps we love the past because it represents accomplishment. It looked like we were really doing something back then. We challenged the status quo. We shook tradition by its tail and developed new ways of looking at everything from skin color to hiring practices. We spoke loudly in the days of our youth—and America listened. At least that's how we remember it.

What happened to the movement? It just faded into the sunset. Can you remember the date that it was officially over? I just remember us settling down and growing older. Now, we collectively appear to walk forward while ever looking backward, resting in the victories of the past.

It's not healthy to live in the past. Living there robs us of the vitality of the present. It shortchanges the future, because all eyes are in the back of our heads looking through the tangled growth of oversized afros. When we live in the past, we stop growing, we stop achieving, and we stop moving forward.

Lord, deliver us from romanticizing the past. We fail to remember its tragic mistakes while gilding the memories of its successes with gold dust. We dupe ourselves into believing that the best has already come and we need not expect anything better. Living in the past can be dangerous.

Many of us can recite the list of the apostle Paul's accomplishments from memory. He was well educated, and wielded a great deal of power in the community. He was on the career track. Yet, even Paul could not rest in the accomplishments of his past.

Paul decided that he really didn't have it made back then. He decided to forget it and press forward. You see, Paul's eyes were on something greater. He saw limitless possibilities of Christ in his future.

Christ is also in your future. Your personal history is waiting to be written. Maybe it's time you forgot your past and moved on.

Threading the Needle

October 10   *Read Luke 18:24-27.*

The use of wealth, for the Christian, has always been a faith issue. In this particular conversation, a young rich man was looking for a painless way to be godly. Jesus' reply was for him to sell his possessions and give to the poor. The poor young man was saddened by this and walked away empty. He was unable to part with all of his wealth. "Wouldn't it," he probably thought, "have been sufficient to just give a comfortable amount to satisfy Christian duty?"

"Indeed, it is easier for a camel to go through the eye of a needle than for someone who is rich to enter the kingdom of God" (verse 25). In order for a camel to thread a needle, it would have to become quite small. Are you small enough to go through that needle?

There are many things that make us big in our own eyes. Some of us are puffed up by knowledge (1 Cor. 8:1). Others of us are puffed up by power and prestige (Luke 6:26). Then, there are those of us who are made big by wealth. The message is clear, those who think they are big must become small to truly enter the kingdom of God.

How could a camel ever go through the eye of a needle? Well, the eye of the needle was a term used for the portals that separated the temple grounds from the rest of the world. They were large enough for worshipers to enter, but low enough to keep camels from wandering in. The only way that a camel could possibly have entered would have been on it's knees. How will you thread the needle? Ask the camels!

Standing in the Heights

October 11   *Read Psalm 148:1-5.*

I often envy the angels. They were created for praise. Their lives are not complicated by such obstacles and by such choices as we have. They seem to be above all the trouble of life.

How nice it must be to live in the heights. I don't think that anyone rings an angel's beeper with the express purpose of pouring out pain and spreading misery. Some days I can get past my own problems to a vision of God; but then here come my neighbors and friends, who are also in pain, needing my shoulder and bending my ear. Then, I am back where I started, longing to see and feel God—wishing I were free to worship. Down here below, where life is so complicated, I must find a vision of God in order to fully appreciate who He is.

Up above life's troubles, it seems as if it would be so natural to praise the Lord. There would be no reason to grumble or to complain. Praise would be as natural as breathing because the only image in sight would be that of the God who created us. How can I get there?

The psalmist hints at the answer. "Praise the LORD! Praise the LORD from the heavens; praise him in the heights!" He was speaking to human beings and to celestial beings. "Praise him in the heights!" What are some of the high points in your life? I am in the heights on those not so frequent occasions when I transcend problems. I am in the heights when the glory of God's presence invades my world and overshadows all else. I am in the heights when I begin to count my blessings. I am in the heights when I make a conscious effort to find, see, and experience God. When are you in the heights?

For some of us, the high places are not so easily found. Oftentimes we must be lifted up to the heights so that we can praise the Lord. Does your life look like a mountain of problems? Stand on top of them and praise the Lord!

They Started It!

October 12   *Read Exodus 2:11-12.*

We somehow have permission to do a whole lot of things if they start it! How many parents have been called to the principal's office when a child was called in for fighting only to hear Johnny say, "Well, he started it!" We adults have been known to refuse to speak to neighbors or family members for an indefinite period of time if they started it! We are capable of keeping a running argument going with a spouse, as long as ten years, if they start it. We even justify half working on our jobs, doing just enough to get by, "because they don't half pay me anyway." You see, they started it!

I am sure that Moses, who understood that he was a Hebrew, must have felt something of this variety of self-righteousness when he saw an Egyptian beating one of the Hebrews. Something inside of him must have risen, stirring him to commit murder in the name of, "they started it!" Was it the actual incident that gave him the reason for murder or was that incident an excuse?

Actually, they don't really start it; they just bump into it. *It* is what happens when bad intentions, motive, and opportunity collide. *It* is what happens when Johnny, who loves to fight anyway, has an opportunity—especially if it is someone he doesn't like. *It* is what happens when we really didn't want to speak to her anyway. *It* is what happens when nations sense a need to flex their muscles in the eyes of the world and impress others with their so-called power. *It* is what happens when a husband is already predisposed to domestic violence. *It* is what happens when we have already made up our minds that we could be persuaded to do the wrong thing.

Today is a day to examine our intentions. Could we be persuaded to do the wrong thing if no one is looking? Are we looking for an excuse to say or do something inappropriate that has been on our minds for a while? If we check ourselves, we can stop *it* before they start it!

Perspectives on Poverty

October 13   *Read Luke 4:18-19.*

What forms the dividing line between being rich and being poor? So many of us confess that we did not know that we grew up poor. I have known adults who were children during the Great Depression and didn't know that there was a depression going on. The thing that makes the difference is perspective.

What is your perspective? Poor health is as much poverty as a poor bank account. Poor situations and poor relationships are forms of poverty. Using these definitions, we are all poor. Yet, not all of us are being set free by God's liberating power. Why? Could it be that we are not free because we have not really identified our needs? Can you see your own poverty?

Luke identifies the poor in many ways. The Old Testament poor were the desperate, the hopeless, the defenseless, and the despised. Luke describes them as prisoners of sin, blind to spiritual things, and oppressed by others.

These people knew that they were in need of relief. The woman at the well, who had been married five times and who was living with a man who was not her husband, acknowledged that she was a prisoner of lifestyle and habit. The physically and the spiritually blind people of the Bible acknowledged that they were previously unable to see or to understand what God was doing in their lives. They came to

Jesus in great crowds because they knew that He had come to help the poor.

Why is it so hard for us to receive God's blessings for our poor situations? Sometimes we remain spiritually poor because we refuse to acknowledge our needs. Our pride often gets in the way—we are ashamed of letting others know our need; and too embarrassed to come before God with our shortcomings. We are often afraid that we will be rejected or ridiculed. But God has promised us that if we call on Him, He will answer us and not despise us.

Poverty. May I offer some closing thoughts? Many who think they are poor are really rich. Many others are poor and do not realize it! Rejoice! The good news of the gospel is for all of us who are poor!

Dust Off Your Head!

October 14   *Read Isaiah 58:3-8.*

Lord,
  We have fasted
    and denied ourselves, they said.
Don't you see
    the ashes on our heads?
Haven't you seen
    our grubby clothes
    and sad faces
        and felt the tremors of our loud weeping?

We have given up chocolate
    and TV and such
    things that are really
        unimportant
            to us.

Trying to catch your attention
    so that we
        could get what we want
        from you
            (for a change).

What else,
    do you want, Lord?

We sat in the ashes of our bedroom fireplaces
    waiting
    impatiently
        for an answer from up there.
In the long silence that ensued,
    we fought with each other
        over the details that
            one of us must have omitted
Because fasting usually works.

Finally,
God broke the fragile silence
    between our belligerent words
        to one another.

"Why do you fast?"
He put the questions
    to us.
"In all your giving up
    and self-denial
You forgot
    to give up fighting.
You kept right on
    misusing your friends
And
Had no mind
    for
        freeing captives
        feeding hungry
        sheltering homeless
            or clothing those without."

"Perhaps,
    If you could
        "give up"
    your own ways and
    examine My ways
You might find no need
    to put so many
        ashes on your heads."

Heaven Must Be Near

The thunderous sound
  of heaven's approach
Roars through our valleys
  and shouts from our mountaintops.

Sick folk are starting to recognize their dysfunction.

They rush to Dr. Oprah
  in droves
  hungry for an end to their misery.
While others
  pick up their pallets and
  limp along in search of a healing pool.

Graveyard dirt
  is etched
  with the signs
  of folk turning over in their graves
Being aroused in their sleep
  as though
  they faintly heard some voice
  telling them to get up.

Lepers,
  with all kinds of diseases
  coming out of their closet colonies
  draw close
  to sites once forbidden,
Harboring thoughts of a coming Cure
  waiting to be discovered
So that they can go home again.

The devils, too
  have seen its invisible form
  on the horizon.
They roar
  with intensity

(while they still can)
knowing that tomorrow
brings silence.

The signs of heaven
Are all around
Proclaiming
That the Kingdom of Heaven
is Near!

Rosa's Feet

October 16   *Read Exodus 1:15-20.*

When I saw Rosa Parks at the Million Man March this morning, I thought of these two sisters, Puah and Shiphrah. What could have killed our baby boys more than the Jim Crow laws of the South and the indifference of the North? Our men were called "boy" then, condemned to a perpetual childhood by the laws of this land. Everytime our grown husbands were called boy, it was like throwing them to the crocodiles of the Nile. But, some of our women feared God more than they feared Pharaoh's law.

Rosa's feet hurt and she refused to give up her seat on the bus one day. Hurt was the reason, feet were the excuse. I think that her heart hurt more than her feet did. I was a child then, not too young to remember that it hurt everyone's heart to see limitations upon liberty, and separation based upon skin color. Rosa's feet screamed at the nation because they were too wide for the narrow path permitted them. They howled with pain because the shoes of segregation never would fit. They protested under the weight of our past. Hurt was the reason, feet were the excuse.

Our young boys hurt more than a mother's, aunt's, sister's, lover's love could ever soothe. Hurt is the reason, gangs and drugs are the result. Their eyes scan through the crowd waiting for a Puah and Shiphrah to say no to the injustice of unwritten laws. We are always so quick to say that they are just looking for an excuse. Well really, they are looking for an excuse to end the pain of slow death.

Shiphrah and Puah said no. They refused with the subtlety of mother wit to participate in the murder plot. "Babies just come so fast that you can't get to them in time to stop them." Murder plots have not ceased, they have just cloaked themselves in fake promises and syrupy plati- tudes. Pharaoh has not stopped symbolically feeding our baby boys to the crocodiles.

Rosa feared God and knew His will for all people. She stands as a sym- bol of those who fear God and continue to stand against injustice and unjust laws. To look on the positive side, sisters, mother wit has not died among us. We have got plenty of reasons. Could it be that we must, with all skill and subtlety, examine our possible list of excuses? Look at your feet, Rosa's daughters, what do they tell you about your walk today?

If You Only Knew

October 17   *Read 2 Samuel 6:16, 20-22.*

Just when did we decide that praise was a thing to be regulated? It doesn't seem to be such a new idea; for here, we see David's wife, Michal, attempting to regulate the way that he gave thanks to God. He was leaping and dancing in the equivalent of his undergarments. He was happy that he had finally made God happy by bringing the ark home. Have you ever looked at this passage and wondered if some other things might have been on his mind?

No one can describe the sick feeling at the bottom of our stomachs when we know that we are hated by someone we have tried to love. David's past was filled with humiliation, for surely the grapevine also knew that Saul hated him and had wanted to kill him for years. He came to power in the midst of scandal. Could he have been thinking about the wars and struggles with his countrymen and women over his leadership? Doubt has a way of creeping in when there is so much opposition. Did the Lord really want me to be king?

For all we know, he could have finally been celebrating the fall of Goliath. He was a mere youth when he felled Goliath with a stone. The people danced and celebrated his fame. But, what did David do? Did he shiver in fear, or hide embarrassment inspired by the crowds. He may have been worrying about how his brothers would treat him after that day. There are many things that may have been on David's mind when he began to leap and dance and praise the Lord in less than his regular clothes.

What goes on in sister's minds, when they, like David, throw back their heads and shout? What thoughts have set fire to their souls? We might not give any of them a sidelong glance again—if we only knew.

Nothing Can Separate Us From God

October 18   *Read Romans 8:31-39.*

This is probably the most exuberant passage that the apostle Paul ever wrote. He celebrates the fact that God has provided all we need to keep us. Nothing can possibly separate us from Him. We are safe and secure in Jesus.

If God is for us, and He obviously is, who can stand against us? Your enemies' efforts are useless. No weapon or mind game will ever be able to separate you from God. God will continue to stand up for you forever, because Jesus is seated at the right hand of God. You are all right!

Paul seemed to be reading my mind when he wrote this passage. When life rushes along all too quickly, and it feels like no one is there to speak up for us, we need to be reminded that no one can legitimately condemn us. The resurrection of Christ means that He is alive and continues to intercede for us. If there are human beings, or even angels or spirits who would dare to condemn or accuse us, Christ continues to speak on our behalf.

Nothing is capable of functioning as a wedge to alienate us from the love of Christ. Paul confesses that hardships, to include distress, persecution, deprivations, or perils shall never separate us from Christ. They cannot stop the victory that has already been secured through the atonement and Christ's continued intercession for us.

Nothing can influence God against us. Death cannot do it. The hardships and failures of our lives cannot do it. Nothing in our present or past will turn God against us. Angels, rulers, the list continues; high things, low things, nothing can separate us from the love of God.

Our place in God is so secure that nothing can convince God that a repentant believer is not justified in His eyesight. Christ, who has been given as a ransom for us, stands ready to refute any accusation against us. Nothing on earth, in hell, or in heaven is powerful enough to override God's provisions for you and for me. If God be for us, who can stand against us?

Prayer: When I feel condemned, Lord, remind me that absolutely nothing can separate me from your love. Amen.

Caught in the Middle

October 19   *Read Genesis 27:41-45.*

Caught in the middle, between two loved ones for whom you are responsible. Caught in the middle between two warring forces. Caught in the middle and trying not to take sides. Caught in the middle when you know blood could be, has been, and will be shed. Caught in the middle and can't share all the details with anybody.

How many times have you been caught in the middle? We don't talk about this predicament in public too often because it is never pretty, and somebody always loses. Yet there are times when we are caught between people who we love who cannot or will not get along with each other.

Are you right in the middle of the mess? Those two people could be two good friends of yours. Or, they could be coworkers. All too often, they are our children or close family members. Big brother hates little brother, or vice versa, and both accuse you of playing favorites. Or your sister hates your father and you are asked to choose to keep the love of either.

God knows this story, too. Rebekah had two sons, for whom she had prayed. Jacob and Esau were her only two children, and they were twins. From the time that they were conceived, they were trouble. Fighting in the womb, fighting in the birth canal, they made both of their parents weary. Now here they were locked in battle again, about to split the family!

They are about to split the family, and you are caught in the middle! They are about to split the church, which side should you take? They are about to start a riot in your neighborhood, how should you advise them? In times like these, there are no easy answers, no easy solutions. Sometimes, all you can do is stand back, and pray.

Prayer: Lord, today I ask you to bring peace to all who are warring with one another. Please cover a multitude of faults with your love. Amen.

We Must Pray!

October 20   *Read Luke 18:1.*

So often we faint and lose heart when we pray. How many times have we heard phrases like: "My prayers just hit the ceiling and fall to the ground again"? Many of us give up before we ever get started because we feel as if we are bothering God. Sometimes we are reluctant in prayer because we feel as if we have been away from the prayer closet so long that we have no right to really expect God's response in this time of crisis. We often feel unworthy and uninvited when it comes to prayer.

Yet, we are reminded that God always hears us. Jesus told the story of a persistent widow. I am sure that she was tempted to think that her prayers might not be answered. The New Testament encourages us to pray. In Peter's first letter he writes, "the eyes of the Lord are on the righteous, and his ears are open to their prayer" (1 Pet. 3:12). The Gospels are filled with portraits of Jesus praying. We see Him praying when He was tired, praying before major decisions, praying when all was well, and praying when He was in trouble.

The Acts of the Apostles describes how believers like you and me prayed. Exciting things can happen when we pray. In Acts, we find that the church was born and empowered in a prayer meeting (Acts 1:14). Saul of Tarsus, who later became the apostle Paul, heard from Jesus when he prayed. He received a vision of Annanias coming to lay hands upon him for his sight while he prayed (Acts 9). As a result of this prayer meeting, Christian history was altered forever.

Cornelius had a vision that led to his salvation as he prayed. Peter also had a vision on the rooftop as he prayed. As a result of these two prayers and these two visions, the church was flooded with the salvation of Gentiles (Acts 10).

Prisoners were released as a result of prayer. Dead were restored to life. Multitudes were healed; the church was spared. There were episodes of prayer too numerous to tell in the Acts of the Apostles. They were people just like us, made bold and powerful through prayer.

Be encouraged today, God does indeed hear our every prayer. But, in order to be heard, we must first pray!

Secret Service

October 21   *Read Luke 8:1-3.*

Unless times were drastically different, the men probably didn't want those women around either. Their deeds are almost mentioned as their excuse for traveling with Jesus and the twelve. Mary, Joanna, Susanna and many others are early members of an elite secret service that has always been vital to the existence of the church. *They* supported *them* out of their own means.

Of the three mentioned by name, Joanna might have been a woman of means. She was the wife of Chuza, the manager of Herod's household. The rest of them were possibly women like you and me—making sacrifices to support God's work.

God has a secret service today. Thousands of women support God's work from pension checks and minimum wage salaries. They do without fast-food lunches and sculptured nails so the rest of us can worship in nice heated and cooled buildings. They hold rummage sales and fry chickens in their own kitchens to raise money. Some of them just give quietly as a private, secret service to the Lord. These are women who will gladly use their teabags twice; and don't always get new dresses for Easter or Christmas. They wear cotton stockings, because they wear longer and smile at us in our finery. You will rarely see a dedication plaque under the numerous donations they make to the church.

Those who study churches tell us that those active church members in the lower tax brackets tend to give more proportionally of their income to the Lord's work; while those in higher tax brackets give as little as 1 to 2 percent of their increase to their local churches. These women of the secret service tithe and then give love gifts. They take care of preachers and take widows to the doctor. The Lord needs more of them, however, because there are many more widows and emotionally orphaned children that need our help. There are so many more dreams of the church that will never come true unless more of us join the secret service. Is God calling you?

Modern day Marys, Joannas, and Susys: please accept our thanks in case the new preacher didn't know. Please accept our gratitude for the things you have diligently done in secret. The church would not be the same without you.

The Fragrance of Worship

October 22   *Read Exodus 30:34-37.*

The proscribed incense, which would characterize the worship of the tabernacle, and later the temple, teaches us a strange lesson about worship. We imagine it to be the most fragrant smell on earth. In actuality, we may also find it to be the most costly.

This incense appears to be an unusual mixture of sweet spices and frankincense. Most of us know frankincense from the gift of the Wise Men to baby Jesus. It is the resin of a tree that grows in Somalia. Frankincense "tears" are obtained by making deep cuts on the trunk of the tree. The milky juice that comes out and hardens becomes the precious substance that we still use in perfumes.

The sweet spices, to which the Lord refers, are also products of struggle and sacrifice. Stacte is known by some as the balm of Gilead. Others think it may be a form of myrrh obtained by tapping or splitting the tree for its resin. Galbanum is a plant resin only available when this beautiful plant is twisted and broken. Onycha comes from grinding the shells of a warm-water shellfish known for purple dye. All of the ingredients of the fragrant incense of the temple have a story to tell. Each spice, each resin, tells a story of brokenness and sacrifice and struggle.

October

The incense of worship that you offer is also costly. Our lives, like these precious substances, also tell stories punctuated by brokenness, sacrifice, and struggle. Perhaps the plant and animal kingdoms have joined forces to teach us mere mortals that worship is most fragrant when offered through our pain. The sweetest thing we offer to the Lord may possibly be the sound of our worship attempts when we least feel capable of lifting up God's name.

Dare we say that the Lord is compounding a fragrance within each of us to be offered in worship? Perhaps it will be composed of the sum total of the grinding, pounding, tapping, and lashing that each of us has endured.

Like Incense

October 23   *Read Psalm 141:2.*

Incense.
Wafting its way toward the ceiling,
spreading throughout the room.
Incense.
Diffusing,
Becoming a part
    Of the very air itself.
What aspirations for my prayer, O Lord!
    Let my prayer today, be like sweet incense;
The kind that freshens a room.
Let my prayer be fresh and
        Pure
            Free
                From any acid undertones.
Let the meditations that flow from my lips
Be like the welcoming smell of frankincense,
        Perfuming my hair
            Filling the air
                With its heady fragrance.
I pray that you might enjoy my prayer, O Lord.
Let it be like the sweetness of Israel's sacrifice.
Let my prayer be your delight.

Let me be your smile today, my God.
Let my adoration linger around your throne and
Remind You that I love You today.
Let it spread,
 Diffuse,
  Fill the heavenlies,
Like incense.
Incense engulfs my room.
It captures the draperies
 Softens the lighting;
Leaving hints and memories of its burning.
May my prayer be like incense and change my soul as well.
The rooms of my heart
 Are often draped with
  fabric that needs freshening.
Soften my harsh vision.
Leave hints and memories
 of this burning prayer
  within my heart
long after I have risen from this posture.
Let my prayer be like incense.

As incense leaves reminders for all,
 Long after it is spent,
Let there be visible reminders of prayer in me.
Let others know that you are changing me,
 Permanently.
Let my children see a new mother, and
 My spouse a new wife.
Let my mother rejoice
 That her prayers are being answered,
My neighbors smile in quiet amazement.
Create in this daughter of Zion a new outlook,
 Full of fresh optimism
  Sweetness
That can only come from your throne.
Bathe me in the fragrance of worship and prayer
 Then
  Ignite me
So I may burn sweetly—like incense.

Seeing the Harvest

When the Lord called us to serve Him in another country, we were overjoyed! One of our lifelong dreams was going to be fulfilled. My husband and I had been praying to teach and preach in Ghana for more than ten years. Though Ghana is not a mission field, they needed extra teachers in one of their old established Bible colleges. Actually, we were looking forward to what they would teach us about being African and Christian—in exchange for the little bit of knowledge we had about the Bible! For us, this was a once in a lifetime opportunity. We were so happy we could barely contain ourselves.

Early in our investigation of this opportunity, we shared our excitement with a dear friend in our church. We invited him to turn flips and dance along with us. To our surprise, he responded with a forced smile and sad eyes that were on the brink of welled up tears. His reply: "There's a whole mission field in this city, you don't need to go to Africa to look for something to do!"

It goes without saying that his words haunted us. Actually his words were a blessing because they forced us to scrutinize this calling we had received. What were our motives? Why were we going? We finally came to peace with the understanding that for some unknowable reason, the Lord needed us in Ghana at this time in our lives. Yet, our calling does not change the truth of our friend's words—there is a whole mission field in this city!

There's a whole mission field in your backyard! By this, I don't mean just your neighborhood. Your literal backyard may be filled with neighborhood children and teenagers who have never really heard or understood the Christian faith. All parents don't force their children to go to church or to Sunday school. Many parents have given up on the church. Who will offer their children an opportunity to make a decision for or against the church? Is it you?

There is a whole mission field on your job! Some of the men and women with whom you work are starving for answers to life's unsolvable problems. They look for spiritual help in times of crisis. They recognize emptiness and are unsure about the way to approach the God that they already believe in. A bit of compassion, a gentle word of testimony,

God's support coming through you at the right time, may be the deciding factor. God may need you right where you are.

Yes, our friend spoke the truth. We are surrounded by people that still need the Lord. There is a mission field all around us.

Looking for the Lost

Marsha found herself standing outside the door of Vickie's house. Vickie had been out of church ever since she and Leona had worked in the kitchen together for the last church potluck. It seems as though Leona said something uncomplimentary about one of the cakes. She didn't know that it was Vickie's sister's cake! Now Vickie was angry and would not return to church. Someone had to break the silence.

This was the last thing that Marsha wanted to do. As pastor of this small church, however, what else could she do? There was no calling committee; there were no old ladies who could discreetly settle the argument. The fact remained that Vickie was missing from their fellowship and needed to come back.

It would never have done to just let Vickie cool off. She was a recent convert from an addictive lifestyle. Her recovery had been greatly accelerated by the addition of this new family of Christian friends. Marsha, to be honest, was afraid to allow her to become isolated. She feared that Vickie might return to her old lifestyle, her conversion was too recent.

She reached for the door-knocker. Before she could knock on the door, Vickie opened it! "Pastor Marsha! I was hoping you would come." In the conversation that followed, Marsha learned that Vickie had already realized that she shouldn't have got mad and blown up at Leona. She just didn't know how to come back—after all, this church life was new to her!

Most sheep know when they are lost. Some of them just need a gentle nudge to come home.

Equal Pay?

It is no surprise that Jesus became unpopular before His crucifixion. He said too many things that rubbed people the wrong way. This parable about equal wages was one of those characteristic statements that Jesus made about the kingdom of God that humankind just didn't want to hear.

Part of the blessing and the curse of the gospel is the tension that it creates. On the surface, the principle of equal pay looks wonderful. By the grace of God alone, we are all going to heaven. There is nothing we can consciously do to earn a higher position there. Even those who accept Christ at the last moment will be our equals. We nod our heads in assent and cheer for justice and equality.

Then, we are confronted with the new songbird convert in the church choir who captures the hearts of the congregation. We resent her voice, her talents, and her not having come up through the invisible ranks that we created for people like her. We resist the new businesswoman who joins the church and immediately assumes a position on the finance committee. We think that she doesn't know us well enough, or hasn't been around long enough to speak for us in such delicate matters. We squeeze out the welfare mother, claiming that we are just being scriptural by "learning those that labor among us." While all along, we are really just suspicious about her morals because of our stereotypes.

The principle of equal pay pinches like a shoe that is too tight because it forces us all to acknowledge that none of us is worthy of the kingdom of heaven. The whole paycheck is just a gift!

For Single Parents

Lord, in this day and age, it really does take more than one person to rear a child. For various reasons, too many sisters have become the only visible parent in their children's lives. Thank you, Parent-God, for being with them.

When they are hidden from public view, left to make critical decisions, be their consultant and their guide. When they are tired and don't need to hear another voice calling for mother's care, help their children to be peaceful. When they are lonely, and feel isolated from social life and friends, be the friend they need for that moment.

Lord, single mothers often become the focal point of criticism, a scapegoat, or a statistic. Hide them in the center of your love from undue public scrutiny. Create in us the kind of surrogate mothers, sisters, and aunts they need. Show us how to support, without meddling, to comfort without crippling. Transform us into communities of faith that will contribute to the wholeness of both parent and child. Amen.

I Am Not Perfect!

October 28　　　　　　　　　　　　　　　　*Read 1 Peter 4:7-8.*

"I am not perfect!" No statement is more true of me, and of you. I am not perfect! In a world that demands perfection, that refuses to overlook or forgive mistakes, these words are often used defensively. These words are usually used as the last shameful resort when honor backs us into the corner, when we miss a meeting, forget a birthday, or say the wrong things. We often hide the last shred of our self-esteem behind the words: I AM NOT PERFECT!

In a world that reminds us daily of our imperfection, we, as people of color, need the Christian community as a place of refuge. If we refuse to accept one another in church, where else will we go? If we throw unwed mothers out of church, where will they go? If we refuse to counsel and teach misguided teens, gangs and drugs may be the only other offer they will receive. If we turn our backs upon those with AIDS, who will teach them of the kingdom of heaven?

The Christian community is designed to be a place where people who are not perfect can come together with a common bond, the forgiveness of Christ. The Christian community is also meant to be a place of forgiveness. It can become a place where we accept others, who like us, are imperfect. Christian communities can truly become places where we live by the perfect law of love—which seeks to bring out the best in every person no matter how far they have fallen.

The good news of the gospel is that Christ died for the imperfect. Jesus died for those who run stoplights, blunder with their lips, or break the Law. While we were yet sinners, Christ died for the ungodly (Rom. 5:8). None of us is perfect. Perhaps that is why Peter, in this passage, reminds his readers that love covers a multitude of sins.

Environmental Concerns

October 29   *Read Proverbs 29:8.*

People in some other countries have an interesting attitude toward the people we regard in this country as a nuisance, people like petty thieves and beggars. In other cultures, people assume responsibility for one another and feel that they, as a community, have failed their brothers and sisters when they are forced to commit crimes to survive. According to this worldview, they, too, are sinners because they created a social environment that offers no other options.

It appears that we have much to learn from the example of other countries. Perhaps one of the more vital questions to ask, as we consider the crime and moral degradation around us, is the part we have all played in creating such an environment. We are not separate from our natural environment. The barrels of industrial waste that we hide during this generation come back to haunt our genes in the next. The waters we pollute today are unable to sustain us tomorrow. The trees we devour take years to grow again.

What about our spiritual environment? Perhaps we should ask ourselves if little ones, who frequently cheat on school exams, are under too much pressure too early in their lives. Is there anything in the spiritual environment that makes drugs, teenage pregnancy, and gang activity such attractive alternatives for our youth? Could it be that we have made it possible for honesty to become our second choice? Our spiritual environment obviously needs help.

Thank God that we are not helpless. God's reconciling activity among us recreates people, places, and even the spiritual climate that makes faith responses possible. Today, as you pray, why not ask the Lord to show you what can be done in your immediate family to re-create an environment of honesty, hope, and trust.

Leaven

October 30   *Read Luke 13:20-21.*

They really didn't want her on the city council. She was a housewife and a mother. She hadn't even gone to college! She was an unknown, which really meant that they did not know if they could predict her votes. And, she was over fifty. How could such a person make decisions for the city? The other city council members were quite disturbed and apprehensive when Ruby joined their ranks.

Ruby was elected because the people knew her; though some wondered if she would really be able to make a difference. They knew that she was a moral woman who did not mind speaking up. They also knew that she would be nearly impossible to bribe. The people of Fernville hoped that her term of office would be the beginning of some changes—if she could endure the pressure.

At first, the other council members did try to ridicule her. After a few shed tears, however, Ruby toughened up and put one of the men on the spot—publicly. "What purpose do you intend to serve by . . . ." He was exposed in the presence of the voters. Like any good politician, he backed down.

Over the next two years, we have no idea what happened behind closed doors. In public, however, we did see a change. It began with the jokes, or should we say the absence of certain kinds of jesting. Gradually, the people on the council seemed to become more sensitive to ways that the city could help the poor folks on the north end of town. Fire hydrants began to appear in remote areas. Crews of volunteers were organized to clean the city's parks. Finally, they began to invite local pastors to their meetings to offer the invocation. All in all, things changed in Fernville—with a little bit of leaven.

God calls all of us to be leaven in this world. Don't despair if you are the only godly person on your job or on your committee. It only takes one to start a *change-reaction.*

Walk On, Walk On

It's just as hard to determine why Peter began to sink as it is to figure out why things may seem more difficult for us this year. Maybe we need to find out what has changed. True enough, the world has changed and things seem harder for everyone. On the other hand, we are one year wiser.

An old woman once said that she had forgotten more about life than I yet knew. At the time, I was offended, because I thought that I knew it all. As the years went by, I discovered how much I didn't know and could appreciate her rebuke. Now, I am approaching a stage of life where I am learning to remember what I have forgotten.

It may sound like double-talk, but think about it. What things have we forgotten that were vital to our well-being? Have we forgotten how to be happy when our bank accounts are empty? Have we forgotten how much we *don't* need to be happy?

Have we forgotten how to look good when we didn't feel so good? The extra preparation often changed a blue day into a forget-me-not day. We learned on those days that we were able to determine, to a great extent by our attitudes, the outcome of the day. Learn to remember what you have forgotten.

Have we forgotten how to walk without a visible means of support? Thats what this incident with Peter was all about. He was out walking on the water with Jesus. Jesus was his primary support. When he took his eyes off Jesus, his rational mind remembered that he was not being supported in the customary ways. That's when he fell. And, that's when we fall.

It's so much easier to live a predictable life. Life, unfortunately, refuses to be tamed and often lashes out at us in unpredictable ways. If we don't keep our eyes on Jesus, most of life will not make sense and its waves will threaten to drown us. The truth is, we really don't make it very well on the visible conventional supports. Our support comes from the Lord, and always has. So, walk on, and don't look down!

November

Yes, Jesus Loves Me

November 1   *Read John 3:16.*

God loves this world. God loves the people within it. Though we have been tragically separated from God by sin, God's love never has been conditional. When we do not know that we are out of order, God loves us. When we do not want God to interrupt the selfish flow of our lives, God loves us. When we do not love ourselves (or anyone else), God loves us. God loves us individually; God loves humankind collectively. We are the part of creation created in God's image—and God loves us!

> Jesus loves me! This I know,
> for the Bible tells me so.

No sacrifice was too costly or precious to restore what God lost when creation was spoiled. Within the divine community of Creator, Christ, and Spirit, what a sacrifice Jesus must have been! Christ was as important to the Divine as children are to their parents. God so loved the world. . . .

> Little ones to him belong;
> they are weak, but he is strong.

Except we come as children, we cannot really see what God has done. We jump in front of the line and beg others to see how we can shine— with just a little bit of help from God. When we come as grown folks, beating our own drum or chairing our own fan club, we shove the power of God, through Christ, into the background.

Except we acknowledge that we are little ones, we will never be great in God's eyes. Those who insist on being big in comparison to others are more like underdeveloped adolescent girls flirting for attention, or like little boys comparing yet-to-be-refined muscles with one another. Apart from God's love, we are insignificant. Yet God, who alone is great, still loves us!

> *Yes, Jesus loves me! Yes, Jesus loves me!*
> *Yes, Jesus loves me! the Bible tells me so.*

One Flesh

November 2   *Read Genesis 2:20-24.*

The sunlight was bright and warm that day. It pierced through the closed eyelids of the sleeping woman. Her eyelids fluttered and finally opened in response. She awakened to see her husband, who had been watching her sleep for what seemed like hours. A serene smile rose in response to his. She seemed to have been responding to everything all of her life. Finally, she spoke.

"Adam?"

"Yes, Eve."

"Isn't this a wonderful morning?"

"Yes, but it's not morning anymore. The sun has been up for hours and I've been anxiously waiting for you to wake up. I haven't seen you for a very long time."

"Really?" She sat up. "I must have dreamed that I was already awake." Have you ever done that? You know, dreamed that you were walking and talking and had even gone to work only later to wake up and discover that you were still in bed? "What did you do while I was asleep— besides watch me sleep?"

"I did everything, Eve." Adam began to tease her. "I said everything, I did everything, I thought everything for the both of us!" By then he was laughing. "Whew! I'm tired!" They both burst into laughter.

"No really, what did you do while I was asleep?"

"I already told you," he had stopped teasing, "while you were sleeping, I did everything for both of us. I think it's time you got up from your dream world to help. Get up, sleepy-head. The day is almost gone!"

"And, what makes you think that I can do so much? Huh?"

"I know what you are capable of doing because God made you and me from the same stuff. Did you forget how you came to be? You are a part of me. Now, let's get back to work—together."

Eve rose from her long nap, and resumed her work, walking by Adam's side. Gradually, she and Adam began to talk together, work together, and even think together—like one flesh. Finally, they began to rebuild together, side-by-side. I wonder if she chose the side with the missing rib?

Take Up Your Bed and Walk

November 3   *Read John 5:2-8.*

I have grown tired
of hearing the same
old complaint
and history of your misery
day after day
time after time
when we meet.

I find it
much more convenient
to avoid your company
and leave you by the poolside
finding other ears to bend
who have not heard the story
of how you came to be
on your pallet
by that pool.

You made your bed
so close
to the healing waters
that you could have
seen your way through
were you not so intent
on making us feel sorry
for you

for your misery
for being well ourselves.

I have
needed
the healing waters
myself
yet chose not to go
because
I just could not
hear
your story one more time.

For thirty-eight
years
you
have been in this condition
refusing God's grace
through angels of mercy.
Preferring rather
the notoriety
of having endured sickness
longer
than the rest of us.

Are you still
lying by the side
of the pool?

I thought
that Jesus told you
to take up your bed and walk!

Tightrope

November 4   *Read Luke 20:24-26.*

As a child, did you ever stretch a rope across the floor and pretend
that you were a tightrope walker in the circus? Perhaps you even bor-

rowed an umbrella and dramatized the danger of your walk across an empty chasm. Maybe what you did was not playing but practicing—life is a tightrope.

Jesus was aware that he lived on a tightrope. As God in the flesh, He was forced to live on the narrow line between two worlds. As Creator, Sovereign, and Christ, He had the right to demand tribute. As a human being, under Roman jurisdiction, He was required to pay taxes. His critics, aware of His controversial nature, wanted to see where He would declare allegiance. If He claimed to be heavenly and exempt, they had Him. If He claimed to be a subject of Rome like the rest of the people, then according to logic, He could not also be heavenly. In setting up this test they hoped to put an end to any sensationalism surrounding Jesus, once and for all.

We, as African-Americans live on a similar tightrope. W.E.B. DuBois called our dilemma "double-consciousness." We are citizens of two worlds, Western and African. As women, we are part of a third world of existence. They all demand tribute from us. We are granted exemption in none of them. We are also citizens of heaven, with all of its duties, rights, and privileges. How shall we resolve such a great series of contradictions?

Look to Jesus for wisdom. Learn to recognize where issues belong, while maintaining personal integrity. It will probably become necessary to pay some form of tribute while you are here.

Partnership

November 5   *Read John 2:7-10.*

From the beginning, we have been partners with Christ. People like you and me were involved with the first miracle at the wedding, which took place at Cana in Galilee. Jesus could have discreetly added wine to the wine barrels without anyone's knowledge of its origins. Instead, Christ chose to establish a future pattern by involving regular, everyday, common people in the process.

What, possibly, can we do in a partnership with God? What did they do? At Jesus' instruction, they filled the water jars with water. They did what they could and Jesus did the rest. The Gospels are punctuated with examples of partnership. Before Jesus would miraculously feed more than five thousand people, He challenged His disciples to do what they could. "What can you find among the people?" he asked. Regular people rolled the stone away from the mouth of Lazarus's tomb. Regular people brought sick people to Jesus for healing. Regular people also came for their own healing.

Perhaps partnership is a precedent to be observed even today. The Lord tends to involve us, in ways that do not exceed our capability, in miraculous works. As you pray for miracles, don't forget to ask the Lord to show you what to do, too!

All Things to All People

November 6   *Read 1 Corinthians 9:19-23.*

Dear Lord,

I am in the process of trying to become all things to all people like Paul did. I am not as successful as I would like to be. Let me give you a few examples of what has happened.

I put on my jeans, in my own little effort to reach the youth group. My own daughter, who is thirteen, told me that no one wears tight jeans anymore, and besides my jeans looked too new for anyone to believe I wore them at any other time. I am grateful she at least talked to me about it. The other girls in the youth group said nothing; they just rolled their eyes and sighed.

Then, I tried to connect with my son's friends. This time I put on my husband's baggy jeans and a big flannel shirt. Things were going pretty well until I said, "Right On!" At that point, I was left out of the conversation. One by one, they slipped out of the room. After they left, my son didn't say much to me—for a week.

When that didn't work, I put on an old dress and went downtown to talk to some questionable looking women. A couple of them saw me getting out of my Benz and laughed! One even asked if I was an undercover cop. Although I know that you have heard it all, I won't tell you what name they called me.

I don't understand what went wrong, Lord. I did what I could to look like I fit in with all of those people. Before I tried anything else, I felt that I should hear from you.

You don't expect me to change my lifestyle or anything, do you?

Respectfully,
Ann

Dear Ann,
Why not?

With all my love,
JC

The Devil Made Me Do It!

November 7   *Read Romans 7:21-25a.*

Josephine was fit to be tied. She worked at the dry cleaners and hated the job to begin with. She was weary of handling everybody's dirty clothes day after day. She was tired of the heat. Her back hurt from standing over the pressing boards. Her feet were often so swollen that she carried her shoes to the car at the end of the day. And, she hated the woman that worked in the area next to hers.

That woman, her name was Belle, kept up more mess! They earned the same pay—minimum wage. How did Belle ever decide that she was Josephine's supervisor? Some days, she took it upon herself to examine Josephine's work. She even had the nerve to report her opinions to the manager! The manager, in turn, was unwise enough to double check Josephine's work, while ignoring the informant. Each day, it took all the religion that Josephine had to walk away from Belle.

Well, one day, as Josephine tells it, something got into her. Belle gave her report to the manager one time too many and Josephine let her have it! We are not just talking about words; we're talking about rolling in the floor! It didn't take long for the manager to get involved.

"Josephine! Belle! What is going on here?" Belle told a very biased story, using the words like an innocent bystander. Josephine attempted to describe how this incident was really just the straw that broke the camel's back. Later, when remorsefully relating the incident to her husband, all she could say was that the devil must have got into her. Why hadn't she held her temper?

Do you also find yourself saying, "The devil must have got into me?" Thank God that Paul was brave enough to write about the struggle that many of us have. It is difficult to hold on in the face of great temptation. We however, are not powerless, unless we try to overcome temptations by using our own willpower. It seems as though the key to victorious living is to truthfully acknowledge that alone, we are powerless. We can only be victorious when we turn our backs on the devil's suggestions, and ask for God's strength, through Jesus Christ.

Don't let the devil make you do anything today!

Living in the Faith

November 8   *Read 2 Corinthians 13:5.*

Paul encouraged some Christians he knew to live in the faith. One would think that the lives of Christians were automatically guided by what they believed, but most of us know this as a goal remaining to be attained. Paul's words could have been written to any number of us today. What does it mean to live in the faith?

Where do I live now? Some days I live in the neighborhood of fear. I am driven by it. On those days, I fear that I may not meet everyone else's expectations. Some days I am imprisoned by a fear that I will be misunderstood. On the days that I live in the New Fear Annex of the city, I fear what others think of me or what others might do to me socially, politically, or emotionally. Yet, in my heart, I know that faith and fear are opposites. How can this place, in which I have taken refuge more than once, be in the faith?

Where do you live? Do you live in the self-pity district of the city? So many of us sisters do. That district has passed an ordinance that encourages complaining and excuses. Any level of despair is acceptable as long as you start your sentence with the words, "I can't because. . . ." Don't you know that moping, depression, and discouragement, have no place in Faith City.

Just where do you and I live? Do we live in that exclusive suburb called Situational Morality, right off Fibber's Highway, where truth-telling is fine only as long as it is beneficial? Do we live on the outskirts of town, where it is okay to cheat for a good cause; or to turn deaf ears or blinded eyes to the sins of those we love?

Faith City has plenty of room. Its hotels always have vacancies. There are plenty of lots upon which to build a new home. The city is character-ized by righteousness, peace, and joy in the Holy Spirit. Its inhabitants are filled with a faith that drives away fear, depression, and torment. After living in Faith City for a time, its inhabitants learn to defend their convictions, even when it hurts, and to face their problems with the assurance that God is with them. I wish I lived there, don't you?

There are so many alternative neighborhoods where Christians choose to reside. Today's passage challenges all of us to live in the faith.

Remember and Thank God

November 9   *Read Psalm 107:1-2.*

Why is it so hard to say thanks? Is it that we are ungrateful or forget-ful? The psalmist in today's psalm is reminding Israel, and us, to give thanks.

Gratitude requires two things: recognition and memory. It's not hard to recognize what God has done for each of us. God has spared us from a great deal of misery. Several college students have, on more than one occasion, shared a secret fantasy with me. Honestly forgetting the pecu-liar dynamic between Black women and White women in America they asked: "Wouldn't it be nice to have been born in pioneer days?" "Think of the neat clothes we could wear. . . ." Each time, I have had to debate with myself. Could I, should I, did I need to remind them that under such circumstances I would have most likely been their slave? At such times, I am forced to recognize at least one thing that God has done for me!

How could our collective memory be so short? We, like Israel, were once slaves. We were hard afflicted. College was out of the question; vacations were a pipedream. Jobs were so scarce that no one would dream of taking the day off to shop! We cried out to the Lord. Just as the Lord sent Moses to the Jews, he sent Martin and Malcolm to us. They were Moses in two bodies, like perfectly matched bookends. One there to remind us of judgment, the other to remind us of mercy. Though life is far from perfect, we do see answered prayers within our reach. Soon, however, even these vivid memories fade and we forget to give thanks.

Can you remember what life was like before your microwave oven? *O give thanks to the LORD!* What were finances like before that promotion? *For his steadfast love endures forever.* How did you feel before your operation? Were you afraid that you might not wake up from anesthesia? Was there a chance that it might be malignant? Did you miss disaster by a quarter of an inch? *Let the redeemed of the LORD say so.*

Are we forgetful, or ungrateful? You decide. Either way, we must recognize what the Lord has done and remember to give thanks.

Jealousy

November 10   *Read 1 Samuel 18:6-9.*

Nobody wanted that giant alive. He was terrorizing the armies of Israel. David had gone from shepherd to champion in just a few hours. The giant was dead, the army was routed, and the people were safe. All was well, except for the fact that the king despised David. Saul became insanely jealous!

What causes some people to become jealous of others? From all appearances, Saul had no real reason to be jealous of David. David was merely a youth. Saul was a large, handsome man who stood head and shoulders above his fellows. He was the first king of Israel. In other words, Saul had it going on! Why would he despise David?

Could it be that he hated David's popularity? Women danced in the streets chanting "Saul has killed thousands, but David tens of thousands." They were making comparisons; and, all of a sudden, people did not admire Saul quite as much as they had before.

Comparisons can be dangerous. They divert our attention from God's blessings. Whenever an exceptional person enters our midst, they do so because God has gifted them in some special way. Some of them may be called to do a job that benefits others, like slaying the Goliaths of our day. Others are called to formulate ideas that we need. At this time, David was a gift from God. Saul could not receive and accept God's gift because he really secretly felt that he already *was* God's gift. Sound familiar?

All good gifts come from God. Air, water, shelter, even helpful people are gifts to the human community from God. When we lose sight of God, the giver of gifts, jealousy can easily creep in the door along with pride. Pride and jealousy are really branches of the same tree. Both the proud person and the jealous person have lost sight of God, who really deserves all the praise.

The next time someone tries to bait you by calling attention to the superlative deeds of someone you know, why not surprise them with a hearty, "Praise the Lord!"

Growin'

November 11   *Read Luke 2:52.*

When we think of personal spirituality, we usually focus on those things that relate to spiritual practices like prayer or Bible reading. We may even focus on how we treat our neighbors in an attempt to live a balanced Christian life. This one scripture, however, seems to point to all aspects of life. As Luke, the beloved physician, describes the "hidden" years of the boy Jesus, he outlines four areas of growth.

The first of these is wisdom. Someone has called wisdom "applied knowledge." Jesus, of course, knew quite a bit. The use of the word wisdom, which parallels the word for Wisdom used in Proverbs, indicates that He knew what to do with His knowledge in order to reach His goal. The Greek word used for growth, in this passage, could also be translated "kept advancing." So, to paraphrase, "Jesus kept advancing in wisdom. . . ." The continued challenge to seek wisdom is one we all aspire to accept.

The next portion of this scripture speaks of favorable relationships with both God and humankind. The challenge comes to be sure that no offense or omission hinders our relationship with either God or with people.

Perhaps a more intimidating area, however, is this last one: stature. It appears that Jesus grew in normal healthy physical stature. The challenge for us, regarding this point, is to pay more attention to our stature. Good health and physical well-being are also important to our spiritual health. This means that overwork and poor eating habits are not compatible with spiritual maturity. OOPS! Why is it so easy to apologize for the abuse that we give our bodies.

Our prayer for today is that we might exercise the same care and concern for our physical health that we exercise for things that pertain to our souls.

The Days of Onions and Leeks

November 12   *Read Numbers 4-6.*

There is something about remembering the "good old days" that brings tears to certain eyes. What are your memories of the past? I remember the days of chittlin suppers and social gatherings in the basement before we were admitted to some of the finer places in town. I remember dressing up for Easter, "doin' hair," and making ice cream in the summertime. I remember hot summer nights before air conditioning, and sitting on the porch naming the stars and constellations. I remember my great-uncles' corny jokes and lightning bugs. Do you remember some good old days?

As horrible as life had been for Israel, they thought of their past as the good old days. They were in transit between oppression and blessing. They still needed to unlearn dysfunctional thought patterns. The uncertainty of the present made their past seem attractive. How could they grow tired of the manna that God rained from heaven every day? All they had to do was gather what they needed! They had amnesia. They forgot hard labor, hard times, and scratching in the ground for onions, garlic, and leeks! Are we like that?

When the present is harsh, we, too, are tempted to glamorize the past.

Our faulty memories tell us that the past was better, the grass was greener, and the days were easier. We forget that chittlins were meant to be
an insult, and that the past is sprinkled with much more difficulty than
we remember. We are also in transit between dysfunction and blessing.
There are many troubled thought patterns to unlearn. If we are honest
with ourselves, we may find that much of our past was filled with
scratching the ground for onions and leeks.

While we are in transit, it's okay to think back on the pleasant days
that God has given. However, no matter how good the past looks in retrospect, it cannot compare with the blessings of the future and the
lessons of the present. God has promised us a land of milk and honey—
not onions and leeks. We can't go back.

Do Something!

In Oklahoma, we had teachers who were very involved in our future.
Some of our teachers had been students in that old broken down school
and were products of what we then considered an inferior education.
They never referred to us as inferior; we were the future of our community. When we got too content, they would challenge us to do something. Even if it's the wrong thing, one of my teachers said, "Do something."

As we read today's passage, I can almost hear Jesus' mother challenging Him to do something! Running out of wine at a wedding was a great
source of humiliation and embarrassment. The family was obviously of
ordinary means and was not prepared for the scores of guests that had
come. Mary was concerned about her friends.

I hoped that you noticed the interaction between mother and son.
Mary ignores Him; pretends that He has not protested. She tells the
servants to do whatever He told them. His mother knew that He was
special. She knew His heart and was certain that He would do something.

Note the ordinary nature of what Jesus told the servants to do: Fill the
water pots with water. Miracles break into our everyday ordinary rou-

tine. Jesus was born to an ordinary young woman. The ordinary shepherds were the first to hear of His birth. Now, this first of many miracles was taking place at an ordinary wedding. And, Jesus gave the servants an ordinary task.

After filling the water jars, they were instructed to draw some out and take it to the head of the banquet. Did you notice that they received two sets of instructions before they actually saw a miracle? We can't be sure if the servants were even able to pinpoint when the actual miracle took place!

Somewhere, while they were in the process of obedience, a miracle occurred. They had enough! They had more than enough! They had good quality wine! The guests never knew.

Somewhere, in the midst of your obedience to what you have understood God to say to you, a miracle is waiting. It may not occur after your first act of obedience. It may not even come after your tenth response; but a miracle is waiting for you in the mundaneness of everyday life. Be like Mary. Know His heart. Sooner or later, He will do something!

Praise God!

November 14   *Read Psalm 100:1-5.*

How exciting it is to read the Psalms! The psalms were actually the hymnbook of Israel. When I need to be in touch with how human I am, I find myself there. The psalmists talk about anxieties, fears, angers, and joys. Today's psalm is noted for its joyous tone.

We are exhorted to shout for joy to the Lord! How is it that we are just a little bit embarrassed when this actually does happen! When we stop to think of the greatness and the uniqueness of our relationship with God, it would seem to be impossible to remain silent.

John, the beloved, was given the rare opportunity to see what happens in the "praise life of heaven." In the fourth chapter of Revelation he saw the twenty-four elders, dressed in white with crowns on their heads. He heard thunderings and rumblings and saw flashes of lightning from the throne. Around the throne were four living creatures; one like a lion, one like an ox, one with the face of a man, and the fourth like a flying eagle.

Day and night they never stopped saying, "Holy, holy, holy, the Lord God the Almighty, who was and is and is to come" (4:8). Simultaneously the twenty-four elders fell down before the throne saying: "You are worthy, our Lord our God, to receive glory and honor and power, for you created all things, and by your will they existed and were created" (4:11).

In the midst of all this excitement, John heard the voices of thousands upon ten thousands of angels saying, "Worthy is the Lamb that was slaughtered to receive power and wealth and wisdom and might and honor and glory and blessing!" (5:12). And the litany in heaven was joined by every creature in heaven and on earth and under the earth and on the sea singing, "To the one seated on the throne and to the Lamb be blessing and honor and glory and might, forever and ever!" (5:13).

Imagine God's invitation to join in the litanies of praise that continue day and night and are conducted by angels, elders, living creatures, and every creature created on earth?

I will enter his gates with thanksgiving. I will enter his courts with praise. I will give thanks to Him and bless his name.

Lamplight

November 15   *Read Matthew 25:1-4.*

Keep your lamps trimmed and burning
Keep your lamps trimmed and burning
Keep your lamps trimmed and burning
Time is drawing nigh!

It's absolute foolishness to try to make it through the night without enough oil in your lamp. Five of these bridesmaids took extra oil, and five of them thought that they could make it with what they had. There are days when I am like one of those foolish bridesmaids, thinking that I am so together that I really don't need any extra help. I always discover, sometimes too late, that I need the oil of the Holy Ghost to maintain my place in God until Jesus returns. Wise woman? Foolish woman? Which one are you?

> Children don't get weary
> Children don't get weary
> Children don't get weary
> Till your work is done.

Keeping a light going in this dark and dreary world is a lot of work. Hold your temper. See things their way. Bend over backward. Turn the other cheek. Look for the lost. Teach your children how to pray. Quit that job if they ask you to lie. When does it ever end! I need something extra in my life so I can live in the faith. Oil of the Holy Spirit, flow over my soul.

> Christian journey soon be over
> Christian journey soon be over
> Christian journey soon be over
> Time is drawing nigh!

While we are waiting for Jesus' return, it seems like the day will never break. It seems as if night will never end. Look at the skies and learn a lesson about God. Night never goes on forever. The sun always rises. It may be obscured from our view by the clouds, but it has risen, nonetheless.

Your life and mine won't always be this procession of struggles. One day, we won't have to work so hard to keep a light shining. For one day, "there will be no more night; they need no light of lamp or sun, for the Lord God will be their light, and they will reign forever and ever" (Rev. 22:5).

> *Children don't get weary*
> *Till your work is done.*

Stepping Out on a Miracle

November 16   *Read Matthew 14:28-29.*

Walking on the water! Peter? Why not? Peter is one of my favorite persons in the Gospels. He is imperfect, like me. He makes mistakes, like mine. He puts his foot in his mouth, just like me. When I see Peter walk on the water, I know that I can have faith too.

The timing of Peter's walk is crucial. They had just been on the mountain with thousands of people. Jesus had compassion upon the crowds who followed Him. He healed their sick and walked among them. Evening had come and they wouldn't go home. He fed them, all of them. They numbered five thousand males plus the women and children that also came.

The story of the feeding of five thousand is familiar. It was a miracle! It followed numbers of miraculous healings. The atmosphere was unnaturally charged with the supernatural!

Peter was right there. I believe that he was an energy-charged boisterous man. He was right there on a spiritual high! Peter was there, and the Holy Spirit was teaching him to believe. Peter was, perhaps, the kind of man who longed to try what he had seen. Peter was so much like us.

Should we make Peter an honorary Black woman? You see, sisters, we are known for our adventurous spirits. We are known for succeeding at the impossible. We are frequent witnesses to the unnaturally charged atmosphere of the supernatural. We love to see God at work.

In this context, it seems most natural for Peter to walk on the water. It is most natural for you, too. Without stopping to consider the dangers, Peter stepped out of the comfort and safety of the boat. He placed the full weight of his trust upon Jesus, and Jesus made a steady place for his feet.

We live in an environment where God is constantly working miracles. Look around you and you will see miracles of healing, of restoration, and of provision. Listen to the testimony of those who have received the compassion of Christ. Finally, when Jesus calls for you to come out of the boat, don't be afraid to put the full weight of your trust upon Him. He is trustworthy. Just ask Peter!

No Right Turn on Red

November 17   *Read Numbers 9:15-18.*

God was acting like a traffic light. When the cloud was over the tabernacle, they did not go forward. Wherever the cloud rested, that's where the Israelites camped. God had freed them and they were happy to obey the signals.

When I was out driving one evening, it suddenly occurred to me that God's direction is like a traffic light in our lives. When I was young, and thought that I knew everything, I was impatient at traffic lights. I felt as if I could see everything ahead without some machine arbitrarily telling me to wait! After a couple of close calls at stop signs, and seeing accidents when some unsuspecting motorist ran a red light, I began to appreciate the wisdom of waiting until directed to proceed.

Traffic laws have a loophole. Normally, if you are turning right, and see no traffic coming, most states allow you to use your own judgment and proceed carefully. Sometimes, however, this is not safe. "No Turn on Red" signs restrict our ability to proceed on our own at dangerous intersections.

Now, I am most fascinated by the "No Turn on Red" signs. When I am waiting for the light to turn green, I try to detect the hidden hazard. Sometimes it is dangerous because vehicles are entering the road from an unexpected direction. Other times there are blind spots or curves. There are times when I cannot detect where the potential problems are; but I am learning to trust that some specialist has seen them and that the sign has been placed there for my safety.

In concept, stop signs, traffic lights, and "No Turn on Red" signs are designed to restrict us in order to keep us safe. This is what God was doing for Israel, and what He really would like to do for us. It is not always safe for us to use our own judgment and proceed with caution. Who knows what dangers lie ahead if we proceed without notice? What may be around the corner traveling at breakneck speed? God knows everything. He sees what we cannot see. Sometimes He must restrict us to keep us.

May the "No Turn on Red" signs in our lives prompt us to listen to God more intently. Have patience, red lights do eventually turn green!

Hidden Heart

November 18   *Read Psalm 139:23-24.*

History records some of the reasons why David prayed this prayer. The indiscretion with Bathsheba, trouble in his household, and division within the kingdom were adequate reasons to ask the Lord to search his heart. David did not have the luxury of contemplating in private. His sins were made public. I feel fortunate to be able to privately ponder the condition of my heart.

There are days when I don't know what is in my heart. These, especially, are the times when I need for you to search my heart, O Lord. Yelling words, angry words, sometimes pour from my mouth and surprise both their targets and me. From where did such wicked sentiments come? Indeed, "The heart is devious above all else; it is perverse—who can understand it?" (Jer. 17:9). Search me and cleanse me, O God.

Other times, it is not the words, but the thoughts that shock me most. When did I develop such a mean spirit? I had a much better upbringing than this. I am thankful that no one around me can hear my thoughts, and I am shamed by the thought that God heard them in an unguarded moment.

The heart is just a house. It is a storing place for that which I am. Out of its storehouses flow an abundance of what is inside. Clean my house, Holy Spirit. Blow even the dust from its rooms so that nothing may pour from this house but remembrances of you.

As I walk with you today, Lord, render me harmless, while you and I work on the fine details of my life. Amen.

Which One?

"There they go again, taking up all the seats in church!" Denise was annoyed at the number of welfare mothers who had begun to come to her neighborhood church. The new minister had preached this gospel of open arms and her arms were tired! "There they go, she thought," with their ratty wigs and their turned-over shoes. What must people think about our church! Her eyes followed one of the ladies to the altar who knelt meekly to pray.

"Lord, thank you for letting me come to your house. The people seem so nice here. I know that I'm not much, but I offer whatever I can do for you. I only pray that the folks here will keep on loving me and keep on working with me while you clean me up and make me what you want me to be."

Denise couldn't hear the young woman's prayer, but she could see the hole in the bottom of her shoe while she was kneeling. It was almost a flashback. Suddenly she was a little girl, looking at a similar shoe—her mother's. Denise remembered her mother's old run-down church. Hardwood floors that needed attention. Pews with attack splinters waiting to snag the visitors. The piano with yellowed keys that hadn't held a decent tune since the Depression. She remembered her mother kneeling at the front of the church in this same meek way, praying for her and her sisters, talking to God about the neighborhood, and thanking God for food and shelter.

Shame flushed hotly over Denise's face. Had it not been for God's grace, she could be kneeling there with a hole in the bottom of her shoe! By now the tears had begun to roll under her chin. Quietly, she slipped out of her seat and rushed to the altar to kneel beside the unknown woman.

"Lord, forgive me," her prayer began. Tell me, which one went home justified?

Prayer: Lord, we have all come from humble beginnings. Help us to learn that your grace erases the lines that separate economic classes, racial groups, and genders. Amen.

No More Tears

November 20   *Read Revelation 7:13-17.*

It has often been said that the book of Revelation is a window. Through it we see pictures of the end times and pictures of heaven. If this is true, who are those people whom we, through the eyes of John the Revelator, see?

We see the saints. Some people call them the ancestors. They are those who have gone before us and stand continually in the presence of God. They live in a place where hunger, thirst, and sorrow have ceased to be distractions. They have the peculiar distinction of having robes that became clean after having been dipped in blood. This is symbolic of the redemption of Christ that purifies believers. Their purification, and the very fact that they have been given the privilege of standing in the presence of God, gives them a reason to worship God day and night within His temple.

There is nothing that they are doing there that you cannot do here and now for the same reasons. You have an absolute right to praise God right now. There is no need to wait. Push past hindering distraction. You have already come through great ordeals and have lived to tell your story! You have been washed and are free from sin. Jesus knows your new name. You have been transformed from a liar to a person of integrity, from a thief to one who builds up the kingdom of God. You have been changed from sinner to saint and need not wait until you become one of the ancestors to worship before God's throne.

So, lift up your hands, your voice, your heart in worship until you finally reach the shore of the land where there are no more tears.

Keeping On

November 21   *Read 1 Thessalonians 5:12-18.*

Today's passage concludes with the words, "for this is the will of God in Christ Jesus for you." I have been looking for a certain way to find myself in the will of God. Have you?

Rejoice always. Pray without ceasing. Give thanks in all circumstances. The verb tenses used in the Greek could have been translated: Keep on rejoicing. Keep on praying. Keep on giving thanks.

Do you find it hard to keep on rejoicing? The epistle writer understood, from his personal experiences, that life seems to try its best to wipe the smile off our faces. Some days it feels like the devil is even after the spring in your step! We would not be encouraged to keep on giving thanks if it were not possible. These words would never have been written if continual rejoicing were a human habit.

Maybe it's easier for you to keep on praying. There are so many reasons to keep on praying. We keep on praying for times to get better. We can keep on praying for loved ones who are distant from God. We can keep on praying for safety in the midst of terrorism. We can keep on praying for a number of things. And, if we could keep on praying, it would be so much easier to keep on rejoicing!

Finally, keep on giving thanks. For what will we give thanks? Thank God for the blessings of the present. No matter how poor we are this Thanksgiving season, we are still considered rich by nearly 70 percent of the world that does not have adequate food, water, or shelter. We have all heard the truism that Americans could feed a starving country on what it throws away!

Give thanks in the midst of trials. Every road eventually ends somewhere, and your long trials will soon be over.

Give thanks that things are no worse. No matter how bad things are, they could be worse. We can always look around us and see that the worst thing didn't happen—we just thought that it would.

If your present situation is not so rosy, and you feel that the worst has indeed happened to you, give thanks for the joy of the past. Even people who have gone through the most wretched circumstances have had at least one instant of joy. Find that moment and remember to give thanks for it.

Keep on rejoicing. Keep on praying. Keep on giving thanks. What pleasant ways to find ourselves in the will of God!

Watching and Waiting

November 22   *Read Isaiah 64:1-4.*

Our most prized kitchen possessions show that we do not like to wait. We press a button and out comes the toast. Wait just a few minutes and the coffee is ready; and how quickly that potato bakes in the microwave! We don't have time to wait. Yet, a great deal of our time is spent waiting. We wait for the school bus with our children. We wait in lines. We wait for returned phone calls. We wait for the letter carrier. We wait up for our teenagers. We wait. We wait. We wait. And we don't like it!

Israel was also waiting. They were waiting for help; waiting for deliverance; waiting for comfort. They had grown weary of the wait: "Why don't you tear the sky open and come down? Come and reveal your power to your enemies. . . ." Is that your silent cry today? We have some enemies. Enemies called poverty. Others called loss, disease, injustice, loneliness. Why doesn't He just come down, throw lightning bolts, tear the sky, or something?

Here we all are waiting—waiting for justice, waiting for our day in court, waiting for a break. How, then, do we resolve the tension between what we see happening every day and what we know God can do? "No eye has seen any God besides you, who works for those who wait for him" (verse 4). We continue to wait because we know who God is, and we know that He is coming.

Israel waited and watched for perceptible signs of God's breaking in upon human affairs. Some died faithfully waiting and watching. Others saw and received the long-awaited promise. That promise marked the first Advent, or coming of Christ. We wait for the second coming of Christ, the second Advent.

This time, between the Advents, is a curious time. Christ is coming, Christ has come, Christ will come again in glory. But, what of those times in between? While we are waiting, Jesus Christ, and his earthshaking power, break in upon us at unexpected times. We see prayers answered. We witness the mountains shaking with fear, and nations trembling at His presence. While we watch and wait for Him, I hear the echoes of the old mothers of the church.

> You can't hurry God,
> you just have to wait
> Trust Him and give Him Time
> No matter how long it takes. . . .
> He may not come when you want Him, but He's right on time.

They seemed to survive the wait, and so will we.

Fire Baptized

John knew that he was not the revelation. He was just there to prepare the way for the Christ. John's baptism was one of repentance. He told his followers that the baptism to look forward to was the one coming with fire. The old folks used to talk about this often. What does it mean to be fire baptized?　Fire wakes us up and catches our attention. It seems that all heads turn when the fire engine goes by. Where is the fire? What is on fire? Are you on fire? Perhaps each personal baptism represents a potential holy bonfire, waiting to be ignited by God. Could it be that the Holy Spirit's fire comes to wake us up to the significance of baptism?

Fire transforms us. Just like fire changes a cake batter into a product that can never be cake batter again, we are changed by the fire of the Holy Spirit. The changes that God's Spirit brings into our lives are permanent. Those in Christ are transformed into a new creation. We become as we have never been. There are so many days that I need this fire.

Finally, fire empowers us. Those with fire are taken seriously. The fiery spirited seldom go unnoticed. They command our attention; we are eager to hear them speak. Those with firepower are sought in times of war. We need them when all around us is dead and needs igniting. We call upon the fiery when the dead debris of traditionalism needs to be burned away. We look for them to light the logs in the fireplace when it is cold and we need warmth. God's fire in them brings power into our helpless lives.

O God, today, I dare to ask to join the ranks of the fire baptized!

Multitudes

November 24　　　　　　　　　*Read Revelation 5:11-14.*

We come from many places to worship Him. Angels, living creatures, and elders are there. Multitudes come to worship the Lamb. All of us are singing at the top of our voices. We are singing the same song in perfect harmony.

Angels from the realm of glory worship at the throne of the Lamb who was slaughtered. Never having sinned they sing the same song. Worthy is the Lamb, their Lamb, my Lamb, your Lamb and ours. They sing it from the heights as they soar in praise visiting places humans never see, singing the same song, them, us, and me.

Living creatures, born God knows where; or were you created? No one here knows your numbers. You defy description. Yet, singing the same song, worshiping the same Lamb, you trumpet "Amen" as we worship the King.

Elders, you and I understand. We know them quite well. Robes dipped in blood, some are martyrs and they sing. Enduring great trials, they have come through tribulation. They met Him in the cane breaks; eyes closed, they saw His face from the lynching tree; they felt His Spirit moving in the brush arbors when no one else would sing. These, too, are singing the same song, gathering at the throne, worshiping the same Lamb, Christ the King.

And, so, here we are, gathering at the same place, after coming from all directions. We are worshiping together, sharing few other experiences; because nothing else matters but the Lamb on the throne.

Wings

November 25   *Read Matthew 23:37.*

I was watching the chickens one day. Several of them had just hatched chicks. One hen had one lonely, noisy chick. Another hen had three. When it was time for them to settle down for a nap, or for protection, it was quite easy for her to gather them underneath her feathers. Still another mother hen had six chicks. I was amazed at the way she was able to fan out her feathers, like lifting a fluffy skirt, to provide a place for her baby chicks to warm themselves.

Then, there was one very unenlightened little chick. He had strayed from his mother, who had gone along without him. He tried to find haven under every mother chicken he met. A perfunctory examination from each hen let him know that he was not hers. Peck! Go away! Peck-Peck! I will not feed you, nor warm you! Peck-Peck-Peck! Don't you have a mother of your own?

I watched this dumb cluck for several hours while I was washing in the courtyard. He even tried to come to me for comfort. It seemed that he did not have a clue as to where he really belonged. I alternated between fussing at him and wanting to cuddle him myself. He seemed to have nowhere to go.

This scripture came to mind. That must be how Jesus feels about us. We have been tragically separated from Him. We don't even know where we belong, and everything in the world seems to reject us. We run from fad to fad, from house to house, from church to church, looking for His comfort. Peck! You don't belong here. Peck-Peck! Find someplace else. Peck-Peck-Peck! We need to settle down with Him!

Well, finally that little chick's mother came along. She seemed distressed that he had been out wandering where a cat or an owl could make easy lunch of him. Just as he had tried every other chicken in the courtyard, he ran noisily over to her, hoping not to be rejected. Reunion! They began to scratch the ground together as though no separation had taken place. Later, I saw him peeping from underneath the skirts of her feathers. It almost looked as if he breathed a sigh of relief!

Do you feel as if life itself pecks you and rejects you? Why not realize where you belong, settle down beneath His wings, and breathe your sigh of relief?

Power Struggle

November 26   *Read John 19:10-11.*

Have you ever been involved in a power struggle? Some people long for power, chase it, and even attempt to steal it. They worry you about the little power that they think you have. Others, like Jesus, just have power. Pilate, frustrated by the fact that Jesus was not intimidated by his presence, used an old power tactic: "Do you know what I can do to you?"

Under such circumstances, another person might have given Pilate a bit more respect. The Romans were in power; and he was, after all, the highest ranking Roman official resident in their area. Jesus was not impressed. Instead, Jesus reminded Pilate of where real power is—in the hands of God.

Is this a lesson that we have yet to learn? If we were to examine human activity, it would become evident that much of what we do revolves around our perceptions of power. Some people spend a great deal of energy looking for power, aligning themselves with power, or usurping what they perceive to be power. Making the right contacts, going to the right places, wooing the right people becomes a preoccupation.

Then, there are those who are not worried about their reputations. They are not worried about the size of their paycheck. They are not worried about shaking the pastor's hand every Sunday, or meeting the mayor when she is in town. They breeze through life with so much less stress. What is the difference?

Perhaps, what it boils down to is understanding where power is. Power is not something that we can chase or for which we barter. Real power comes from God. If you allow Jesus to live through you, you already have all the power that you need.

Bigger than Life!

What would you say if you were ninety and you heard God say that you were going to have a baby? It would be bigger than my faith! Sarah and Abraham obviously had the same problem. Let's just face it, they were old! Old people don't have babies. Old men may manage to have a child, but old women are out of the question. Sarah relied upon what she had seen in the past to govern her response to the present and to fuel her hope for the future. She had seen old men have babies, not old women, so she did the only thing that she understood, gave her husband permission to pursue God's promise with a woman who was yet able to produce a child, Hagar. We all know that she missed it. It was perhaps the biggest mistake of their marriage. But, even in the mistakes of the faithful, we find encouragement for today.

God made a promise that was bigger than both Sarah's and Abraham's dreams; in spite of the error of the century, they were going to have their own child! I am encouraged when I read about these faith struggles, because I certainly have faith struggles of my own.

Some days my dreams are almost nonexistent. Some days your dreams die before your head leaves the pillow. The condition of our dreams does not stop God's promise. You may feel that some major mistake in life has caused you to forfeit God's promise, but that does not have to be true. One of the reasons that we continuously read the accounts of God's dealings with humanity, as recorded in the Bible, is to discover what God is like. This story teaches us that God is not prohibited by human mistakes.

The Lord made a promise to Abraham and Sarah that was bigger than their faith, and bigger than their mistakes. Eventually, Isaac arrived, as promised. Nothing and nobody could stop God from doing what He wanted to do in their lives! In the same way, nothing and nobody can stop God from fulfilling His desires for you. God's plans for you are bigger than life!

Thanksgiving Remembering

Everyone looks forward to Thanksgiving at our house. Some of my fondest memories are of preparation for Thanksgiving meals. We baked for weeks in advance!. In many of your homes, as in ours, this time of the year continues to be one of the most exciting times of the year. On Thanksgiving Day, family and friends would come from far and near to grace our table. After the big meal, we would share childhood memories and funny stories. We just spent time enjoying one another's company until the wee hours of the morning. For most of us, Thanksgiving is one of the seedbeds of family tradition, a place to share heirloom recipes, and a touchstone for fond memories.

The first Thanksgiving, as historians retell it, came at the end of a time of trials. The early pilgrims and their Native American neighbors came together to celebrate survival, and God-given abundance. That first Thanksgiving was bittersweet. In the living memories of each who had survived was the remembrance of others who had not. Within the context of the celebration of abundance came also the tacit acknowledgment that others were in want.

As we look around our cities, as we look at the plight of the inner city, our memories become bittersweet. Our neighbors are poverty strickened and lonely. Some are hopeless and helpless. Can we even understand their thoughts at this time of the year! For the homeless, Thanksgiving could become a time of bitterness. The widowed, divorced, or recently bereaved find this holiday particularly challenging. Others find this a very depressing time because they have no one with whom to make memories. We, in all of our enthusiasm, often overlook the needs of those who suffer.

This year, we will probably continue to share our holiday with family and friends. We will continue to look at the meal and its preparation as an opportunity to build new relationships and to reinforce old ones. We will do all of this as the bittersweet acknowledgment of those in need nags us and tugs at our hearts.

In spite of our realizations, our rituals will probably continue because we do not really know how to reach out to others. They are helpless, and we are afraid, but prayer is a starting point.

Prayer: Lord God, we hear you continuing to speak through your Word. Your Word teaches us that you are an advocate for those in need. We also care about our brothers and sisters in need, but we do not begin to know what to do in order to show that care. Show us tangible ways to touch lives and to meet needs. Let Thanksgiving become a memorable day for those who suffer. Amen.

For Those Who Have Suffered Loss

November 29

Lord,

Grant your peace to those women who have lost lifelong partners, O God. Help them to embrace comforting memories of their companion-lover-confidant-best friend. Grant our sisters peace as they make casket selections and final arrangments. Prepare them for our awkward expressions of love.

Walk with our sisters after the ceremonies end, Lord. When friends have ceased to make phone calls, and when family members have returned to their hometowns, walk that unfamiliar road with our widowed sisters, we pray. Fill the lonely hours, that will inevitably come, with your presence, Lord. Be, for them, that unseen companion who accompanies them to the church social, to the doctor's office, and to the grocery store.

We also ask you to strengthen those women who live in fear of widowhood;

For those women whose husbands are fading into eternity through terminal illness;

November

For those women whose husbands are no longer the same person because of Alzheimers;

For those women whose husbands no longer recognize their familiar touch;

We ask you for grace.

Create in us a welcoming circle of friends that will, for them, become living reminders of comfort and love. Amen.

Night Angel

November 30   *Read Psalm 134:1-3.*

I saw you last night.
You were in an old dress,
   Working and
      Singing
   While the rest of us
   Watched television and
      Talked to our girlfriends
         On the phone.

You were there
Until well after midnight,
Preparing the church for the rest of us.

   Did I forget to say that
   I heard you last night?
   Praying for my son,
      Who could have gone to jail.
   You were praying and
   Rocking in that old chair of yours,
   While I walked the floor
      And wept
      And swore that
         I should have taken more skin off his backside.

   Did we forget
   To say

Thank you
For baking all the pies
    For the church social?

We were too busy, you see.

But,
We sure do like it
When you remind us
Of the deserts
    Our mothers tried to teach us to bake.

Did Pastor forget to thank you?
You pretended not to notice.
I know that the mothers
Really appreciated
    The way you took on
        All the costumes
            For the Christmas program.

We were so busy,
Getting ready for Christmas that
    It must have slipped our minds.

You are the one who
God applauds.
You minister by night
In the house of the Lord.
Sometimes you are there
Cleaning or
    Cooking.
Other times you are there
Praying for the health of the church or
For the things that we are
    Too upset
        To pray about.

You are up until the wee hours of the morning
On Sunday
    Seeing to it that the
        Ushers look good and that the
            Choir robes are ironed.
You even worry about the snacks for Sunday school.

You are a Night Angel.

Sometimes you get tired.
And,
Sometimes, you get
    A little disgusted
        Because we don't help you.

But,
God applauds you.
He sees your weariness and
He applauds your faithfulness.

This psalm is for you
Who work in the church kitchen
    While others listen to the sermon
        In the sanctuary.
Lift up your hands
In your personal sanctuary and
    Praise the Lord.

You,
Young mother
In the nursery,
        Rocking my child
            While I try to get my life together;
Wave your hands to the King of Kings!

And you,
Ms. Dickens,
    Home until your foot swells,
        Baking all the pies,
            Wave your spoon,
                Shout hosanna, and
Step that old mother's step for the Lord!

Receive God's benediction for all of his hidden workers.
Accept God's blessing for all of His Night Angels.
May the Lord,
"The Maker of heaven and earth,
    Bless you from Zion"
        Amen.

December

We're Having a Baby

Who doesn't love babies? Even the most difficult person seems to melt in the presence of a newborn. Babies seem to bring out the tenderness and compassion in most people. Babies, however, are also demanding.

They change our lives; they are supposed to. They need space and time. There are things that most of us need to do before receiving a child into our lives.

Babies change our schedules. Their priorities eclipse ours. Two o'clock feedings become substitutes for the Late Show. Afternoon show-and-tell walks replace idle time. Our whole worldview changes when children come into our lives.

Our dreams also change when babies come into our world. Pregnant women almost always daydream about their baby's future. Perhaps she will be a doctor; maybe he will invent something new. Those who are parents know that making those dreams come true involves endless sacrifice, effort, and sometimes frustration.

Accepting Christ into our lives is, in a sense, much like accepting a new baby into the family. There are some major changes that need to take place in our lives. Some of these changes are pleasant. Others, at first, are frustrating.

Jesus needs space in our hearts. So often, we crowd Him out with the cares of this world. Selfish interests often eclipse His. Have we really made room for Him?

Have you given the Lord time, lately? Your best friend would put you down in the face of neglect. Have you unconsciously neglected the best friend that you could ever have? Take time to know Jesus. Do your part to nurture friendship with the Divine. Give Him your old recycled dreams in exchange for His, which are much more pleasant.

What shall we do with the child that God has given us? Shall we ignore Him, or adore Him? Shall we restrict time for Him to Sunday mornings at 11:00 A.M., or shall we make room for Him in our hearts?

For a child has been born for us,
a son given to us;
authority rests upon his
    shoulders;
and he is named
Wonderful Counselor, Mighty God,
Everlasting Father, Prince of Peace. (Isa. 9:6)

Truthful Tears

December 2   *Read Matthew 5:4.*

We deceive ourselves more times that we would like to admit. Have you ever convinced yourself of something about yourself, only to discover later that it was not quite true? Tears, by contrast, have a way of telling the painful truth. Sometimes, tears are the vehicle that the soul uses to remind us of where we are in life.

Tears are like a wake-up call. When tears come involuntarily, we are presented with several options. We can either ignore them, suppress them, or interrogate them. If we choose to ignore tears, they may intrude again at a time we consider less appropriate. If we suppress them, they may leak in ways that resemble anger or resentment. What happens when we interrogate the tears that roll down our faces seemingly without cause?

"Why are you here, Tears?" Had you convinced yourself that those ugly comments about you did not hurt? You may have told yourself one thing, but those tears are saying something else. To experience some hurt, sometime, is just human. Maybe the tears have come to remind you that your feelings do count.

"Tears, why am I crying?" Are you disappointed, disgusted, or depressed? Be reminded that there are some human emotions that will not go away completely until they are honestly acknowledged and their source examined. When we are stuck, the tears often come to speed the process along. Like good friends, they want the best for us, don't despise them.

Tears are like headaches. They are just symptoms of the deeper realities that we often hide from ourselves. If you should find yourself tearful, seemingly without cause, muster the space and the courage to interrogate your tears. God has made a promise to the tearful ones who dare to acknowledge their pain. Fear not, you will work your way through this, with God's help. "Blessed are those who mourn, for they will be comforted."

Love Came Down and Lived with Us

December 3   *Read 1 Corinthians 13:4-7.*

Christmas preparations are driven by love. Much of what we do for the holidays is driven by our need to show our love to others. Our gifts are often the loving reflections of a good listener. We purchase gifts we feel our loved ones want or need. We hope they will remember us as they use them. We attempt to impress others with our extravagance, hoping that they will think our love for them is equally extravagant.

In reality, our gift giving rarely has the power to accurately reflect our real feelings. Things cannot convey real emotions. Gifts just cannot do what we want them to do.

Love is such a hard thing to pinpoint. Love is something you feel and something you do. Love is abstract. When we try to explain what love is, we find it easier to say what it is not. The writer of 1 Corinthians 13 found it easier to say what love is not. He said that love is not envious or boastful. Love is not rude or proud.

Nearly two thousand years ago, God showed us His love. Jesus Christ, God Incarnate, came to reveal the love of God to human hearts. God's gift to us was the loving reflection of a good listener. He heard what humanity needed, and His response was Jesus! Jesus told us, and He showed us, the God kind of love. In our abstract way of sensing things, we feel God's love for us. The more that we learn of Jesus, the more fully we understand God's love for us.

Jesus also provides a yardstick for us to use in measuring our love for others. If we look at the extravagance of God's gift, we only begin to see the greatness of His love. Before we purchase holiday gifts, let's accept the challenge to measure our relationships with others by the yardstick of Christ's love. The love chapter, 1 Corinthians 13, offers some convenient measurements. Try these out in your own private prayer closet: Is your love patient? Is it kind? Does it envy? Boast? Is it proud? Is your love rude or self-seeking? Easily angered?

Love came down and lived with us. Jesus is the visible image of the invisible God. Jesus is the one who shows us how to love, because God is love.

Someone Else Knows

Mary wasn't alone. The angel Gabriel had given her an awfully difficult assignment. Who would understand; how would she explain the swollen belly that was certainly coming? The angel told Mary that Elizabeth was also going to have a strange baby. Mary's relative, Elizabeth, was old and barren, but she was also going to have a baby. The people in her neighborhood certainly knew that she was pregnant by now, because she was in her sixth month.

The Gospel writer relates that Mary hastened to her relative, possibly the only other person on earth who would understand what she was about to go through. And, Elizabeth seems to have been waiting for her. Elizabeth knows. Even the baby in Elizabeth's womb knows that Mary has been given a special burden and privilege by God.

While we are not expecting another virgin birth, we do have times when God does things in our lives that are hard to understand. We pack up our children, leave good jobs and relocate; we change careers, or refuse promotions. We let a supposedly good man's proposal for marriage slip by. You know some of the peculiar things we do. Some of the things in your heart today may be even more strange to onlookers. How can we know if they are authentic?

Mary needed verification. God was gracious. He told Elizabeth, whom she knew and trusted, and gave Mary a measure of comfort.

Has the Lord told someone else about your challenges? He would tell someone who cares about you and someone that you could trust. Have you received understanding of another sister's secret blessing? Have you told her? Does she need to know that you know?

For Mary, it was critical to know that she was not crazy. Elizabeth, her kinswoman, who was older and wiser, could comfort and perhaps defend Mary. Mary stayed with Elizabeth several months while she adjusted to the idea, then she faced the world. Life might have been unbearable had Mary never discovered that someone else knew and shared her challenges.

The Body of Christ is a community of believers. God intended for us to need one another. We learn, in the prayer closet, about one another's struggles in order to be supportive. Just as Mary needed Elizabeth, it may be a turning point in some woman's life to hear some knowing words of encouragement from you. Won't you share them today?

Nobody's Business, Everybody's Fault

December 5   *Read Judges 19:25-30.*

"Joe, stop it!" The woman next door was screaming again. It seemed like Lula and Joe fought all the time. Every weekend, Joe would drink cheap bourbon until he passed out. Hours later he would wake up in a rage and beat Lula until she passed out. It was the same every weekend.

"Aw Joe, what have I done to you . . ." Joe yelled back at her words not suitable for this page. The neighbors could hear her ample body hit the wall for the umpteenth time. Then the usually muffled sobs followed as he told her the same things he told her every weekend.

"I am a man. I will drink as much as I want to . . ." His script had become familiar to the entire neighborhood. The way Lula responded made one think that he was punctuating each major thought with a jab or a punch in some part of her body that was probably sore from last weekend's beating.

"Joe, please stop, you are hurting my head." The man must have once wanted to be a boxer and a wrestler the way he handled his wife. He alternated between beating this part and yanking another part; the whole neighborhood could visualize what was going on. Everybody visualized what was going on, yet nobody said a word to the police. They didn't even discuss it with one another because it wasn't their business.

The day that Lula died, they had all visualized her death. They heard the awful clang when her head finally hit the steel radiator. All of them heard Joe tell her to get up—but she couldn't. Still nobody called the police because it wasn't their business.

It was nobody's business and everybody's fault. Consider it, take counsel, and speak out.

A Man!

December 6   *Read Numbers 23:18-19.*

"Do you think that Stephen King was trying to say that God is a Black woman?" It was breakfast time, and I wanted to give my youngest son a hard time after viewing the last evening's marathon of Stephen King's *The Stand.*

"Mom, what do you mean, God can't be a woman. It's against nature!" My question so caught him off guard that he was unable to see the mischievous twinkle in my eyes.

I repeated my question, "Do you think that Steven King was trying to say that God is a Black woman? After all, Ruby Dee was the chief spiritual figure in the movie." He couldn't hear my question, and we were off to the races. What I had intended as a vehicle to poke fun at my youngest son, turned into a deep philosophical conversation about the gender of God.

In all of our fuss about the gender of God, all of us have forgotten that God is not like a human being. God indulges us by allowing us to make descriptions using human terminology. We talk about the eyes of God, the hand of God, the mouth of the Lord. The Ewe people of Ghana, West Africa, call God *Ataa Naa Nyonmo,* which means Grandfather/Grandmother God. Precolonized Africans often have concepts of God that are either genderless, or gender inclusive.

In actuality, God is a Spirit (John 4:24). As such, God is neither male nor female. God is just God. Those who worship God must do so in spirit—the gender of God has very little to do with it.

How did my son and I settle the dispute that arose? He called my attention to something very simple. "Mom," he said, "you have always taught me that God was male because when we pray we always close our prayers with A-Man!" After that, I was silent.

Finding Rest

December 7   *Read Matthew 11:28-30.*

Camra tossed and turned all night long. It seemed as though her bed was stuffed with doorknobs. She searched every inch of that bed; sleep was nowhere to be found.

"What is wrong with me," she asked herself? "I just can't seem to sleep anymore." She shrugged her tense lean shoulders. "Life is such a pain in the neck," she thought, as she tried to rub the crook out the right side of her neck.

Her thoughts drifted to her mother in Mississippi. Why wouldn't her mother come to live with her? She had been worried about her mother's blood pressure for weeks. Mother, of course, being independent, saw no need for worry and kept on salting the collard greens. Camra just couldn't seem to understand the choices that her mother was making.

She almost dozed for a moment, when her thoughts turned toward her little sister. Nina was two years younger and had always been the adventurous kind. This time, however, caution would have served her better. Nina was shacking with a married man and Mrs. Married Man had sworn to kill her. "Is that girl going to get some sense before she gets hurt?" The thoughts nagged Camra like an old headache. She decided to pray.

"Lord, what shall I do with my family? They just don't want to do right." Tears welled up in her eyes as she continued to stalk the sleep that eluded her. In the stillness of the early morning, these words crept into her restless thoughts: *Come to me, all you that are weary and are carrying heavy burdens, and I will give you rest.* Minutes later, the much sought after sleep followed.

There is rest today for all weary souls who take their problems to the Lord and leave them there.

A Modern Dilemma

December 8   *Read Luke 1:26-38.*

"Poor Mary, what will she do? You know Joe says it ain't his baby—you think he will divorce her?"

"Her momma says she came home with some story about an angel and a ghost—sounds like drugs to me."

"Maybe she got tangled up in some cult business. Poor child, she was such a good girl."

Not everyone understood Mary's story—her untimely pregnancy—God coming into her life in this unique way. Not everyone understood. And, they talked. Yet, nearly two thousand years later, we understand, and we admire Mary for the courage it must have taken to bear a special child when no one understood her story. She was courageous enough to watch this unusual child grow into manhood and become so unpopular. With a broken heart, she stood by, watching His crucifixion. After His death, it still was not over, for her baby remained the subject of much controversy.

It seems as though women of all colors have always had to be strong. The Lord chose Mary to bear Jesus the Christ because He knew that she would not be crushed under pressure.

Bible heroines like Ruth, Esther, and Deborah have proved that women are able to withstand great pressures and triumph against odds. Most of you can tell stories of strong praying mothers and grandmothers who stood against odds and held the family together through our turbulent American past.

So what happened to the frail fragile woman who always faints at the sight of blood, freezes in times of disaster, and does not know how to manage the daily affairs of her life? We find that in the realm of our daily experience, that woman does not really exist. What we really have is a whole list of women of color, women like Mary, who work hard, get little recognition, and bear a great deal of pain in silence.

In your day's encounters with these women, our women, I encourage you to whisper a silent prayer of solidarity and encouragement for them. I encourage you to let your eyes say, "I understand," and your smiles say, "I love you."

A Tale of Two Daughters

December 9   *Read Matthew 21:28-32.*

Once upon a time there were twin daughters, Elaine and Bobbi Jean. Some folks thought that Bobbi Jean was the better girl between the two. She brought home good grades, kept her curfew, and baby-sat for the neighbors without accepting payment. She said "yes ma'am" and "no sir." Bobbi Jean never seemed to give her parents a moments trouble.

The other daughter, Elaine, was quite the opposite. She was known to dye parts of her hair bright green. She struggled with math and English, had been known to drink wine, and often wound up grounded for being out too late. "Ma'am" and "sir" were not in her vocabulary, and she didn't seem to care what anyone thought. Elaine was a free spirit.

As circumstances would have it, the twins' parents were required to leave town for a family emergency. It was finals week, and the two seventeen-year olds didn't need the long trip to Georgia or the three day absence from classes. So the parents grit their teeth, closed their eyes, and prepared to trust them alone—with each other.

The girls were grilled again and again with a long list of expectations. no parties, no booze, no boys—no. "Do you expect me to live like this?" Elaine asked. When her parents said "Yes!" she didn't even bother to respond. Bobbi Jean just smiled, in an angelic way, and said, "Trust me!"

Before her parents' car had gone down the street and turned the corner, Bobbi Jean was on the phone. She called her boyfriend. She called two girlfriends. She called the pizza delivery number. Nobody was looking —for a change. She was having a party and her boyfriend was staying over!

Elaine, whose bangs were pink today, looked at her sister in disbelief. "I don't believe you!" she said, as she spun on her toes and returned to her room. For the entire weekend, Elaine only came out for more microwave popcorn, while Bobbi Jean and her boyfriend played house.

Perhaps the moral of the story is a question. Tell me, which girl was the good girl after all?

House Divided

December 10   *Read Matthew 12:25.*

I met an African lady at a dinner party one evening. She was proud and majestic. I made sure to say, "Yes, Ma'am" and "No, Ma'am" as we held a conversation. I avoided using my left hand, and did not challenge her eyes.

In my efforts to connect with her, I mentioned the names of some people I knew from her country. They were important, and she was important. Perhaps they knew each other. Yes, they knew each other. Her reply, "They are Gikuyu, we are Masai!" The conversation ended.

It did not matter to me that they were from different tribes. I protested without an audience. They are Africans from the same country. Why aren't they more united?

I have been surprised by the Africa I encountered. It is so much different from the Africa of my dreams. In the Africa of my dreams, all Africans are united. Tribal distinctions do not exist. The color of sun kissed skin ties us all together.

The real Africa is quite different. Ethnic loyalties continue to be strong. People groups, those the missionaries called tribes, band together.

Outsiders are easily identified and must often prove themselves before being admitted beyond the borders of polite conversation.

"African-Americans are one big ethnic group," I mentally boasted. We are one, because we are Black I mused. When I thought about the real Black community, sadness overcame me. In the absence of ethnic groupings, we have substituted divisions of our own.

"They are from uptown, we are from the high-rise."

"They are light skinned, we are dark skinned."

"They eat beans, we eat steak, and don't cook no chittlin in my house!"

We are people with a split personality. We love one another in front of other people. But behind closed doors, we bite and devour and undermine one another's success. Sadly, we are just as divided as our brothers and sisters across the ocean.

In this, we mirror people all over the world. Human beings are tragically separated, by sin, from God and from one another. The words of Jesus make a great deal of sense at this point. We need the Lord, or none of us will stand.

Somebody's Child

December 11   *Read Proverbs 19:17.*

Mamie does some of the strangest things for this day and age. She is as poor as a church mouse, yet she insists on putting her loose change into all those little displays—you know, the ones in the stores that raise money for this charity or that boy's ranch. I asked her once why she does it, when the charity ought to be giving to her. She just said, "They raising money for somebody's child. You never know when somebody might have to raise money for my child."

The beggars on the street know Mamie. When they are down to their last they can always count on her for a quarter toward a sandwich or fifty cents for a pop. "Mamie," I said, "you better keep some of that pop money for yourself. You po as them." She didn't pay me no mind at all. She just mumbled something about "somebody's child."

Well, Mamie sees somebody's child just about everywhere we go. Somebody's child is in the hospital. Somebody's child is in the jailhouse.

Somebody's child is trying to go away to school. Somebody's child died and the family didn't have enough money for the funeral. To have her tell it, you just can't get away from running into somebody's child.

Maybe Mamie has it all figured out. The poor, the homeless, the sick, and those in prison, really are somebody's children.

Wonderful Memory!

December 12   *Read Luke 1:11-13.*

Remember the stories of the faithful. By the end of the year, we are tired and worn. We need to remember someone whose prayers were answered and someone enthralled by the wonder of God's grace.

Look at the people described in today's reading. They were two very godly people: Zechariah, whose name means *Jehovah has remembered*, and Elizabeth, whose name means *oath of God*. They were ordinary church folks. Zechariah was a priest, and Elizabeth would have been called the preacher's wife in our day. They led long faithful lives and choked back the pain of being childless.

In a time when being childless was presumed to be a curse from God, two godly people had to struggle with the same questions that we ask at times like these: "Why do the wicked prosper?" "Why do child abusers get to have children?" "We have such a good home to offer, why are our arms empty?" So many women with empty arms suffer silently because we don't know how to share that pain with them.

Zechariah in his bitterness, could have asked: "Remembered what?" Elizabeth's situation was no better. Her name was supposed to remind her of God's promise. Can't you hear the folks in the neighborhood whispering: "God must not love them like He loves others. I wonder what they've done?" By this time, they had given up on ever being parents.

In the midst of their pain, an angel spoke: "Do not be afraid, Zechariah, for your prayer has been heard" (verse 13). In other words have no fear Zechariah, *God remembers.*

How often have you felt that God forgot about you? God has a wonderful memory. He always answers our prayers at just the right time. If Elizabeth had not been childless, John the Baptist would not have been so special. There are so many special blessings reserved for each of us. We just have to wait for some of them.

As you enter your Advent meditations, why not take these words to Zechariah as your own: "Have no fear, God remembers." God has a wonderful memory; He never forgets.

Don't Be No Stumbling Block

December 13   *Read 1 Corinthians 8:7-9.*

Paul seems to be reminding the Christians in this passage that they are being watched. Take care that this liberty of yours does not somehow become a stumbling block to the weak. These words were couched in a conversation about non-Christian practices. Some new Christians were wrestling with the symbols of their old lifestyle like meat offered to idols. Others, who had never worshiped those idols, did not regard the meat in the same way. The question became, "Do I have to deal with another person's symbols. The meat is nothing to me."

The same is true today. As we wrestle with the lists of do's and don'ts that vary from church to church, the real issue is what the prohibition represents—its symbol. For example, at one time, no church women were allowed to wear pants. Some felt that pants represented loose lifestyles and overly progressive trends. Others simply saw comfort, warmth, or protection for old knees. Still others saw a way to keep their daughters out of short skirts. Do you remember the confusion that resulted? Perhaps the real issue was never the pants, but their symbolic meaning.

There are other intriguing symbols with which we wrestle. Some believe that eating meat is wrong. Others feel that strong drink only leads to sin. How will we ever wade through these issues? Returning to today's passage, we see that Paul was not concerned with correcting symbolic meanings. He dealt with people where they were. If meat offends you, then I will respect your symbol, sister, and will not become a stumbling block by eating that meat in your presence. We are encouraged to respect other people's symbols and not cause them to sin.

You never know who is watching you, especially in a small community. Christians are perhaps the most watched people on earth. Non-Christians are watching us to see how the faith works in hard situations. It's the closest thing they have to test driving a car. Other Christians watch us too. Some are new in the faith and want to imitate your mature walk. Others are old in the faith and watch vigilantly to ensure that careless Christians do not misrepresent the entire group.

When people see you, what do they see? Like it or not, you are probably being watched. Don't be no stumbling block!

"Is This You?"

December 14   *Read Matthew 2:13-18.*

When Jesus was just a baby, it looked as if everything and everyone were out to get Him. If someone were going to cause a miscarriage, wouldn't they put a young very pregnant teenager on the road to Bethlehem from Judea? Were you that teenage girl? If someone wanted to ensure a germ filled environment where would they place a baby?—a manger of course! Were you that baby? If the evil forces of this world wanted to stop the unstoppable ones and beat those destined by God for greatness, would not they attempt to stop them before they ever got a chance to shine? Was this you?

There are so many times life does not make sense. There are times when the most beautiful flowers in the garden are trampled and crushed. Is this you? Why has it been so hard? Why is it so unfair? Both Moses' and Jesus' mothers could have asked those questions. Something unseen out there seemed to want to destroy their beautiful baby boys. Life was lumpy, unpredictable, hard to swallow. Are you that mother?

When we look at the plight of our children, we have to wonder which are destined to be the next Tubmans or Mandelas. It seems that life tries so hard to stop them. Listening to them, seeing their eyes, and hearing their sighs, we wonder: Little Baby, is this you?

How else do we explain our common struggles? We are both blessed and cursed like Mary. We are blessed to be chosen for greatness and cursed because others do not seem to understand. We are both Mary, narrowly escaping and sometimes barely making it, and Rachael, weeping for our sons and daughters innocently slaughtered.

But the angel of the Lord appeared to Joseph in a dream! God knows and understands our human dilemmas. The Lord appeared. God provides directions for an escape plan and guidance that preserves our lives. The Lord appeared to Joseph. Others may be involved in God's plans to save us.

The Lord appeared to Joseph in a dream! What redemptive dreams are you dreaming? How has God planned to use you? What part are you chosen to perform in the great cosmic drama? Is this you?

For Women in Prison

December 15

Sometimes, Lord, we are so involved with our petitions for the brothers behind prison bars that we forget that many sisters are also in prison. Be merciful, we pray, to our sisters incarcerated both justly and unjustly. Enable them to experience your love and forgiveness. Assure them of restoration. Give them courage to walk on holy pathways.

Be merciful to their children, O Lord. There are babies that have been deprived of their mother's love, and teenagers who are unable to hear their mother's advice. These children are often forgotten, often ashamed, and need your grace.

We pray for the sisters, grandmothers, aunts, and best girlfriends who have assumed unexpected parenting responsibilities. We pray that they might be able to feed, clothe, and nurture the children that have been placed in their care. Have mercy upon them, Lord, and bless them for being there for these children in a time of great need.

Have mercy, O Lord, upon the brothers who are waiting for their wives' return. When their hopefulness begins to sag, build them up. When they are tempted to abandon their children, give them strength and courage. We pray that fragile marriages might be able to weather the storms of separation and stigma.

Finally, Lord, we pray that we might be a part of our sisters' healing. Teach us how to be the supportive community that our sisters need while in prison and when they return. Amen.

Star Struck!

December 16   *Read Matthew 2:1-2.*

> We three kings of Orient are;
> Bearing gifts we traverse afar,
> Field and fountain, moor and mountain,
> Following yonder star.

The wise men from the East were actually Gentiles. They were star-gazers, astrologers, and philosophers. They took what they knew, the stars, and were led to the Christ Child. We assume that they were three because of the number of the gifts they brought: gold, for a king; frankincense for a priest; and myrrh, often used in those days for embalming, for a sacrifice.

"For we observed his star at its rising, and we have come to pay him homage" (verse 2). Nowhere else in the Gospel accounts of the nativity is there mention of the star. The Jews were not looking at the skies for a star. The shepherds were told of the new baby by a band of angels. We must conclude that God, in His love and mercy, chose to speak to these Gentiles who knew nothing of prophecy, and little if anything of Israel's history, through the means that they did know—the stars. There must have been some kind of disturbance in the stars.

What did they see in the stars? Regardless of what it was, they saw something, and this led them to the feet of Jesus. God indeed works in mysterious ways. Perhaps these ways are so mysterious to us because we fail to recognize that God wants to save all who are lost. God reaches into the signs and symbols of our everyday world and speaks to each human being in meaningful ways. This is His divine effort to bring all nations, kindred, tribes, and tongues into His family.

May I invite you to be alert to the many ways that God is reaching into your world to speak to you? One of the joys of the nativity and Incarnation of Jesus Christ is that God reached into many worlds to carry the message of redemption. Perhaps the old saying is true: Wise men and women do follow the star!

> O star of wonder, star of light,
> Star with royal beauty bright,
> Westward leading, still proceeding,
> Guide us to thy perfect light.

New Clothes

December 17   *Read Colossians 3:12-17.*

Do you think we have become too touchy these days? It seems as though we have forgotten how to put up with one another. Paul had to remind the church at Corinth of their need to bear with and love one another.

As African-Americans, we inevitably find ourselves in tension with American culture. All around us the culture speaks individuality and isolation. We are taught to do our own thing in elementary school. The media encourages us to have it our way. By contrast, African culture teaches us to work together for a common cause, and to prefer group goals to personal gain. Stay together, work together, build together. For some of us, especially this generation of youth, the tension has been insurmountable. Some have been forced to decide between individuality and community. Could it be that those things we perceive as offenses are really just excuses to isolate ourselves? Isolation is less complicated than learning to live with one another.

The Bible seems to lean more toward maintaining community. We need one another. We cannot grow in some areas of our lives without growing through the offenses that often separate us. At the time we run away from one another, what we often need most is to learn to work it out.

God's solution? New clothes. When you were little, remember how different new clothing made you feel? "Dressed up" clothes encouraged "dressed up" behavior. New clothes, in some ways, often help us feel new. We are invited to clothe ourselves with compassion, kindness, humility, meekness, patience, and love. With all those new clothes we are bound to need to take off something that we were already wearing. How about removing some grumpy socks or griping pantyhose? Get the picture?

Breathe on Me

December 18   *Read Genesis 2:7.*

Today's verse reminded me a great deal of making rolls for the holidays. It takes concentration, for me, to make sure that the yeast does not get too warm or too cold. It takes rhythmic care to knead out the air bubbles and to knead in just enough flour. Fashioning them into a finished product that looks like something is akin to a work of art. Yet, the Creation was more personal than baking rolls.

The Creation, by James Weldon Johnson, gave me my very first visual image of God making humankind from the dust of the ground. In it, I saw God bent over, kneading out the lumps and imperfections. I saw God fashioning us in His image and likeness. We were not created by the wave of a mighty hand or the blink of an eye. Creation was a very sacred and personal process.

It was sacred because God did it. He made us Himself. Some children look like their fathers, and God made us to look like Him. We were close enough to feel God's breath. The original language suggests the phrase: "The Lord God breathed in Adam's face." Yes, creation was much more personal than baking bread.

When you feel like dust has become your new dwelling place, remember that you did not just happen, you were created. When men and women call you everything except a child of God, remember that you are created in God's image. When you feel frayed and ragged around the edges, be reminded of the great care that the Lord has taken in making you.

Prayer: On the days that I feel like I have returned to the dust prematurely; when I feel like there is no life in me; Spirit of God, breathe in my face.

Spiritual Hunger

December 19 *Read Matthew 5:6.*

I have yet to meet a single person who is absolutely satisfied with their spiritual development. Everywhere we look, we women are acutely aware of our need for more of God.

When we say *more of God*, we mean a variety of things. *More of God* means more *like God*. *More of God* means more of *God's will becoming evident* in our lives. *More of God* means *making more impact upon the world in which we live*. *More of God* means *more understanding about who God is and what God wants* from each of us. We are haunted by our need for more spirituality and more of spiritual things in our lives.

Jesus' wisdom shines through his use of the word *hunger.* Hunger is time-less. Hunger is genderless. Hunger is classless. Everyone understands what hunger is. Hunger is one of those last powerful human motivators that we have not been able to tame. The pharmaceutical market may offer a tempo-rary remedy to curb hunger, but, true to its nature, hunger will not be denied.

God says that your spiritual hunger will not be denied. Just as you con-fidently rely upon God to fill your empty belly, rely upon God to fill your soul. Just as you know that physical hunger needs must be met several times a day, remember to turn your hunger toward God who will meet your spiritual needs all through the day. Spiritual satisfaction does not come to remain, it comes for the moment. We are designed to need more.

Today, if you are hungry, regard it as a good sign, it means that you are alive and growing. Most people only lose their appetites when they are sick.

A Few Good Friends

December 20   *Read Luke 5:17-20.*

Sandy didn't know quite how she felt about this prayer meeting. It was impolite, she had always been taught, to refuse prayer. Otherwise, the Women's Prayer Band would never have been given permission to invade her bedroom.

Sandy was a private person. Having cancer was a private kind of thing. She felt that people would treat her differently if they knew that she had been diagnosed with such a disease. The doctors said that they had caught it in time. With the proper treatment, and regular checkups, she should live to be a hundred. She wished that she had kept it to herself, for now the Women's Prayer Band had camped on their knees at her bed-side.

The Women's Prayer Band was a group of older women within Sandy's home church. They prayed, *hard,* and all the time! They were the last resort group, often called in when parishioners were declared terminal. Having them come, in such numbers, made Sandy feel nervous and embarrassed.

There they were, kneeling the old-fashioned way, and moaning until the floor seemed to vibrate. Try as she could, Sandy had seemingly been unable to reassure this group that she was going to be fine. They had come to pray heaven down and were determined to do just that. They started a familiar, old-style, long meter hymn, just as their mothers before them must have done. The low notes growled and roared in Sandy's belly.

Seeing that there was no more she could do, she shut her eyes and tried to pray along with them. Before long, the long, slow, hymn gave birth to rhythmic prayer. Unconsciously, she tuned into its familiar cadence and found herself anticipating the familiar phrases that rose from their lips.

"Come by here Lord, Come by here." The pictures on the wall seemed to fade into the background. Sandy began to reflect that it had been a long time since she had taken the time to attend an old-fashioned prayer meeting. The women's fellowship, to which she belonged, chose innovation over tradition. Perhaps, every now and then, she thought, she should stay in touch with some of the old ways.

"Our sister needs you, Lord. You are a doctor that has never lost a case. . . ." The prayer band had increased its intensity by this time. "Yes, Lord, I do need you for more than a quick fix or a broken body. I have so many questions that need to be answered." Sandy was more involved in this prayer than she had planned to be.

"We need your help! We need your help! We need your help!" With reverent lips, Sandy formed the words, "I need your help" as the power of God blanketed the room.

Sometimes, we just need a few good friends to help us touch the Lord.

What Child Is This?

December 21   *Read Luke 2:1-17.*

There is nothing more natural than having a baby. The cycle of life involves babies. Babies come and babies grow up to have babies. And, of course, there is no baby as beautiful as our baby. Some babies really catch our attention—for a little while.

Who would ever have thought that this baby would create such a stir? This baby was born to a teenager who had not exactly been with her husband yet. This tragic scene is replayed thousands of times a year in a thousand American cities. Who would think that we would remember such a child? What was so different about this child?

The whole world was waiting for this child. This child would save us from terrible times. This child would grow into manhood and change the face of human history. This child would teach us His Father's ways. This child would heal the sick and raise the dead. This child would rule with diligence. This child? Mary's baby?

Two thousand years later, the world is still talking about this child. They are still talking about Mary's baby, who happens to be the Son of God. Twenty centuries later, this child is still saving us from terrible times. This child is still teaching us His Father's ways. This child is still healing the sick and raising the dead. This child, grown into manhood, seated at the right hand of God, continues to change the face of human history.

Strong men have died defending His name. Nations are still fighting because of Him. His very existence is still discussed in the best and worst of places.

> What child is this who, laid to rest,
> On Mary's lap is sleeping?
> Whom angels greet with anthems sweet,
> While shepherds watch are keeping?
> This, this is Christ the King,
> Whom shepherds guard and angels sing;
> Haste, haste to bring him laud,
> The babe, the son of Mary.

What Do We Really Need?

December 22   *Read 1 Samuel 8:19-20.*

> Gimme, Gimme, Gimme
> Why do we always want
> something we do not have
> or really need
> when we see someone else with it?
>
> Gimme a new house
>   like Sally Sue's.
> Gimme something else.
>   (The commercial said this one won't do.)

> Gimme a break.
>> Gimme a chance.
>> Gimme, gimme, gimme something please.

Samuel's Israel was intent on having a king like the other nations. They were unaware of the responsibilities that came with having a king; but they wanted one anyway. Having one proved disastrous.

Are we like that too? Do we want cars that we could never afford to service or houses that we don't have time to clean? Do we covet responsibilities for which we have no training or giftings for which we have no anointing? It is far too easy to admire things from afar and wish that they were ours.

> Lord, you know what we best need.
> When the world is
> dissatisfied with
> ten varieties of bread,
> teach us to number ourselves
> among the fortunate
> who have any bread at all.
>
> When our culture becomes
> self-serving,
> competitive and
> vengeful,
> give us clean hearts and
> pure thoughts.
>
> When we are lured by the
> demands of a
> world that cries
> Gimme!
> Give us wisdom, and
> show us how to use what
> we already have.

Family Picture

December 23   *Read Mark 3:31-35.*

Wilma was a long way from home. She had moved from Small Town, Texas, to Big City, California, with three small children hoping to find work. She had a good job, and her neighborhood was safe enough, but she sure did miss the folks back home.

Wilma and her mother were like sisters. She missed their long talks together. Wilma and the mothers of the church were good friends. She longed for the wisdom that spilled from their mouths in casual conversation. Wilma loved her sisters' company, and her aunt's peach cobblers. How had she ever left them? She felt financially stable and emotionally bankrupt.

"It is so tempting to leave this job," she thought, "I need to go back home where my roots are." But, what about work? She had been an unsuccessful job hunter before—six months and no suitable employment. "Lord," she prayed, "help me to make it just a little while longer!"

The following Sunday, the Lord answered Wilma's prayers. She met Sister Catherine Caldwell who was returning to church after a long absence. Immediately, Sister Caldwell reminded Wilma of the women she had left back at her home church in Texas. She lived alone, and had no family in the area either. Wilma and her three children reminded Catherine of her own children and grandchildren who lived far away. Before long they became each other's family away from home.

Catherine and Wilma were about as family as family could get. They started having Sunday dinners together once or twice a month. Catherine baby-sat for Wilma from time to time, while Wilma did daughterly chores for her newly found second mother.

After a while, they stopped going to visit their biological families so often and began spending some holidays at home—as a family. Did you see their snapshot in the church's family album?

Modern culture notoriously isolates us from our biological families. Don't worry. No matter where you may find yourself, God has a family for you!

Entertaining Angels

December 24   *Read Hebrews 13:1-2.*

No one knew the bronze skinned man with the silvery hair, who sat in church on Christmas Eve. He sat beside Carol in the back of the church. With her last two dollars in her purse, Carol and her boys had taken the church van to Christmas Eve service so that they could thank the Lord for lights, heat, and enough food.

Who was this unknown visitor? Visitors often came to Carol's church, but this man stood out in a crowd. He was handsome, dark bronze, and he glowed. The twinkle in his eyes as he sang the hymns betrayed the fact that this man knew the Lord. He reached to Carol with smooth, manicured hands when the pastor made room in the service for greetings.

The visitor faded into the scenery of the sanctuary as Carol reflected upon the blessings God had given her in the last year. She had been reunited with the church. She had seen her sister's life improve. Though there were no gifts at home for the boys, they were all together as a family with something to eat and a warm place to live. Last Christmas, things were not so pleasant. Tears rushed down both sides of her face in Thanksgiving. When offering time came around, without hesitation, she put in her last two dollars.

The worship service climaxed with the traditional singing of "Silent Night." Carol joined hands with her oldest son on her right and the silver haired stranger on her left. The organ stopped playing in the middle of the song as worshipers savored the beauty of hundreds of voices offered in praise. *Sleep in heavenly peace, sleep in heavenly peace.* A prayerful benediction was offered.

As they all gathered their coats to leave, the unknown visitor shook Carol's hand. He gave her a simple, "God says enjoy yourself" and a folded piece of paper. Carol smiled in response and said, "Thank you, Merry Christmas!" At first, Carol thought that the paper was a business card or an advertisement of some kind and paid it very little attention. She was preoccupied with T.J., who already had a runny nose, and needed his hat before he ran outside to be with the other boys his age. Before she put on her coat, she glanced at the paper given her by the stranger—it was twenty dollars! When she looked for the stranger to thank him, he had disappeared into the night.

How many times might you and I have encountered an angel, unawares?

One of Us

December 25—Christmas Day   *Read Matthew 1:23.*

What must it have been like, Jesus, to leave your home in glory to come to a place like this? When you were born, did it hurt more

December

emotionally or physically, to come into this cruel world? Did you notice that your family was poor? Did the smell of the stable offend you? What were your impressions of human life on that first Christmas morning?

You came to be with us. You were ordinary and unique at the same time. It was a long time before I knew that I needed you. Forgive me, for not recognizing you sooner. No angel interrupted my workday to announce your coming. Had I known that you came *just for me*, I wouldn't have turned you away. I would have rushed to the gate to meet you, on that first Christmas morning.

What must it have been like, Jesus, to limit yourself to flesh? After being Spirit for all of that time, how did it feel to hunger, to weep, to plead, to bleed? You walked up and down dusty roads, slept on the ground, and prayed all night long *for me*. I thank you for tasting a multitude of miseries so that you could really understand my petty moans and complaints.

Thank you, Jesus, for enduring a family that often did not understand you, and for enduring the rejection of hometowns. I even thank you for letting them call you crazy! Now, I don't feel so alone. Lord, thank you for loving Peter, and reclaiming Mary of Magdalene. In them, I am reassured of your love for me. Thank you for opening eyes that had been sightless, and for restoring the sick to their families. Thank you for raising dead folks like me. Thank you, Jesus, for coming to us on that first Christmas morning.

Most of all, Jesus, I thank you for not letting that be all there was of you. You were human and you are spirit. You are faultless. Once dead, you are alive. And, so also shall I be, because you became one of us on that first Christmas morning.

Kwanzaa: *Umoja* (Unity)

December 26   *Read Luke 9:43b-46.*

Isn't it just like human nature to miss the point of the discussion? Jesus was telling His disciples that He was about to die through betrayal. He was preparing them to take over the mission. They, in response, were more concerned with determining who was the greatest!

We have not changed. Jesus is still attempting to prepare disciples,

both male and female, to carry on the mission. And we are still responding with the same argument: "Who is the greatest?"

Our lifestyles are built around competition. From early childhood, we
are taught to win the race, beat the other team, or capture the flag. Bigger is better; faster is better; more is better. We learn early in life to
regard each person as a potential contender for the glory that we covet.
Never tell your secrets—that very person may use them against you!
Don't let them take your job!

While the world around us encourages us to compete, the Bible
encourages us to work together. Love one another; pray for one another;
defer to one another's needs. Build together. The watchword from the
Bible is not compete—it is cooperate.

In order to cooperate with one another, we must learn to love and trust
again. Our communities are betrayed and about to die. Our sad response
has been, "Who is the greatest?" Perhaps competition, instead of coopera-
tion, is one of the reasons why our neighborhoods are disintegrating.

Getting God back into our communities is more important than race,
gender, money, or popularity. We have never needed God's guidance as
desperately as we need it now. Today, if you should find yourself tempted
to make comparisons with someone, why not whisper this prayer: "Lord,
is there some way this person and I can work together for your glory?"

Kwanzaa: *Kujichagulia* (Self-Determination)

December 27   *Read Genesis 17:15-16.*

Everybody's getting their names changed these days. Actually, the
concept is not new. It has always been customary in the United States
for a woman to change her name when she gets married to signal a
change in outlook and a change in relationship. Martha Jones becomes
Mrs. Martha Smith. Her identity changes; we look at her differently; and
ultimately, she begins to think of herself in different ways.

Others of us have changed our names to reflect similar realities. Isabel
Bumfree, whom we know as Sojourner Truth, changed her name to

symbolize a mission in life. It was a religious experience; it was a permanent change. Some receive a new name when completing female or male rites of passage. Once again, the person is presumed to have changed and we are also invited to acknowledge that change by addressing them in different ways.

So it was with Sarah. After years of trials and testing, God changed her name from Sarai, which meant my princess, to Sarah, which meant noblewoman. Things had changed. No longer would she just be Abraham's wife; she would become a mother of nations. Abraham, whose name had also been changed, had to acknowledge this change. God commanded him to address his wife by the newly given name.

You have a new name; so have I. God has a new way that He regards us. We are no longer to be thought of as mere sinners. We are the redeemed of God by Christ Jesus. We are not liars or gossips. We are holy people because we belong to a holy God. We are not castaways or misfits; we are part of God's family. Could this mean we must change the names that we call ourselves?

Sarah's name change was public. God wanted her to think of herself differently and commanded Abraham, her husband, to call her by her new name. I have learned that many people may never really understand a legal name change, but they do understand change. Perhaps it is time for a public acknowledgment of the changes that God has effected in your life. For you, it may not necessarily mean a legal name change, but it can mean a change in attitude and outlook. Changes in the way you think of yourself will eventually influence the way that others relate to you.

If you have legally changed your name and find that people are having a hard time adapting, don't despair. The real issue is not what others call you; nor is it even what you call yourself; it is the new name written in heaven that counts. What does the Lord call you?

I told Jesus, it would be alright if he changed my name . . .

Kwanzaa: *Ujima*
(Collective Work and Responsibility)

December 28   *Read Matthew 5:14-16.*

When I was a child, one of my earliest memories of church songs was of "This Little Light of Mine." In my mind's eye, I could see a tiny little birthday candlelike light, needing to be cradled. I secretly harbored a fear that Satan, like an unexpected gust of wind, would blow it out before it got a chance to shine and please Jesus.

However, when I reread the Sermon on the Mount, I saw that we are like a light for the whole world. Another Bible translation says that we are the light of the world. I have often wondered how to translate my early childhood concept of a hand held birthday candle into a light that would light the world.

This is not an easy concept to grasp—that is if we think of lighting the world single-handedly. But, compare the child's birthday cake with your grandma's. Some of us may feel like our light is small, feeble, and in danger of being blown out, but joined with others, we become a bonfire!

Together, we are more than birthday candles; we are a shining star. We were not meant to shine alone. We are a city set upon a hill that lights the way for travelers who are lost—when we shine together.

When we shine together we are bright and cannot be hidden. Sister, when we shine together, it doesn't matter who thought they were the brightest. When we shine together, no one is out in the cold, and we are all warmed. When we shine together, other little lost candles can see where to run for safety and protection. When we shine together, it takes a mighty gust of wind to blow us out. I believe that we can't all be put out. Of course, that is when we shine together.

Kwanzaa: *Ujamaa*
(Cooperative Economics)

December 29   *Read Luke 19:28-32.*

Did you ever wonder why you have so much stuff? Most of us have things we will never use. We neatly tuck them away in drawers and closets. Some of us are waiting until we have a new house, a bigger table, a good reason, an appropriate occasion. Has it ever occurred to you that you might just be holding onto certain items until the Lord needs them?

I wonder if the owner of the donkey realized what he was doing. He had a colt that had never been ridden. Had it never been ridden because the man was too busy? Perhaps it had never been ridden because he had plenty others to ride. Whatever the reason, he was really nurturing that donkey for the Palm Sunday ride into Jerusalem.

Somewhere in his being, the owner of the donkey knew that Jesus needed the donkey. He released it without any recorded controversy. Will there be controversy in our hearts when the Lord needs some of our stuff?

What might the Lord need from us? When a house burns to the ground, or a flood comes and sweeps a family's possessions away, the Lord already knows where all of their necessities are. You may have a coat that has never been worn, or dishes in the basement that the Lord has need of. When a neighbor runs out of groceries before the end of the month, her sustenance is in your cupboards and mine.

We are all merely caretakers of God's overflowing abundance. He gives many of us more than we can possibly use; so it must be for someone else too. Wouldn't it be wonderful if we could all look at the extra stuff in our lives and ask: "Lord, who am I keeping this for? I know that you have a need for it somewhere!"

Kwanzaa: *Nia* (Purpose)

December 30   *Read 2 Kings 2:11-14.*

Second Kings 2 is the classic picture of the prophet Elijah passing the mantle to his friend and protégé Elisha. The condition of the blessing was simple. If you can see me leave this world, you can have the blessings and the responsibilities that were mine. If you can see me leave this earth.

Can you see them leaving sisters? Fannie Lou was here and now she is gone. Can you see that one day Coretta and Rosa will fade away as Mary Bethune eventually did? Can you see them leaving?

Elisha had to study Elijah. He had to walk those last days with him. He had to study in order to learn what made him successful in God's service. Reread the story. Elijah was almost tired of being followed so closely—or was he testing his protégé? Seems to me, girlfriend, that we have a lot of studying left to do, because the older sisters are marching into history and we have so much left to learn.